The Ethics of Engagement

The Ethics of Engagement

Media, Conflict, and Democracy in Africa

HERMAN WASSERMAN

OXFORD
UNIVERSITY PRESS

OXFORD
UNIVERSITY PRESS

Oxford University Press is a department of the University of Oxford. It furthers
the University's objective of excellence in research, scholarship, and education
by publishing worldwide. Oxford is a registered trade mark of Oxford University
Press in the UK and certain other countries.

Published in the United States of America by Oxford University Press
198 Madison Avenue, New York, NY 10016, United States of America.

Library of Congress Cataloging-in-Publication Data
Names: Wasserman, Herman, author.
Title: The ethics of engagement : media, conflict, and democracy in Africa /
Herman Wasserman.
Description: New York : Oxford University Press, 2021. |
Includes bibliographical references and index.
Identifiers: LCCN 2020025324 (print) | LCCN 2020025325 (ebook) |
ISBN 9780190917333 (hardback) | ISBN 9780190917357 (epub)
Subjects: LCSH: Social conflict—Press coverage—Africa, East. |
Social conflict—Press coverage—Africa, Southern. |
Journalistic ethics—Africa, East. | Journalistic ethics—Africa, Southern |
Press and politics—Africa, East. | Press and politics—Africa, Southern.
Classification: LCC PN5450.5.E18 W37 2020 (print) |
LCC PN5450.5.E18 (ebook) | DDC 303.609676—dc23
LC record available at https://lccn.loc.gov/2020025324
LC ebook record available at https://lccn.loc.gov/2020025325

DOI: 10.1093/ oso/ 9780190917333.001.0001

1 3 5 7 9 8 6 4 2

Printed by Integrated Books International, United States of America

For my parents, who taught me ethics.

Contents

Acknowledgments

Work on this book started during a sabbatical leave period spent at the Ludwig-Maximilians Universität (LMU) in Munich, Germany, in 2018, funded by a Georg Foster Research Award from the Humboldt Stiftung. I am very grateful for this grant, which gave me the opportunity to spend time in a wonderfully stimulating academic environment. I am especially indebted to my generous hosts at LMU, Thomas Hanitzsch and Bernhard Goodwin. I also thank the University of Cape Town for granting me research leave.

It was again in an office in the Oettingenstrasse, during a subsequent visit to LMU in June 2019, that I sent off the last chapter of the manuscript to my copy editor, Simone Chiara van der Merwe, whose careful and patient editing I appreciate very much. That draft received an unusually thoughtful and thorough review from the anonymous reader, whose suggestions I am very grateful for. The review prompted me to make further revisions. Just as I was finalizing these, the Covid-19 pandemic broke out. The final manuscript was sent to my editor, Dave McBride, while we were both in lockdown on different sides of the world. The extent of the impact of this global catastrophe and the ways it would change the global economy, political landscape, and scholarly teaching and research were still very unclear when I submitted the final manuscript in April 2020. It was strange to think about conflict at a time when, despite the devastation wreaked by the virus, the initial global response was one of coming together and an outpouring of solidarity in many unexpected ways. As the disease was unfolding at the same time as the manuscript was wrapped up, it was not possible to consider the ways Covid-19 might impact our understanding of the media's role in conflict and democracy in a future world other than an odd footnote or two. There is no doubt that the global media's response to the pandemic will still provide much cause for important research in the years to come.

My interest in the role of media, conflict, and democratization is largely linked to my earlier participation in an EU-funded project, Media, Conflict and Democratisation (www.mecodem.eu) under the leadership of Katrin Voltmer (grant agreement no. 613370). Although this book does not draw extensively from the data generated in that multicountry study, many of the insights I lean on in this book and some of the case study material derives from that project. Katrin Voltmer's work is seminal to the field of media and democratization studies, of which this book is a very small part. The results of the Mecodem study are published as Voltmer, K., C. Christensen, I. Neverla, N. Stremlau, B. Thomass, N. Vladislavljevic, and H. Wasserman, eds. 2019. *Media, Communication and the Struggle for Democratic Change: Case Studies on Contested Transitions.* New York: Palgrave Macmillan.

Other case study material leans on two previous publications:

Wasserman, H. 2013. "Journalism in a New Democracy: The Ethics of Listening." *Communicatio* 39 (1): 67–84.
Wasserman, H. 2015. "Marikana and the Media: Acts of Citizenship and a Faith in Democracy-to-Come." *Social Dynamics* 41 (2): 375–86.

These are drawn on with permission.

As always, my greatest thanks go to my family: Helena, Lukas, Daniel, and Sophie. Not only do they have to put up with my frequent traveling, but also they give meaning to my life in ways that no academic project ever could.

I dedicate this book to my parents, Herman and Marietjie Wasserman. They have instilled in me the importance of ethics, listening, and care for others from my earliest childhood recollection, and they continue to demonstrate those values in their lives every day.

1

Tear Gas, Rubber Bullets and Democracy

Introduction

More than twenty years into a democracy that has been hailed worldwide as a triumph over racial oppression and the beginning of a transformation from authoritarianism to inclusive democracy and social change, South African students embark on nationwide protests to demand free education. Although "born free"—having never personally experienced the brutal system of apartheid—it is still mostly black students who continue to bear the brunt of tremendous sociopolitical inequality and are excluded from higher education because they can't afford it. In a movement dubbed #FeesMustFall, students close down campuses, march on Parliament, and block roads. These protests frequently result in conflicts as students clash with police and security forces, are sprayed with tear gas, and are shot with rubber bullets. Responses to the students' actions vary—some hail the movement as an inspiration, a sign that young people are willing to take on the government to ensure their right to education. Others condemn the students for disrupting the academic program, damaging property, and acting violently and threateningly. Why, this argument goes, do the students not exercise their democratic agency at the ballot box to vote out the African National Congress (ANC) government if they are dissatisfied with their policies? Why raise your voice in protest when you should rather improve your rational argument in democratic debates in the media?

In Kenya, the popular opposition leader Raila Odinga was defeated in the 2017 elections, which were marred by irregularities and eventually nullified by the Kenyan Supreme Court. He withdrew from the second election, and violent clashes erupted between his supporters and the police, sparking fears of a repeat of previous bloody ethnic postelection conflicts (Moore 2017;2018; Wadekar 2018). His supporters then arranged an alternative "inauguration" ceremony for Odinga in the capital, but the government responded by shutting down news broadcasts, leaving only online and international channels to report on the event. Were the protests and alternative "inauguration" an

The Ethics of Engagement. Herman Wasserman, Oxford University Press (2021). © Oxford University Press.
DOI: 10.1093/oso/9780190917333.003.0001

example of the vitality of Kenyan democratic culture despite an increasingly intolerant government displaying creeping authoritarian tendencies? Does the nullification of the first election by the court demonstrate the strength of the rule of law and the separation of powers, or is it a worrying sign that Kenyan democracy is on the retreat? Does the conflict resulting from Odinga's defeat in a flawed election signal citizens' resistance against electoral corruption or a sign of sustained or increasing social and ethnic polarization, often mirrored in the country's ethnically aligned media?

These examples show how transitions to democratic societies often result in ongoing struggles for greater recognition of identities and rights, redistribution of resources, and rebalancing of power relations. These struggles often result in conflicts, many of them violent. The world has seen an increase in such conflicts over the past decade. Although there has been a decline in conflicts between states, there has been a strong increase in internal conflicts due to terrorism, the increase in the numbers of refugees, and violent clashes between protesting citizens and their own governments such as could be seen in the much-publicized protests in Hong Kong (Voltmer 2016, 11). Growing hatred based on ethnicity, race, and religion as well as xenophobia fomented by populist politics have contributed to the growth of internal conflicts and the fragmentation of social cohesion in countries worldwide (Voltmer 2016, 11).

Paradoxically, shifts to democracy often increase the likelihood of conflict. Political and social instability is notably higher in countries characterize by so-called hybrid regimes, that is, countries emerging from authoritarianism into democracy that experience lapses back into authoritarianism or remain in a contested, unstable, and dangerous zone in between (Voltmer 2016, 11). In other words, the transition to democracy in many parts of the world has often led to an increase in conflict rather than the growth of peace, as when election contests deepen social polarizations or turn violent, or when the media promote one side over another and amplify pre-existing tensions (Voltmer 2016, 12). Conflict is often seen as a threat to these democratization processes, a negative dimension of political life and a force that threatens to disrupt negotiations or democratic deliberations. Yet conflict is also an inevitable part of life and all human relationships and cannot be avoided completely.

This book is about this phenomenon.

Despite the commonly held view that conflict is a destructive political force that can destabilize democracies, the argument in this book is that while many conflicts can become violent and destructive, they can also be managed in a way that can render them productive and communicative to democracy. African countries have certainly seen many examples of the former type of conflict, continuing from the violent conquests of the colonial era and the subsequent clashes between liberation fighters and government forces to the oppression and authoritarianism that often marked the postcolonial era. However, instead of dreaming of an ideal political environment where conflict would be entirely absent, conflict can also be accepted as an integral part of democratization processes that should be managed rather than avoided. When conflict is viewed in this way as "communicative contestations" (Voltmer 2019, 1), it becomes possible to read conflict not merely as a threat to democracy, but as a characteristic thereof. During democratization processes, political antagonists "compete for hegemony over the definition of reality" as they disagree on the way that the transition from authoritarianism to democracy should unfold and on how to evaluate the past dispensation while developing democratic norms for the future, as well as decide on who would be the best to lead the country into the new era and how to balance competing interests and identities as the new dispensation is negotiated (Voltmer 2019, 2–3). As politics become increasingly mediated, including on the African continent, the media is the terrain where these conflicts are fought out (Voltmer 2019, 3). In some ways this assumption revives long-standing questions about the relationship between media coverage and violence, but it also raises new questions such as how political debates are moving to online spaces, how journalism frames democratic change, who the participants in these debates are, and how media spaces may serve both as instigators or promotors of conflict and as facilitators of constructive dialogue, listening, and de-escalation of tensions.

Conflict, Democratization, and the Media

Broadly defined, conflict is a serious disagreement between parties whose demands cannot be met by the same resources simultaneously; it is a struggle, an antagonistic state or action, or hostility arising from incompatible goals (Frère and Wilen 2015a, 1; Meyer, Baden, and Frère 2018, 4; Wallensteen 2007, 14). Conflict does not necessarily have to be violent to be defined as such,[1] although some type of confrontation, struggle, or clash over the distribution of power is usually a dimension of conflict (Frère and Wilen 2015a, 1;

2015b, 1). Conflict is sometimes used as a means to an end, and in some cases conflict itself becomes the goal (Frère and Wilen 2015a, 2). In other words, "conflict" is a wide term that encompasses a variety of disagreements and struggles, which range from discord about political or social arrangements, policies, or processes to violent clashes that leave death, destruction, and trauma in their wake.

As we will see in greater detail in the discussion of conflict in the next chapter, some level of conflict can be considered to be an inherent part of life, a feature not only of all human relations but also of healthy democratic life. Conflict does, however, become problematic and disturbing when it involves violence, instability, and trauma. Violent conflict and war have led to unspeakable pain during the course of history but have also given rise to inspirational stories of transformation, reconciliation, and truth telling. Conflict confronts us with deeply human questions about truth, justice, forgiveness, reconciliation, and peace. These questions are asked time and again in literature across the ages. We may have experienced such conflict in our daily lives and relationships or due to tragedies that have befallen us. However, even if we are not caught up directly in violent conflict, we are today probably more aware of such conflict as a result of the increased mediatization of conflict globally. Like the troubles in Northern Ireland, African conflicts such as the genocide in Rwanda and South African apartheid, as well as their de-escalation and aftermath, were brought to the consciousness of global audiences through the new media. War and conflict occupy a significant place in the history of news media, given the important role that media plays to inform audiences about the developments of conflict, what their governments are doing about it, and what the prospects for peace might be (Obijiofor and Hanusch 2011, 131). Extensive scholarship in media studies has consequently sought to establish what the impact of media coverage might be on the escalation or resolution of war and conflict, and what the ethical orientation of media should be in times of conflict, given this impact. The genocide in Rwanda, the Iraq War, and the US intervention (Operation Restore Hope) in Somalia are some of the examples that have become iconic in scholarly debates about the media's role and influence in conflict, peacebuilding, and policymaking.

Hoskins, Richards, and Selb (2008) refer to the work of Shaw to sum up the presence of war and conflict in the collective imagination. They observe that where in the past major world conflicts would intrude into people's lives perhaps once or twice in a lifetime, there now seems to be a "continual stream of wars demanding our attention" (2008, 5). These are often marked by a lack of resolution, with the threat of danger, risk, and terror having become ubiquitous. This sense of living in a "risk society" (Beck 1992) is largely due to a climate created by the media.

Even if we are not physically close to conflict, our awareness of conflicts, however remote, makes a moral appeal on us as media consumers. How are we as media consumers meant to respond to the images of violence, destruction, and war that we see on our screens? Should we engage with social media trolls who circulate extreme speech or racist, misogynistic, or homophobic content? Should we consume media content that show us gory details of crime, war, and humiliation? How can we avoid being sucked into "filter bubbles" that confirm our own political, cultural, racial, ethnic, and gender biases?

For media practitioners, the coverage of conflict raises similar questions. When does media coverage become voyeuristic? Will coverage of conflict lead to further violence? Should journalists actively try to de-escalate violence when reporting on conflict? If so, what is the best way of trying to do that? Furthermore, when we examine conflict in relation to democratization—as we do in this book—the questions multiply to include aspects of media's role in political participation and citizenship, the mediatization of political processes such as elections, and the coverage of politics in ways that are substantive rather than merely spectacular.

These questions are all related to the negative aspects of conflict and the problems it raises for the media. However, if we accept that conflict is an inevitable part of human life and a key feature of healthy, agonistic democracies (as we will discuss in Chapter 3), then the questions about media, conflict, and democracy can also be turned around: We can ask how this relationship can become productive. How can an analysis of media, conflict, and democracy help us understand wider claims made by media about their role and place in society? Can the ethical questions raised by the mediatization of conflict tell us something about our identities and responsibilities as citizens of mediatized societies? And—especially when we consider how exceptionally vividly the relationship between media, conflict, and democracy is illustrated in transitional democracies, such as those in Africa—what can we learn about media in a globalized world undergoing rapid social, political, and technological change?

This book approaches the topic of media and conflict from the angle of democratization and transition. As Voltmer (2013, 1) points out, the collapse of authoritarian regimes and the transition to democracy have become significant global phenomena that have shaped political life around the world in the past decades. She mentions (2013, 1) the fall of the Berlin Wall as the start of a process that continued to play out for the next thirty years in places such as Tunisia, Syria, and Egypt. Similar transitions to democracy have also occurred in sub-Saharan Africa, mostly as part of a wave of democratization in the 1990s, followed by a postcolonial era that has often been marked by regressions to authoritarianism. These democratization processes have not only often been marked by conflict but also frequently regressed into new forms of authoritarianism or antidemocratic tendencies. This book focuses on these processes as they played out in the context of sub-Saharan Africa. As elsewhere, the media has played an important role in the conflicts arising from both democratization processes and their subsequent reversals in this region, although the specific ways in which it did so may differ.

If It Bleeds, It Leads?

The global media has undergone rapid development in recent decades, with the emergence of digital media and the expansion of the global media industry into a 24/7 machine with rolling deadlines and an insatiable hunger for stories that will appeal to audiences in an economically competitive environment. Regime change, protests, conflicts, and upheavals remain high on the news agenda (Voltmer 2013, 2). The cliché "If it bleeds, it leads" is familiar to media practitioners everywhere. Since conflict is a long-standing criterion for news selection and attention (a so-called news value), it is usually assumed that media will pay attention to violence and conflict, whether it occurs on an interpersonal or political level, locally or globally. This interest becomes significant and sustained in the case of international conflicts, especially wars and conflicts involving large-scale violence such as humanitarian crises or civil wars (Vladisavljević 2015, 15).

One of the first questions we should ask, therefore, is how this inherent orientation of the media toward conflict of various sorts shapes the public's world view and even constitutes publics by calling communities of interest into being. A conflict between "us" and "them" already interpellates an audience to identify with a particular position and calls a public into being. The media is therefore key to identity politics and struggles for recognition, from the racial politics of #BlackLivesMatter to the feminist agency of the #MeToo movement, from the rise of the populist right wing in the United States and

Europe in recent years to the struggles of the #Occupy movement and the student protests in South Africa and elsewhere around the world.

Media coverage can also influence how people see their place in the world and navigate their everyday lives. People get their information from the media, but it is also the place from which they derive their fears. Hoskins, Richards, and Selb (2008, 5) point out that the rapid increase in the number, range, and scope of news outlets and providers—all competing for audience attention, often by providing as much spectacle and sense of threat as possible—as well as the development of media technologies that give audiences on-demand access to such information and the ability to produce and circulate content of their own "have ushered in a new connectivity, immediacy, and, at times, intimacy to the mediation of conflict."

Media coverage is a key component of the broader public discourse in which information about conflicts is constructed, shared, and interpreted. This discursive construction of conflict takes place on at least four levels, as follows (Baden 2014, 2):

1. Establishing conceptual categories to identify objects of concern, main actors and groups, relevant acts, and imbuing these categories with value (good vs. bad, us vs. them, etc.)
2. Making evidential claims about the world, current events, and possible future developments
3. Suggesting interpretative frames to make meaning of events, ascribe responsibility or blame, and recommend courses of action
4. Constructing conflict narratives that link actors and events in a chain and justify agendas for a particular outcome or resolution of the conflict

Politics enters the consciousness of audiences through similar discursive strategies, and how political matters are constructed influences the way in which publics engage within the political sphere. The increased mediatization of politics also means that political conflict, even if nonviolent, is increasingly a part of our everyday lives. Political contests such as election campaigns, as well as protest action and civil society activism, provide a sense of spectacle. When reporting on politics, the media frequently employ a "game frame" in which politics is covered similar to sports—with an emphasis on personalities and conflicts, with less attention paid to substantive issues, policies, and strategies, and more of a focus on candidates' strategies and the likely outcomes of the election-as-race (Vladisavljević 2015, 15). The mediatization of democratization conflicts therefore raises ethical questions, not only in terms of how participants in these events are represented, but also regarding how the mediatization may influence and affect the course of such processes and events. As Voltmer (2013, 2) observes: "The fact that the whole world is watching shapes the behavior of the actors involved in the process and thus the dynamics and the eventual outcome of uprisings against authoritarian regimes."

While the reporting of democratization conflicts by mainstream media has become a central feature of these political shifts globally, participants in these processes are no longer merely passive observers of such portrayals. The development of digital media technologies has given participants in democratization conflicts—activists, politicians, and citizens—the means with which to communicate their messages, mobilize support, and orchestrate events, as well as engage with mainstream media agendas. This has changed the landscape of media and conflict in fundamental ways. Voltmer (2013, 3) remarks:

> The availability of ever more sophisticated communication technologies has expanded the repertoire of strategic choices for both democracy activists and the ruling elites, who are trying to preserve their grip on power. Activists have quickly learned how to utilize, sometimes even manipulate, the media for their own purposes. And political leaders and governments have followed suit. At the beginning of the twenty-first century, the internet and mobile communication technologies have complemented traditional channels of mass communication and are about to reconfigure the strategic arena of political change yet again. In particular, the new ways of interaction, networking and information-sharing opened up by Web 2.0 have added a fresh dynamic to the interplay between democratic change and the media.

The growth of social media platforms—such as Twitter and Facebook, and especially the messaging platform WhatsApp—in recent years has led to even further development of these communication and mobilization capabilities. There has been an increasing focus on WhatsApp's role in influencing politics and protests. This platform is now the biggest messaging app in Africa (Dahir 2018), where it is seen to have an influence on political processes (Mohammed 2015) and protest action (Jacobs and Wasserman 2018). As has been the case elsewhere in the Global South (see Udupa 2017), the platform also has a "dark side," namely that of facilitating extreme speech and unverified rumors (Muendo 2017) that often lead to violent conflicts.

Conflict therefore provides us with a lens through which to examine the media's relationship to publics, politics, and society in a globalized world. This relationship raises important ethical questions as to how the media can influence the unfolding of conflicts and their outcomes, affect the dynamics of democratization processes, and provide agency to those working for social and political change. While there are similarities in the ways that the mediatization of democratization conflicts plays out in different global settings, the specifics of different localities, histories, and societies have to form the departure point for any analysis. In the case of this book, that departure point is Africa. It should be noted, of course, that Africa is by no means monolithic, and that while certain trends can be noted in various African countries, the specificity of particular contexts should always be borne in mind when analyzing the relationship between media, conflict, and democratization. Moreover, this book focuses only on Anglophone Africa, with a more specific focus on East and Southern Africa. This focus should not be misread as an intention that the specific countries are stand-ins for the whole continent. For media and conflicts in Francophone Central Africa, Marie-Soleil Frère's work (e.g., Frère 2007) remains a standard point of reference.

Africa as a Perspective

As Africa has been one of the major areas in the world where post–Cold War conflicts have taken place (Thussu and Freedman 2003, 1), it makes the continent an appropriate geographic point of focus for an investigation into media and conflict. The growth of multiparty democracy on the continent provides further opportunities to consider the links between media, conflict, and democratization in ways that could have broader relevance for transitional societies elsewhere.[2]

Furthermore, the fact that the widespread democratization processes in Africa happened alongside the liberalization and growth of the media on the continent provides us with ample opportunity to analyze the links between media and democracy, as do the subsequent regression and setbacks suffered by both democracy and media freedom on the continent, which have often resulted in renewed and ongoing conflicts. Several African countries have backslided into authoritarianism after their earlier transitions to democracy, and the mediation of conflicts has also been hampered by recurring state interference in the media, elite dominance over media discourses, and, lately, the rise of disinformation and "fake news" in Africa (Wasserman and Madrid-Morales 2019).

This ebb and flow—between democratization and media development on the one hand and democratic regression, the shrinking of media spaces, and renewed conflict on the other hand—can clearly be seen in many African countries. Focusing on this region can therefore illustrate how democratization is a multidimensional, multilinear process that cannot be adequately understood through simplistic narratives of democratization as teleology, media "effects," and technological determinism.

Although a focus on democratization, media, and conflict in Africa can be particularly productive, the aim of this book is not to provide a contribution to the study of Africa in the vein of "area studies."[3] Rather, the rapid development of a pluralized media industry and the extensive take-up of digital and mobile media technologies on the continent—coupled with the transitions and regressions of democratic culture, often giving rise to conflict—can provide us with a useful springboard into broader debates about media, conflict, and democratization as they occur globally, especially in transitional countries.

It is, however, also the case that there has been a close association between Africa and conflict in historical narratives about the continent, ranging from colonial discourses featuring tropes of Africans as violent and irrational to more recent media stereotypes that tended to paint a pessimistic picture of Africa as a hopeless, violent, and desperate place. An analysis of media, conflict, and democracy in Africa, such as this book seeks to undertake, should therefore first take care not to provide further fodder for such simplistic discourses through broad generalizations. However, it is also important to critically interrogate those same discourses, as they provide us with a vital perspective on how Africa and the Global South are located within global media narratives and scholarly discourses. A book on media, democratization, and conflict in Africa therefore also activates a variety of other issues for analysis.

The Focus of This Book

The main focus of the book is on conflicts that have arisen as a result of transitional processes in Africa, mostly involving a transition from authoritarian regimes to democratic states (although, as will be discussed again later, this process has been far from uniform or linear). In addition, the book considers the role that the media—again, a wide category that we will define in due course—has played in these transitional conflicts. Lastly, the focus is defined largely in terms of an ethical perspective: Of interest in these discussions is not in the first place the empirical details of how these conflicts have been mediatized; rather, the pertinent questions concern the normative dimension of this mediatization. In other words, the book's perspective is informed by a curiosity not only about how transitional conflicts in Africa were mediatized but also about how such conflicts could be mediatized better. Africa, while the point of focus, is not treated in isolation from global democratic processes, nor is it treated as a case study with which to illustrate theories developed elsewhere. Rather, it provides a lens through which to view ethical theories and a point of departure from which to engage global debates about media ethics, conflict, and the media's role in democracy. Because it provides such a suitable example of the nexus of these various processes, a study of the media in Africa can contribute to a better understanding of these issues globally.

The various components mentioned previously will be defined in the course of this book, starting with a more detailed explanation of the different types of conflict that usually dominate media agendas, and the different types of media involved in the mediatization of conflict, in the next chapter. Later on we will focus in greater detail on the political and ethical dimensions of mediatizing conflict.

From the outset, however, some initial thoughts on the book's various points of focus, namely the mediatization of conflict, democratization in Africa, and media ethics, may be helpful as a means of orientation.

The Mediatization of Conflict

Conflict is a key news value, and news reporting on conflict always attracts audience interest—"news is largely about conflict, and conflict is always news" (Thussu 2003, 117). There seems to have been not only an increase in

the number of "multi-layered and complex" armed conflicts globally in recent years but also a change in the ways these conflicts are communicated and
the importance of such communication (Meyer, Baden, and Frère 2018, 4).

The technological advancements of digital media have made it easier for
anyone to communicate conflict, from anywhere. News about conflicts are
now produced not only by journalists but also by citizens, bloggers, nongovernmental organizations (NGOs), diasporic communities, civil society organizations, development agencies, and other stakeholders, resulting in a more
porous and multidirectional flow of communication (Meyer, Baden, and
Frère 2018, 4; Scott et al. 2019). On the other hand, commercial pressures and
the increasingly competitive news environment have often had a detrimental
influence on the coverage of conflicts, as demands for round-the-clock live
reporting have created imbalances in terms of which conflicts can be accessed
and covered quickly. Together with cuts made by news outlets to their foreign
correspondence budgets, this has often led to superficial coverage (Hawkins
2002, 228).

Although the public discourse around conflict is made up of a variety of
actors, including NGOs, that can act as information brokers (Fröhlich and
Jungblut 2018, 86), this book focuses on the media—itself a wide category (see
discussion of definitions in Chapter 2). Despite widely held beliefs about the
media's contribution to peacebuilding, the media is often part of the problem.
Media coverage can shape the way publics think about and respond to conflict, but it can also contribute to the development of conflict (Hoxha and
Hanitzsch 2018, 46). The media is "undoubtedly the most accessible and the
most universal" source of information on political matters, and failure to perform this role adequately undermines the viability of participatory democracy (Voltmer 2013, 27). Although the media frequently claims to work in the
public interest by providing information that aids citizens' political choices
and keeps power interests to account, the media is also often viewed with mis-
trust, as its obsession with violent events is seen to serve its own cynical commercial interests. Social media, while making it possible for a greater variety of
actors to participate in the communication of conflicts, is also often criticized
for their potential to amplify social polarization and intergroup tensions.

The role of the media in communicating conflict should be seen as more
than mere "coverage" of conflicts, in the sense of reflecting events to audiences
as if it were a mirror or a neutral conduit for information. The media is a role
player in conflicts, and its presence in conflict narratives has been viewed
by different scholars as having a range of potential impacts on conflict itself.

These may range from having a direct influence on policymaking, changing the behavior and eventual outcomes of the conflict, shaping political discourses and processes, and entrenching and amplifying social and political polarizations. There have been various attempts at theorizing the impacts and influences of the media's role in conflict, including terms such as the "CNN effect," "mediatization," and the "politics–media–politics" cycle.

Democratization and the Media in Africa

Since the 1990s, the African continent has seen the widespread implementation of democratic politics marked by multiparty elections, a major feat given that most of these countries had been in the grip of authoritarian single-party regimes and violent dictatorships for decades (Frère 2011, 13). Coupled with this wave of democratization, we have witnessed the development and liberalization of African media. The former media landscape, where most media were state owned and controlled, evolved into a vibrant one marked by the rise of private and independent newspapers, private radio and television stations, and, increasingly, digital and social media, the latter facilitated by the phenomenal penetration of mobile phones. This period also saw significant advances for media freedom in sub-Saharan Africa, including the Windhoek Declaration in 1991 by African journalists calling for greater freedom. This agreement was later endorsed by UNESCO and is seen as a turning point toward greater media freedom in the region.

The diversification of the media sector across sub-Saharan Africa was accompanied by better legal and institutional frameworks in support of media freedom. The new constitutions adopted in the region in the last three decades have all enshrined some right to the freedom of expression, although many constitutions still retain subclauses that impose excessive restrictions on that right related not only to national security but also to public order, morality, insults, or other murky or vague notions that have been used to criminalize critical journalism (Wasserman and Benequista 2017, 3).

The impact of this greater freedom on political processes in sub-Saharan Africa leads Frère (2011, 13) to observe: "Not only are there more elections than ever before in Africa, but these elections are being reported and discussed in an unprecedented fashion." In these fragile contexts, the media have had the opportunity to act as either "warmongers or peace-builders" (Frère 2011, 13). As in pluralist democracies around the world, the media's role in the establishment and deepening of these political processes includes providing the public with information on parties and candidates, as well as the electoral process itself, and playing a monitorial role to ensure fairness and accountability (Frère 2011, 14).

The role of the media in democratization processes in Africa has, however, not been simple or free of problems. The positive developments relating to the media and democracy seen in Africa have undergone significant regression in recent years. Democratic institutions in the region have steadily been eroded by colluding political and economic elites in what has been referred to as a "democratic recession" (Wasserman and Benequista 2017, 4). As a result, media freedom across the region has declined. Even where the laws and treaties guaranteeing media freedom remain in place, they are increasingly being violated in practice (Wasserman and Benequista 2017, 54). The African media landscape can therefore be seen to have "mirrored the ups and downs of democratization processes" on the continent (Frère 2011, 20).

Despite greater protections for press freedom, the harassment, imprisonment, and disappearance of journalists remain a feature of the media in Africa. Media houses still suffer from deficiencies in funding, management skills, and capital, and journalists often lack proper training (Frère 2011, 20, 21). Media sustainability in the region is low, with many media outlets struggling to keep afloat, and the few big media houses frequently becoming the targets of political interference (Wasserman and Benequista 2017, 6). Media freedom on the continent also continues to be hampered by the criminalization of libel and defamation; inadequate protection for whistleblowers; threats to and intimidation of journalists; repression under the guise of antiterrorism laws; commercial competition, concentration, and conglomeration; and the use of the media to fight factional political battles regulat (Wasserman and Benequista 2017, 10). Many of these obstacles to media freedom also have an element of conflict, such as the harassment of journalists. As such, a focus on conflict also provides us with an entry point into wider questions on the media's role and position in African democracies. When considering the role of the media in democratization processes in Africa, we have to avoid overly celebratory analyses that might arise from a comparison with colonial and postcolonial authoritarian periods, when the situation was worse. Instead, the questions this book will be asking include how the media may contribute to a deepening of democracy in actual African contexts marked by pressures and constraints that may be absent from idealistic conceptions of democratization. Most analyses of media and conflict tend to focus on journalism as a professional occupation. However, the notion of journalism as a profession not only is analytically problematic, as will be discussed in more detail later, but also neglects the increasingly participatory character of journalistic practices. This book considers the mediatization of conflict in such a participatory way—not only is it more accurate not to limit the analysis of the media's role in conflicts to "professional" journalists but to include bloggers, social media users, citizens using mobile phones, and so forth as cocreators of information, but also, from an ethical point of view, such a more inclusive perspective is crucial. When the mediatization of conflict is understood as participatory and inclusive, the ethical imperatives to de-escalate conflict, engage in listening across divides, and imagine peaceful outcomes become a collaborative effort where media users cocreate alternatives instead of leaving it to a "professional" class of media creators to make ethical decisions.

Moreover, the guiding principle of cocreation and collaboration is also relevant when considering democratization in Africa in broader cultural and social terms than merely the formal political ritual of multiparty elections. While these events are important in terms of the shift from authoritarianism to multiparty democracy, they are not a sufficient measure of levels of citizen participation, deliberation, and recognition in African societies. Structural conditions continue to militate against the greater involvement of all sections of African societies in the democratic public sphere. Often, this sphere is divided, with elites having access to the media's agenda and the policymaking processes of formal politics, and the rest remaining on the margins, struggling to make their voices heard in the media or to be taken seriously by politicians outside of election times—a situation that has been typified as the "bifurcation" of the public sphere (Heller 2009). While the unmet needs and expectations of those on the margins of emerging democratic politics in Africa have often led to frustration and disappointment, the new democratic environment has also emboldened citizens to make these frustrations heard. While access to the mainstream media sphere remains difficult to negotiate for these marginal citizens, the booming digital and mobile media environment has provided them with new tools to express themselves and demand greater accountability from democratic governments. Consequently, democratization processes in Africa have often given rise to renewed tensions and conflicts, as citizens felt left out of democratic processes in between formal election periods. These frustrations frequently are expressed in the form of protests, marches, or boycotts, amplified by social media platforms. Any consideration of the ethical dilemmas attendant upon the mediatization of conflict therefore has to encompass not only formal political processes and rational debate in the Habermasian sense but also the language of outrage, frustration, and impatience. Similarly, the analysis of the relationship between media, conflict, and democratization in Africa therefore has to stretch beyond static categories of journalistic professionalism and formal political processes to include the multitude of ways in which African media users enact their citizenship in creative, dynamic, and inventive ways in everyday life.

The "ethics of engagement" this book is interested in is one that takes into its purview the variety of political practices and the wide range of mediatizations available to African media users, including but not limited to "professional" journalists. When considering ways in which the mediation of conflict can lead to constructive, peaceful, and collaborative outcomes, the ethical perspective of "listening" will be used as a guiding principle in this book, and also receive more elaborate discussion later on. Listening as an ethical stance presumes relation, interaction, and mutuality—principles that assume collectivity, collaboration, and inclusivity. This ethical approach is the appropriate one to guide democratic media practices that are open, collaborative, and attuned to difference in contexts of conflict.

Media Ethics

This book deals primarily with normative questions about how the media engages with democratization conflicts. The increased political and commercial pressures on African media, as mentioned earlier, create challenges for ethical media practices. Journalists in many African settings find it difficult to act independently while their industry is commercially weak or unsustainable, giving rise to phenomena such as the acceptance of "brown envelopes" (see Lodamo and Skjerdal 2009); others may find their reporting increasingly characterized by superficiality, scandal, and spectacle instead of the substance that audiences may need to make sense of and navigate important conflicts. As journalism becomes more oriented toward elites and lucrative audiences, the existing social and economic marginalization of poorer audiences may be exacerbated, with a negative effect on African public spheres. In turn, the political pressures on African journalists working in unfree, partly free, or nominally free environments may make it difficult for them to maintain an outspoken, independent, and critical position.

The politics of identity, race, culture, gender, and ethnicity can be amplified and exacerbated by journalists in divided African societies, leading to biased or partisan mediatization that is ethically unjustifiable. The fact that the mediatization of conflict is no longer limited to journalists but involves a wide variety of actors, as mentioned earlier, has also raised ethically complex issues. The use of social media in particular has created new types of conflicts and social polarizations, often exacerbating existing social tensions.

Apart from the practical ethical dilemmas raised in these contexts, more substantive normative questions also arise, for instance:

- Does the media have an ethical responsibility to help de-escalate conflicts?
- Should the media contribute to peacebuilding, and if so, how?
- Should the media maintain an "objective" distance from conflicts or intervene and get involved?
- How can the media encourage citizens to participate in peacebuilding and the de-escalation of conflicts?
- What should the media do to better hear and amplify citizens' voices?

These questions go to the heart of normative frameworks that provide guidelines as to what the appropriate approach to conflict should be. This book will consider these ethical issues, as well as a range of approaches that have been developed in scholarship on media ethics and media and conflict.

Global media coverage of African conflicts raises other ethical questions as well. Conflict has historically been a staple of global media's stereotypical portrayal of Africa as backward, dangerous, and uncivilized. These representations of African conflicts and politics often repeat colonial tropes that have been complicit in the subjection of Africans and undermine their human dignity. The consideration of media ethics and conflict in the African context therefore takes place against the background of colonial histories and continued unequal global power relations in the media.

Key Arguments

This book will be making three key arguments:

- The first argument is that conflict is a feature of democratizing processes and should be engaged with constructively rather than wished away. This argument assumes that conflict does not necessarily have to be devastating or destabilizing for new democracies but can be thought of differently. Conflict, when approached ethically, can contribute to a political environment where opponents engage in adversarial debate without becoming enemies intent on destroying each other. Such a view relies on the assumption that democratizing conflicts can be harnessed for constructive, positive ends and de-escalated before they turn violent or destructive. This idea will be developed in more detail when the work of Chantal Mouffe is put in dialogue with the literature from journalism studies.

- The second argument deals with the nature of democracy in Africa. When considering the case studies of democratizing conflicts that will be touched upon during the course of this book, it should become clear that democratization is not a process that is rolled out uniformly across contexts; nor are democracies delivered to countries as complete packages to implement. Democracies are made, undone, and remade through ongoing negotiations and contestations, through discursive struggles in the media, and through protests in the street and heated policy debates in Parliament. Democratization is not teleological, nor does it look the same around the world. In African contexts, the democratization process often moves in cycles of progress and relapse, forming hybrid regimes where democratic institutions and patrimonial networks may coexist.

- The third and central argument is that media ethics should be thought of in cultural terms as collaborative and dialogic. The media is a very important democratic institution, but they are not—as journalistic hyperbole often likes to claim—the sole protectors of democracy. The media is not democracy's center but are part of its coming into being, making democracy substantive and sustainable only if they manage to do in relation to and in collaboration with other citizens. This relationality of the media is the premise upon which this book builds its ethical argument. An "ethics of engagement" implies mutuality, dialogue, and listening, but it does not exclude adversarial sparring or the robust exchange of ideas; nor does it assume consensus or agreement as a prerequisite for ethical communication. It is, however, committed to nonviolence and peacebuilding: this distinction between conflict as a dialogic possibility in democracies and violent conflict aimed at destruction and exclusion of the other is crucial. The ethical orientation developed in this book is therefore based on the assumption that mediatization of conflict should be multifarious and inclusive, ensuring that a range of voices, experiences, and perspectives are being heard and are being amplified via the media. In making this argument, the book draws on cultural studies to approach media ethics from the point of view of media users and audiences. Instead of viewing media ethics as a set of codified guidelines for professionals, a user-centric, cultural approach considers media ethics to be open, contested, and dynamic. While rooted in norms such as truth, dignity, and nonviolence that exist cross-culturally, the view of media ethics taken in this book assumes that these protonorms are interpreted and applied in specific contexts. This means that deciding on the ethical response to conflict within emerging democracies in Africa will be influenced by culture, history, and sociopolitical factors. Creating an ethical space for communication during periods of democratic transition and consolidation and within situations of conflict is therefore a collaborative act that cannot be done by journalists alone but rather in conjunction with media users and audiences. What counts as truth, what democracy should look like, what is permissible in arenas of contestation, and what is out of bounds—these are all ethical decisions that should be cocreated between producers and users of media rather than imposed from up high. Journalists do, however, as a result of their occupational position, have a key role to play as interpreters of events and framers of debates. For this reason, they bear a particular ethical responsibility. This responsibility is best encapsulated by the literature about listening. In the final chapter of this book, the arguments developed will find culmination in a discussion of the ethics of listening. This ethics asks journalists to invert the power relationship between them and their publics so as to find their identity not in the first instance as "givers" of voice but as listeners, partners, and collaborators. This is a radical ethical stance that requires a rethink of the role that journalists play in democracies and during times of conflict.

Conclusion

Conflict provides us with a point of entry into a wide range of issues and debates pertaining to the media's role in democratic societies, politics, and human relationships. Narrowing the focus to conflicts emerging from media and democratization raises a further set of questions pertaining to the media's role in politics, participatory citizenship, and regional and global geopolitical relations.

The ethical considerations related to the coverage of conflict can provoke new ways of imagining journalism's current and future position in a changing media environment and an interconnected world. In a globalizing world, conflicts tend to span "national, racial, religious and ethnic boundaries," raising questions of "who is responsible for recurrent indignities and violence and what might be a responsible response to them" (Zelizer 2017, 6).

The consideration of the moral dimensions of media coverage of conflict has implications for the way we think not only about media ethics but also about the very nature of ethical questions and moral values in a global context where a multiplicity of subjectivities and normative frameworks coexist and compete. The global nature of media has brought into vision a variety of possible moral stances and has necessitated "new, less binary, more nuanced ways of envisioning the moral charter connecting the news and its multiple publics" (Zelizer 2017, 7). In this environment, conflicts can provide a useful and important lens through which to rethink media ethics in a globalized context. A reliance on professional codes of ethics is no longer sufficient to address the moral quandaries arising from the media's relationship to conflicts that cross national and cultural borders and to a changing media environment that assumes a much greater level of participation for media consumers. Furthermore, in transitional and developmental contexts, the media has the potential to play a much more active role in facilitating civic dialogue than is normally envisaged in ethical codes based on the assumption of more homogenous publics in established liberal democracies.

The way these contestations play out in Africa can provide us with a platform from which to view the ethics of media engagement with conflict in a much broader sense. This book's focus on media and democratization conflicts in Africa should therefore not be seen as a narrow preoccupation with a specific region in the way that area studies tends to do, but as a valuable entry point into global debates about the media, politics, and, especially, how we can think about these questions in a responsible, ethically committed way.

2

Characterizing Conflict, Defining the Media

Introduction

Even in African countries that have undergone formal transitions from authoritarianism to democracy, conflicts continue to flare up. Sometimes these conflicts are violent, as has been the case with the severe postelection violence on at least two occasions in Kenya (2007 and 2017). These conflicts can take the form of clashes between citizens and authorities, or between citizens themselves. They can take the form of clashes between protesters and police, for example when activists march on public buildings or blockade streets, which has become routine in South Africa, where communities have demonstrated their dissatisfaction with the slow pace of economic reform or improvement to their daily lives since the end of apartheid. Often the media have fanned these conflicts by only paying attention to them when they turn violent-prompting protesters to resort to visual spectacles such as burning or blockading in order to catch the media's eye. Social media has become another terrain where conflicts play out. Ethnic and racial tensions and polarizations are a key feature of African societies, and ethno-politics driven by populist politicians have often benefited from polarizing media discourses (Kalyango 2011, 30). As the uptake of platforms such as Twitter, Facebook, and WhatsApp has increased rapidly in African countries, these pre-existing racial and ethnic tensions have often found further expression and have circulated widely. In some cases, these digital platforms have assisted in the outing and persecution of perpetrators of hate speech (as the White South Africans Penny Sparrow and Adam Catzavelos found out when they took to social media to spew racist commentary about their Black compatriots). In other cases, the closed loop of group communication on WhatsApp, now the most popular messaging app in Africa (Dahir 2018), has enabled the spread of misinformation, hate speech, and antagonistic political

The Ethics of Engagement. Herman Wasserman, Oxford University Press (2021). © Oxford University Press.
DOI: 10.1093/oso/9780190917333.003.0002

messages in countries such as South Africa, Kenya, and Tanzania. And while the widespread democratization in African countries in the 1990s was coupled with liberalization of the legacy media of broadcasting and print media, which entailed the opening up of the media market to private ownership and the loosening of controls over freedom of expression, many governments remain hostile toward journalists and intolerant of criticism. Moves toward greater democratic accountability in the African region have frequently occurred side by side with the continuation of patrimonial networks, while new freedoms of expression have often lapsed into renewed authoritarian tendencies. As has been noted in a variety of other global settings (Hughes and Vorobyeva 2019), such hybrid regimes are often very dangerous for journalists and other media producers, as the formal commitment to freedom of speech and democratic norms on a national level is not backed up by protections on the regional or local level, and weak systems of accountability allow for corruption, intimidation, and harassment to continue and even grow.

Before we can start to explore the relationship between media, democracy, and conflict in transitional African societies and the ethical questions emerging in this regard, some key concepts need clarification. Without agreement on what we understand under "conflict," "media," and "democratization," normative discussions may take place at cross-purposes. There has also been much contestation about the normative frameworks within which ethical questions are embedded. Questions about the applicability of normative frameworks inherited from established Western democracies to African societies have been integral to debates around the media's role in postconflict and postauthoritarian African societies.

This chapter will explore some of these key concepts. The next chapters will deal with various core aspects of the media-democracy-conflict relationship in African societies. These are

- the political dimension, pertaining to issues around media and democratization (to be dealt with in Chapter 3);
- media ethics, how it relates to practice, and the debates around "professional" practice and ethical codes (to be discussed in Chapter 4); and
- various normative frameworks for guiding the media's ethical reflection and practices, and an evaluation of which of these frameworks is the most appropriate media in conflict situations arising out of democratization (the focus of Chapter 5).

Defining a Scope

When we consider the increased mediatization of conflict, both in the conventional, legacy media and on new digital and mobile media and social platforms, a number of general questions about the ethical imperatives and different types of engagement between journalists and other participants in conflict discourses arise. These include the perennial, practical questions such as whether journalists should take sides in a conflict, how to make decisions about potentially offensive or shocking content, and how to avoid reporting in ways that escalate tensions. The changing global media landscape and the particular challenges posed by democratization processes in African countries have also raised more substantial issues, such as What is the ideal role of media in African societies? How should journalists engage audiences to ensure that all voices are being heard? How can "professional" journalists best collaborate with other producers of media such as nongovernmental organization (NGOs) and government communicators to ensure pluralistic yet trustworthy and accurate information?

These questions about the media's engagement with conflict takes on a particular resonance in African contexts, where transitions to and regressions from democracy have often coincided with conflict stemming from particular colonial and postcolonial histories, ethnic identities, and socioeconomic inequalities. The African media's engagement with conflict in these situations also often has broader implications for other transitional countries where the appropriate ethical approach to reporting on conflict is also being negotiated.

The central research question of this book is therefore a normative one: How should media engage ethically with African democratization conflicts?

Before we can tackle that central question, other questions need to be clarified first:

- What do we mean by "the media"? What forms of communication will be included in and excluded from our purview?
- What do we mean by "conflict"? How is conflict defined? What types of conflict will be identified for the purposes of our analysis?
- What are the links between media and conflict? Is there a causal relationship between the mediatization of conflict and its outcomes?
- What are the links between media and democratization?

We will proceed to answer these questions as a starting point for the more in-depth discussions that are to follow in subsequent chapters.

Defining the Media

Although it is important for delineating our focus and scope, defining the contemporary media is not easy. Significant shifts have taken place since the time when formal media outlets such as newspapers, radio stations, and television stations had a monopoly over the information that reached the public sphere. While the legacy media of radio, television, and newspapers remain more dominant on the African continent and elsewhere in the Global South than is the case in the Global North, social media platforms have been thriving in Africa and play an increasingly important role in journalism (Paterson 2013, 1). In fact, the rise of digital media may even strengthen the position of legacy media; for example, the position and penetration of radio in Africa have been boosted by the migration to digital platforms (see Mano 2012, 102). The rapid and wide uptake of mobile phones in Africa has been an especially important facilitator of these participatory and sharing platforms, and there has been "mounting evidence that the technology is being used, to varying degrees, by citizens to contribute to news-making and information exchange in influential ways" (Paterson 2013, 2).

Despite much optimism about the potential of social media to democratize information, encourage wider participation in political discussions, and facilitate peaceful dialogue, there have also been various African examples of the darker side of these digital media platforms. The ability of social media to provide weaker actors with more opportunities to compete with their opponents has been particularly useful in African countries where social movements resist authoritarian governments, or where grassroots organizations need to disseminate information to their constituents that does not reach mainstream media agendas. It has, however, also become evident that social media's ability to facilitate extreme speech and provide extremists with supportive virtual communities (Wolfsfeld 2018, 107) applies to African societies as well. One example of this is the divisive Twitter campaign on "white monopoly capital," driven by British public relations company Bell Pottinger using fake accounts to sow racial division in South Africa in service of a political agenda. Social media in that country has also served as a platform for racist rants that went viral (see Wasserman 2017). However, there are also cases where social media played a more positive role by enabling conflict victims to find support, facilitated the exchange of information in crisis times, and helped to contribute to peacemaking efforts by encouraging dialogue. Social media can be especially useful where legacy media fail to do so or are restricted (as in the case of the postelection violence in Kenya in 2008 [see Mäkinen and Kuira 2008]).

"Media content" is also a term that encompasses a wide range of aspects, which can include news reports, text messages, videos, and sound clips, and which can take the form of serious reportage, gossip, jokes, and rumors, all of which shape the everyday media interactions of Africans (Willems and Mano 2017).

As is the case around the world, media in Africa is increasingly produced by a range of actors, which includes professional journalists (often working under precarious political and economic conditions) but also citizens on social media and NGOs that produce strategic communication material and news content that are taken up in public discourses in and about conflict settings (Fröhlich and Jungblut 2018, 86). NGOs have become increasingly visible in media discourses on conflict. They have an especially important influence on foreign policy, public perceptions, and political agendas because of their credibility and networks of contacts that provide trusted information, and because global media outlets cannot afford permanent foreign correspondents anymore (Herrero-Jiménez et al. 2018, 68; Meyer, Sangar, and Michaels 2018, 149, 152).

Given this wide range of media products and media producers that shape discourses on conflict in Africa, a too narrow definition of "media" would not be useful for our discussion of democratization conflicts on the continent. Since this book is not aimed at providing an empirical analysis of particular media formats, but rather an exploration of the normative issues underlying such discourses, it opts for an inclusive definition of media. However, the orientation is toward media that contribute to journalism as defined by Krüger (2017, 24), namely "the social practice whereby information and ideas of civic importance are gathered, processed and distributed on a range of media platforms." Journalism has historically been the principal conveyor of news, information, and interpretation of conflicts (Cottle 2006, 3). For this reason, a too rigid distinction (such as the one Krüger goes on to make) between "journalism" and forms of expression classified as "entertainment" or "advertising" is not helpful, given that entertainment and advertising also have public, political, and social implications of civic importance,

while journalism also often seeks to entertain. Avoiding a too narrow definition of "media" and "mediatization" allows for ethical issues to emerge from
the "messy," loose web of discourse taking place across the various sites of
civic interaction in African societies (Krüger 2017, 27). This distinction between formal *media spaces* and more general, and also informal, *mediatized*
spaces is becoming more and more difficult to uphold in the current context, where the range of platforms and participants in mediatized discourse
is wider than ever before. Social media, for instance, are seen to have an increasingly important influence on political agendas, foreign policymaking,
and political communication, including in Africa, even if not all exchanges
on platforms such as Twitter, Facebook, and WhatsApp would necessarily be
classified as "journalism" (Herrero-Jiménez et al. 2018, 69).

The debate regarding what defines "citizen journalism" and who qualifies
as a "journalist" is one that has been raging for years, as the change in the
media environment has called for a reconceptualization of the notion of a
journalist on practical, ethical, and legal grounds (see, e.g., Knight, George,
and Gerlis 2008; Singer 2006; Ugland and Henderson 2007). This debate is
too wide to go into here, especially since our primary aim is not to delimit
the boundaries of what counts as "journalism," but to widen them—at least
to the extent that such a definition is manageable. Even where social media
primarily serve an entertainment or socializing rather than information-
providing function, they can still shape discourses on conflict and democracy in important ways. This is especially true in the African context, where
the formal media landscape is often restricted due to political or economic
reasons. In these circumstances, it could even be argued that social media are
vital in performing the work of democratic political communication, even
in the form of satire, jokes, and rumor (for Zimbabwean examples, see Mare
2016; Willems 2011).

For this reason, this book mostly uses the broader term "media" and
"mediatization" to include this broad range of practices. Even though the
focus does fall mostly on journalism and news media, these terms are broadly
conceived, in recognition of the fact that the boundaries of "journalism"
have become porous.[1] Today, journalism "reflects many contradictory sets
of people, dimensions, practices and functions" and should not be reduced
to only one variant of journalism, namely "hard news in conventional legacy
establishments" (Zelizer 2017, 12).

Why this emphasis on the definition of journalism, who counts as a journalist, and the importance of including a variety of media practices in our

analysis of the mediatization of democratization conflicts in Africa? Because, as indicated in the first chapter, the idea of cocreation and collaboration is a guiding principle in this book's exploration of the ethical dimensions of media engagement in democratization conflicts. Not only is democracy seen as a collaborative effort involving all citizens, but also "truth" about conflicts, the interpretation of conflict events and their significance, the space where mediatization takes place, and the arenas where democratic values are being contested and negotiated are understood to be collaboratively and mutually constructed. These assumptions will eventually lead us to consider ways in which media ethics itself can come into being as a co-constructed, open project where listening and reciprocity are the foundational principles.

Ethics and Evil

Conflict is part of the human condition. Not all conflict is destructive, however, and some degree of conflict may even be productive—disagreement and dispute, for instance, as we will see later, can be considered an inherent part of democracy. However, conflict can also escalate to disastrous proportions, causing pain, death, and destruction. The inhumane treatment of fellow humans has been a part of history throughout the ages. When we allow ourselves to consider the fear of Jewish prisoners arriving on the train to Dachau, the screams of women being raped in Nanjing, the sight of the bodies of Tutsi children floating down the Kagera River in Rwanda, or the sound of gunfire outside the police station in Sharpeville, we may despair at what we could think of as evil: the destruction of people's inherent human dignity, collective humiliation, and death (Hamelink 2016, 1–2). However, if evil seems to be an inherent part of humanity, so does, fortunately, human beings' ability to reflect on the ethics of their actions: "The human species is locked into recurring waves of gross immoral conduct and refined moral reflection" (Hamelink 2016, 138).

One of the guiding themes in this book is that, while conflict is inevitable, it is transformable. To expect that human relationships could function without conflict would be a "fallacious utopian construct" (Hamelink 2016, 139). While conflict in the affairs of humans may be inevitable, the cultivation of a moral sensibility about how to respond to conflict is a realizable ideal. The focus should therefore not be on the avoidance of conflict, but on how conflict can be de-escalated and reshaped into a productive, democratizing force.

Escalation and de-escalation are broad concepts, but the de-escalation of conflict can be seen as a reduction in the intensity of the conflict behavior, a decrease in the level of stress, a decrease in the number of parties involved in the conflict, or the move toward a settlement of the conflict through mediation, bargaining, negotiation, and other similar activities (Frère and Wilen 2015d). Another way of thinking about de-escalation is changing the character of conflict from a destructive to a productive force. This could be made possible by redefining participants in a conflict as "adversaries" rather than "enemies," for instance. This distinction, which can shift discourse in the media from polarization to critical dialogue and listening, will be discussed in more depth in the next chapter, with reference to the work of Mouffe (2005).

Instead of trying to avoid conflict or thinking about conflict "resolution"— instead of assuming that the situation can be reversed to what it was before, or that there can be a winner and a loser—it may therefore make better sense to think about conflict "transformation." In this way, conflicts can be turned into opportunities for better understanding, connection, and relationship (B. Brown 2017, 79, 82).

What remains important for the discussion of conflict in this book, focused as it is on questions of democratization and transition in Africa, is that conflicts go through different stages and, depending on how they are constructed, are categorized under different "policy paradigms," such as prevention, crisis management, peacemaking/peacekeeping, conflict resolution, and reconciliation (Meyer, Baden, and Frère 2018, 10). The media's role in these various stages may differ, and therefore the emphasis on ethical values may fall differently. In some cases a monitorial, watchdog role may be most important, for instance, to ensure that governments remain accountable to citizens in wartime or that elections are transparent and fair in order to prevent conflict from erupting if the results are disputed. In other cases, a more appropriate ethical role for the media may be that of listener and facilitator, for instance, to enable conflicting parties to engage in dialogue or to amplify the voices of the poor and the marginalized when they protest against exclusionary policies. In some instances, however, even attempts at applying certain ethical notions such as "objectivity" or "independence" may be out of place.

We will return to different ethical frameworks for dealing with conflict in Chapter 5. At this point of our conceptual exploration of different types of conflict, it is important to take care to distinguish between different types of conflict, as these different conflicts may require different ethical responses from the media. Only once we have a clearer view of how we define conflict and how to evaluate it will we be able to arrive at a more nuanced consideration of possible ethical responses to it.

Conflict Phases and Types

Various types of conflict can be identified in the literature, and therefore it is not easy to prescribe a simple, uniform ethical response on the part of the media's role in relation to these conflicts. Conflicts are embedded in social constructions—they "are made sense of discursively and culturally" (Cottle 2006, 5). Conflicts can differ in duration and scope. Some conflicts flare up intensely; others simmer for many years, across generations. Some are interpersonal, some localized, and others take on a global and geopolitical dimension (Cottle 2006, 5).

The different phases that conflicts go through have been described as a curve, starting with the absence of conflict, moving on to latent turmoil, and then visible turmoil in the form of an open dispute. This can then escalate into a crisis, which in itself can be characterized by different levels of violence, before it reaches a stalemate stage, at which point a de-escalation phase may commence (Frère and Wilen 2015c). These phases do not, however, always follow each other in a linear trajectory. Some phases may be repeated, some may last longer than others, and at some point the process may not be moving along at all (Frère and Wilen 2015c).

Noting different phases may be useful in deciding which type of intervention efforts would be most appropriate, and how the media may best respond to a conflict at particular stages of its development. A recurring criticism of the media's response to conflict is that it only becomes aware of or interested in a conflict when it reaches a manifest stage of dispute or full-blown crisis. As a result, some alternative normative frameworks have been suggested to guide media toward a longer and deeper engagement with conflict (to be discussed in Chapter 5).

The literature on conflict identifies a range of different types of conflict that feature in the media (see, e.g., Cottle 2006; Hamelink 2016; Thussu and Freedman 2003):

- Extreme speech/hate speech
- Xenophobia, racism, identity conflicts, and struggles for symbolic recognition

- Violent suppression of protest and activism
- Resource conflicts
- War, military conflict, and terrorism

Although these conflicts may not always have to do with transitions from authoritarianism to democracy, they can manifest in such transitional situations and then be considered democratization conflicts. In other words, democratization conflicts can manifest in different forms and with various levels of intensity.

Extreme Speech/Hate Speech

Speech acts that cause hurt, antagonize, or marginalize people based on their identification with particular groups can be defined as hate speech (Elliott et al. 2016, 2) and can be seen as examples of conflict in and of themselves or can cause the escalation of conflict.

The term "extreme speech" (Pohjonen and Udupa 2017, 1174) is preferred by scholars who emphasize the contextual situatedness of speech and how it is used. The complexity around definitions of hate speech or extreme speech becomes especially "contentious and problematic" in contexts of democratization (Elliott et al. 2016, 2). This is because, while the social volatility in these polarized contexts makes some sort of provision for harmful speech necessary, the importance of freedom of expression in transitional, postauthoritarian countries can also hardly be overstated, given that these countries have usually emerged from periods where such freedom had been severely curtailed. Harmful, extreme, or hate speech therefore has to be distinguished from those speech acts that can contribute to a pluralistic debate on issues of importance for the development and deepening of democracy (Elliott et al. 2016, 2)

One of the major ethical conundrums for the media in contexts of conflict, especially when the democratic rights are new and nascent, is how to balance freedom of speech with the principle of human dignity. Free speech acts— allowed in the interest of establishing and deepening a pluralistic democratic environment—are usually circumscribed by limitations aimed at preventing the eruption of violence (Elliott et al. 2016, 5). However, deciding when to allow potentially harmful or divisive speech in the interest of establishing a culture of tolerance and free speech remains difficult and highly contingent upon context.

These decisions are made all the more difficult in African contexts, given that the literature on hate speech, especially within the legal domain, is dominated by perspectives from the Global North and influenced by a history of thought and philosophy linked to Northern, liberal-democratic constructions of democracy, freedom, personal liberty, and freedom of expression. In African societies—such as South Africa, with its history of racism and deep social polarization, and Kenya, where ethnic divisions were exploited during elections, leading to violence—some suppression of freedom of expression in favor of the protection of human dignity and the safeguarding of peace may be necessary (Elliott et al. 2016, 6).

There is a growing anxiety over the role that online media may be playing in promoting extreme speech, leading to social polarization and conflict. It is perhaps not surprising that in African contexts these polarizations regularly occur around questions of identity. We will consider this wider category of conflict next.

Xenophobia, Racism, Identity Conflicts, and Struggles for Symbolic Recognition

The media has emerged as a key player in the cultural politics of recognition and respect that has been on the rise in Western societies in recent decades. In the struggles for a "difference-friendly world, where assimilation to majority or dominant cultural norms is no longer the price of equal respect" (Fraser 1999, 25), social media has emerged as a contradictory space. As digital platforms provide amplification to hate speech, bigotry, and trolling, they have also managed to set an agenda for social change by mobilizing activists and creating online communities to challenge political or social authority. There have been several recent examples of how social media, especially, can set an agenda for conversations around these issues and, eventually, contribute to social change. Recent "hashtag activism" movements in the Global North, such as #BlackLivesMatter and #MeToo, have refocused media attention on identity politics and notions of intersectionality, reminding us that the personal is still political (Sanders 2018). These campaigns have used online media narratives to frame offline protest and create networks for mobilization (Yang 2016, 13). A recent

African example of such "hashtag politics" is the student movements in South Africa to demand the "decolonization" of tertiary education, tied to broader issues of racial exclusion and social inequality (Bosch 2016; Luescher, Loader, and Mugume 2016).

The media can, however, also contribute to the continued marginalization and silencing of those positioned as "Others," portraying them as deviant from "our" norms and values and ultimately engaging in a process of symbolic annihilation (Cottle 2006, 183, 192). There is a vast literature on the media's role in conflicts, suggesting that the media has an ethnocentric bias in the coverage of conflicts. This translates into a loss of critical distance, the privileging of in-group sources above those from an out-group, and assessing the former more positively.[2] Reporting on immigration and refugees often falls into the trap of scapegoating these groups for socioeconomic problems such as crime, health problems, or housing shortages (Cottle 2006, 55), often linked to urban conflicts over scarce resources (Hamelink 2016, 103). Such xenophobia has been at the root of very violent clashes in Africa as well, which continue to flare up regularly. Populist leaders around the world often exploit these identity politics.

In Africa, colonial governments often co-opted patrimonial leadership structures and benefited from a divide-and-rule approach to political organization, thereby entrenching the power of particular communities and patronage networks (Cheeseman 2015, 14–15). The patrimonial networks thus amplified by colonialism remain widespread in the contemporary postcolonial era. Traditional forms of government, based on family loyalties or ethnic communities, are fused with modern political structures in systems of "neo-patrimonialism" (Cheeseman 2015, 14).

Violent Suppression of Protest and Activism

In general, news reporting of protests tends to emphasize spectacular events—the more violent and conflictual, the more likely they are to receive coverage—rather than provide an explanation of the causes and the possible solutions that might be reached (Cottle 2006, 38). Democratic protests therefore tend to be covered as conflicts, sometimes even as "riot porn" (Duncan 2016, 147), that emphasize criminality, foreground official sources, and present protests as unrepresentative of a broader public opinion, as "irrational" or a threat to public safety.

The media's focus on the conflictual and violent aspects of activism and protest action may direct attention away from the everyday, "slow violence" (Nixon 2011) that people experience. Ironically, it is usually this very slow, everyday structural violence that has led protesters to express their outrage in a more spectacular and sometimes violent manner. In the South African case, for instance, it has been shown that communities experience their inability to access basic services (water, sanitation, shelter, health care) and to navigate complicated legal and political systems (which alienate them) as a source of frustration and indignity (Pointer et al. 2016, 7). We will return to the example of South African democratization protests later.

Resource Conflicts

Conflicts that are frequently framed in the media as "ethnic" or "xenophobic" in character often have their roots in contestation over scarce resources, where the ethnic or racial "Other" is presented as the culprit for the lack that is being experienced.

The violent xenophobic attacks on Black immigrants from other African countries that occurred in South Africa in 2008, and which continue to flare up regularly, can also be seen as having their roots in a contest for scarce resources. Although these conflicts raised issues around nationalism and citizenship (Neocosmos 2010), they were not directed at wealthy White immigrants or middle-class African immigrants, but largely at poor African immigrants accused of competing for low-paying jobs in the context of severe poverty and inequality in the country (Dodson 2010).

A similar example can be found in the protests around basic services in the South African city of Cape Town in 2018. Residents of an informal settlement, Siqalo, which was formed when vacant private land was occupied a number of years previously, demanded that the provincial government provides electricity, water, and sanitation. The government refused, on the grounds that the land could not be used to build houses, as it is on a flood plain, and that the provincial administration could not provide services to private land (Cebulski 2018). Protesters blocked roads and damaged property, and when the protests turned violent, police fired rubber bullets and stun grenades in the area. Tensions then flared up between protesters from the informal settlement, who were largely (in apartheid nomenclature) "Black, African," and Xhosa speaking, and residents from the adjacent

"Colored" (Afrikaans- and English-speaking) township, Mitchells Plain. At public meetings, as well as on social media (especially WhatsApp messages circulating during the conflict), inflammatory racial rhetoric was used to pit residents of the formal township against those of the informal settlement. "Colored" nationalism (claiming primacy over the land) was used to denounce the "African" incomers.

The water crisis in one of Africa's major cities, Cape Town, is another, more recent, contest over resources. This situation has not yet developed into violent conflict, but it has shown how contests for resources can show the fault lines of race, class, and ethnicity in a transitional African context. This crisis, resulting from an unprecedented drought and inadequate water reserves, has come to epitomize the combination of climate change and political mismanagement (Poppick 2018). Because of its roots in both environmental changes and the dynamics of urban growth and migration, the Cape Town water crisis is likely to be a harbinger of the type of resource conflicts that may become increasingly frequent in the future, as forecast by the United Nations Development Program (UNDP; see Hamelink 2016, 112), in other parts of the continent, such as areas along the Nile, Niger, Volta, and Zambezi deltas.

The water crisis was also constructed as a threat to social stability and peace, one that might have to be controlled by the police and the military (Pijoos 2018). Although the water crisis in Cape Town has not yet resulted in violent conflicts, it has generated much media coverage, both locally and internationally, and has seen a great deal of political conflict and strong differences of opinion about who is to blame.

To these conflicts over natural resources one can add the struggles over land. While territorial conflicts are as old as time, the struggle for natural resources linked to changing climate conditions may exacerbate pre-existing conflicts over the access and use of land and bring historical inequalities and injustices relating to land into sharper relief. South African media debates in recent years about the expropriation of land without compensation (for a brief overview, see Stoddard 2018) as a way to redress historical imbalances of land ownership resulting from colonialism and apartheid have frequently taken the form of conflicts over identity, race, and belonging. Similarly, the water crisis highlighted the persisting social inequalities, linked to the country's history of racial discrimination and unfair and unequal access to land (Davids 2018). Several observers (e.g., Mathekga 2018; Roberts 2018) have pointed out that lack of access to water has been an ongoing feature of poor South Africans' daily existence despite the advent of democracy, and that media attention to "Day Zero" spoke more to the fear of suburban residents than to their own experience.

Because the struggle over resources in African societies highlights long-standing racial and ethnic divisions and socioeconomic inequalities, and because they articulate frustration and discontent with the dividends of democratization processes, resource conflicts in Africa can also be seen as democratization conflicts.

War, Military Conflict, and Terrorism

Wars are "quintessentially newsworthy," as they satisfy conventional news values such as conflict, violence, deviance, drama, and spectacle (Cottle 2006, 76). War reporting is also a good example of the symbiotic nature of media's relationship to conflict. Not only have media over the course of history brought information about wars, military conflict, and acts of terror to their publics, but also these conflicts have enabled the news media to construct a professional identity for themselves in the role of "eyewitnesses." By portraying themselves as first responders to a conflict, especially when live coverage became an increasingly central part of television broadcasts, journalism could claim a sense of importance and significance that served its orientation as a public service (Zelizer 2017, 15).

A discussion of war coverage raises several ethical issues. Apart from the perennial, yet very important, questions about how to represent violence and suffering (we will return to this question of "proper distance" in Chapter 4), war coverage also exemplifies one of the key normative roles that can be played by media in democratic societies, namely a collaborative one (Christians et al. 2009, 196). Despite their claims to independence and holding power to account, mainstream national media have been found time and again to oblige, by supporting their national governments and cooperating with them in the coverage of war (Cottle 2006, 80).

A particularly complex area of analysis pertaining to the relationship between media and armed conflict, and one that has been of rising importance in the media's coverage of African democracies, is that of terrorism.

Critics argue that, despite some attacks having occurred in African countries such as Kenya, Somalia, and Egypt, the risk of terrorism in Africa has been exaggerated to fit into a global security agenda set in Washington after the 9/11 attacks (Obi 2006, 89). The global media discourse of Islamic terror, it is argued, has often provided justification for the "securitization" of the continent and a move away from seeing the continent as primarily a recipient of development and humanitarian aid to viewing Africa as belonging to the category of risk, fear, and threat (Abrahamsen 2004). Paterson (2018) shows how US military expansion in Africa, ostensibly within the framework of "antiterrorism" efforts, has largely gone unscrutinized by the mainstream media and only came to light after investigations by online publications. The militarization of the continent, Paterson (2018) suggests, may increase as a result of US mercenaries working for China in African countries, and the Trump administration giving more power to the US military in Africa to escalate its activities without seeking permission from Washington. In addition to these efforts being underreported, the lack of media scrutiny has allowed official narratives to hold sway in terms of the framing of these activities as related to "antiterrorism" initiatives rather than expansionist efforts by the United States.

The mediatization of "terrorism" and the global response to such events not only provide us with an example of how African conflicts are implicated in global media narratives but also raise important ethical questions, to which we will return in subsequent chapters.

Democratization Conflicts

Democratization conflicts arise from disagreements not only about the character that the new democracy should take but also about the place and role of the media in the new political and social dispensation. One of the key arguments of this book, as stated in Chapter 1, is that democratization is not a uniform process across all countries and regions. As Voltmer (2013, 14) points out, although the notion of democracy has found wide resonance and appeal, the interpretation and practice thereof, as well as the way democratic transitions and deepening happen, differ depending on context. In Chapter 3, we will discuss the contestations around the nature and meaning of the concept of democracy as well as the place and role of the media in democratization.

Another key argument running through this book is that, by reflecting critically on their ethical responsibilities when reporting on democratization conflicts, the media can contribute to the harnessing of conflict in ways that can de-escalate violence, help facilitate peacebuilding efforts, or help transform these conflicts into constructive opportunities for the building of an agonistic, pluralistic democracy.

The democratization process may be preceded by a conflict—for instance, a civil war or violent repression of insurgence—that is then de-escalated and transformed into a democratic transition. However, often the conflict-ridden transition from an authoritarian system to a democratic one again brings about new types of conflict, arising from continued social (including racial and ethnic) polarization, different claims to particular outcomes of the democratization process, unequal access to resources, or the continuity of elite domination of the public sphere.

In all these situations, the mediatization of the transition and the conflict is of crucial importance. While the media often claims to make a vitally positive contribution to democratic transitions and democratic culture itself, this is not always the case. The media can also exacerbate conflicts and contribute to the widening of gaps between conflicting parties. By looking at these conflicts from the perspective of media ethics, we can consider the various normative frameworks that the media may use to guide their actions, and evaluate which of them may be most appropriate in various conflict situations in African contexts.

The Links between Media and Conflict

Media frames, agendas, and information claims can shape the cognition, attitudes, and behaviors of actors in conflicts (Meyer, Baden, and Frère 2018, 5). The media can play the role of critical observer or publicist, or be a battleground in itself where war is played out.

Historical examples of the media's role as *critical and adversarial observer* suggest that the media can play a role in forcing governments to be more transparent about military operations and be accountable to their citizens. The many examples of the media's role as a jingoistic *publicist* of its governments' military actions are, however, a reminder that the media is often quick to sacrifice its independence and collaborate with governments during times of war and conflict The observation that the media is a *contested space* where conflicts are fought and experienced by people from a distance (Thussu and Freedman 2003, 7) is evident in some of the more robust democratic spaces in Africa, where the media is in a symbiotic, cyclical relationship with politics (Wolfsfeld, Segev, and Sheafer 2013, 120).

For the media to assume such a civic or political role, the first assumption is that people would be able to access, use, and engage with it. However, access to the media is unequally distributed in African contexts. Socioeconomic inequalities and a lack of resources hamper the efforts of the poor and the marginalized to make their voices heard in a media landscape that is often dominated by and oriented toward an elite, especially during and after political transitions (Sparks 2009). This is especially evident in democratization struggles that might not take the form of an all-out war or violent clashes, but play out over the course of smaller conflicts that are not as visible in media agendas, such as protests by communities or social movement activists. Given that the cards are stacked against them, activists from marginalized communities often engage in a range of activities that could either attract the attention of the mainstream media (such as blockades, arson, and vandalism) or appropriate the means of communication in often inventive and creative ways. The "resource poor" in these contexts have therefore "become adept at deploying resonate symbols and cultural myths or performing stunning media events—'dissent events'—to attract the media spotlight" (Cottle 2006, 2). This creativity is often on display in African societies, where activists have used a range of "nanomedia," such as dancing, performance, songs, and the symbolic use of clothing, to bring their message across (Bosch, Wasserman, and Chuma 2018).

The obsession with causality—to what extent media can influence the outcome of conflicts—is not the most important question from an ethical perspective. It is understandable that this causality would be an issue on a continent where Rwanda's Radio Télévision Libre de Mille Collines broadcast incitements to the genocidal killing of Tutsis by the Hutus, similar to incitements issued in neighboring Burundi a few years before, and where, in Côte d'Ivoire in 2002, the stoking of ethnic hatred led to a civil war, or where in Kenya during the 2007–2008 elections, the media was drawn into the ethnic tensions and polarization that descended into violent conflict (Hamelink 2016, 51–52). Yet the discourse of "media complicity in political incitement" (Hamelink 2016, 45) is not sufficient to capture the range of ethical dilemmas arising from the mediatization of conflict. At stake in the first instance are not the causal consequences of the mediatization of conflict themselves, but rather the set of norms, values, and principles underpinning the mediatization of conflict. In other words, the hateful messages spread by Radio Télévision Libre de Mille Collines would have been unethical because they infringed on the dignity of fellow human beings and dehumanized them in acts of discursive violence, regardless of whether it could be proved that they directly caused the genocide or not.

In Chapters 4 and 5, these ethical issues and normative frameworks will be investigated in greater detail. In the current context of discussing the links between media and conflict, some further exploration of different theoretical approaches, and the implication they have for media ethics, may be useful.

Media, Culture, and Structure: Theoretical Approaches

How we evaluate the ethics of the media's engagement with conflict depends to a large extent on how we see the broader relationship between media, society, and democracy. How we see the media's role in conflict is therefore influenced by the theoretical lens we apply. Let us look at some of these paradigms that may influence the way we evaluate the media's ethical responsibilities during periods of democratization conflict.

The Critical Paradigm

Certain normative approaches, especially those coming from a tradition of deliberation, may create the impression that conflict is merely the result of a lack of communication or understanding, and that its resolution lies in consensus, which can be reached by means of rational deliberation in which various options and consequences for decisions are weighed up. From the perspective of critical theory, the problem with the mediatization of conflict is not so much that the deliberative process itself is flawed, but that the de-escalation of conflicts requires more than an attention to the quality of discourse. Ethical critiques of the media informed by critical theory would therefore evaluate the extent to which such reporting identifies and examines the structural conditions that underpin the disagreements and tensions in the first place and the way these or other structural conditions may determine how these conflicts are mediatized. From this perspective, conflicts have their roots in structural and material conditions, such as the allocation of scarce resources, and will not necessarily be solved by more communication. In fact, more communication may even exacerbate conflicts, as the channels for such communication (such as the media) are themselves skewed through political and economic factors to favor a particular participant or outcome

in a conflict (Magder 2003, 30). Instead, a critical approach may demand political activism aimed at achieving social change through the redistribution
or reorganization of the structural conditions that caused or exacerbated the
conflict. A critical ethics would also take into account how the economics of
media production, distribution, and consumption influence the perspectives
and frames of media reports on conflict. These political-economic factors
include asymmetries in levels of access to the media, and economic factors
impacting the ability of journalists to practice ethical journalism (for instance, the economic pressures that give rise to practices such as "brown envelope journalism" in many African countries [Skjerdal 2010]).

Attention to these structural issues would help explain why certain
conflicts are covered better than others; why dominant views, values, and
voices in conflicts tend to get more attention; and why oppositional voices
usually get marginalized—not always as a result of intentional imbalances
imposed by actors in the media sphere, but as the outcomes of market forces
and economic structures that skew coverage toward elite perspectives (Cottle
2006, 14, 15). It is this critical perspective that underpins one of the three
guiding arguments in this book, namely that media ethics in the context of
democratization should be thought of as participatory and collaborative.
Limiting media ethics to professional codes of ethics can reinforce especially
commercial media's orientation to an elite. Instead, a participatory, open, and
collaborative media ethics would prioritize the media's service to the public
interest in its broadest possible sense. This would include paying particular
attention—listening, as we will go on to explain in one of the book's other
key arguments—to the voices of the poor and the marginalized who often
do not reap the economic dividends of democratization to the same extent
as elites, and who also lack the same level of access to the media agendas and
representation.

In Kenya, for example, the corporatization and financialization of the
media have had a significant impact on journalistic practices in conflict situations, which in turn can be seen to be exacerbated by ethnic allegiances and
social polarization (Wasserman and Maweu 2014a). In South Africa, differ-
ential access to the media during community protests has resulted in skewed
reporting that favors middle-class audiences and that has led protesters to escalate the violent and destructive aspects of protests to gain media attention
(Wasserman, Bosch, and Chuma 2016, 2018). The poor are often reported on
in media debates about social and economic issues from an elite, suburban
perspective (Friedman 2011) rather than appearing as agents in their own

stories. Instead of listening to those with lived experience of poverty, academic or NGO "experts" are called upon to explain the "politics of the poor" (Pithouse 2007).

The Media Contest Paradigm

Not all citizens benefit equally from democratization processes. As we have already established, a process of "elite continuity" often results in large sections of the population remaining socially and economically marginalized and politically disconnected from the levers of power. This also includes the media. Even after democratization, which in many African countries included liberalization of the media and the loosening of the state's grip over public sector media, not everyone has equal access to media agendas and platforms. Instead of seeing these marginalized actors as powerless, attention could rather be paid to the ways in which they challenge and contest the terms of their inclusion, or their total exclusion, from mediatization processes. This *media contest paradigm* (Cottle 2006, 20) focuses on the ways in which various groups and individuals (increasingly aided by new technologies that facilitate their participation in the media sphere) compete for dominance over the media narrative. The media's orientation toward a political and economic elite has the consequence that weaker, marginalized actors have to devise ways of getting the media's attention—if they can't enter through the "front door" as authorities in the same way that elites do, weaker actors have to use the "back door" of protest, civil disobedience, or even violence (Wolfsfeld 2018, 109).

In African postauthoritarian democracies, the state and civil society actors are frequently seen to compete for control of conflict narratives. While the state may lay claim to the authoritative version of events through state media channels, citizens (often the youth who are internet savvy and know how to use digital platforms to good effect) increasingly use alternative channels to challenge these views. The Kenyan government's blackout of television stations in January 2018 to prevent them from covering an informal "inauguration" of the leader of the political opposition, Raila Odinga, as "the people's president" (BBC 2018), referred to in the first chapter, is a case in point. Many of the blocked channels continued to stream their broadcasts online and citizens used social media to disseminate their own views (Bocha 2018; Clarke and Duggan 2018). Similarly, in Burundi in 2015, the government tried to quell protests against President Pierre Nkurunziza's bid to run for a third term by banning radio stations from reporting on protests, while young people took to social media to coordinate protests and spread information outside the country's borders (Dimitrakopoulou and Boukala 2018, 126). Social media, in particular Twitter, was also used by the Burundian presidency and its spokesperson to counter protest narratives (Dimitrakopoulou and Boukala 2018, 126).

The methods used to challenge dominant media frames may be unconventional. They include what has been referred to as "nanomedia" (Pajnik and Downing 2008): small-scale media, including community radio or video, as well as popular songs, dances, street theater, graffiti, and modes of dress. In South Africa, the use of *toyi-toying* (a militant marching dance), the blockading of roads, and sit-ins can also be seen as a way for social and political actors to contest the dominant mediatization of conflicts in which they are involved (Bosch, Wasserman, and Chuma 2018; Chiumbu 2015, 3). This can be done either by using these channels to distribute alternative representations or counternarratives or by mobilizing for direct activism, for instance, protest marches. In African contexts especially, these digital technologies are often combined with other forms of communication, such as door-to-door campaigning and the distribution of pamphlets or items of clothing, to amplify messages and give activists a broader communication repertoire (Chiumbu 2015; Wasserman 2007).

The democratic role that digital media can play in African societies, however, remains limited by various social and economic restraints. Apart from social and economic hurdles to access, we can also note political restraints, such as the recurring shutdowns of the internet in African countries by governments in response to citizen protests. In recent years, these include disrupted internet services before elections in Uganda, antigovernment protests in Ethiopia, an internet blackout in Cameroon, and the shutting down of the internet after protests against the president of Togo (Dahir 2017). Shutdowns have been used several times by the government of the Democratic Republic of Congo, and here, as elsewhere, the threat of misinformation during elections has often been used as an excuse ((Marchant and Stremlau 2020, 4330). After the Zimbabwean High Court ruled in 2019 that an internet shutdown by the government in response to protests was illegal, it continued to block social media like Facebook, WhatsApp, and Twitter even after internet access was partially restored (AP 2019). Internet shutdowns in Africa take a variety of forms, and although the government is often assumed to be the main actor, non-state actors such as militant groups, hackers, foreign governments and tech companies are also sometimes responsible for shutdowns or cyber-attacks such as a distributed denial-of-service (DDoS) attack (Marchant and Stremlau 2020, 4330).

While social media therefore has the potential to provide alternative discourses to mainstream media, social media is also a contested terrain where struggles for discursive dominance can play out.

The Media Culture Paradigm

African journalists often find themselves faced with competing loyalties to contradictory communities. On the one hand, their membership of the interpretive community of journalists may demand of them distance and objectivity, while on the other hand, their national, ethnic, or cultural community demands of them solidarity (Hoxha and Hanitzsch 2018, 48; Wasserman and Maweu 2014b). The *media culture paradigm* (Cottle 2006, 25) is helpful in understanding the various social, cultural, and ethnic positions from which practitioners and users engage with the media. This cultural approach enables us to see the media's ethical role in the first place as one characterized not by certain "professional" obligations toward a public, but as a culture— a "complex web of meanings, rituals, conventions and symbol systems" (Zelizer 2017, 194).

This focus on cultural identity is of particular relevance to African conflicts, which often have their roots in colonial histories of divide-and-rule, which amplified ethnic differences and set up polarized relations to power. Recent examples of such ethnic conflicts include the clashes between the Hutus and Tutsis in Rwanda and the postconflict violence in Kenya in 2007–2008, in which political tensions between the supporters of the two presidential candidates became articulated in tensions between Luo, Kalenjin, and Gikuyu. However, to avoid falling into the trap of essentializing ethnic differences in Africa and thereby repeating colonial tropes of "tribalism," it should be emphasized that these ethnic conflicts are usually based on material issues such as land inequality and regional imbalances rather than on identity per se (Nyambura 2017).

The media has been seen to play a role both in fomenting these identity conflicts and in providing ways out of them. It has often been the case that political elites "hijack news media to manipulate public opinion and mobilize one ethnic group against another" (Zenebe 2012, 8). While the availability of affordable media technologies, such as SMS tools, has made it easier for extreme speech to circulate faster and wider, these new digital platforms have also been used to appeal for peace and the transcendence of ethnic identities. This was the case in Kenya, where SMS messages implored Kenyans to declare "I Have No Tribe . . . I am Kenyan" (Barber 2017, 145). When considering the role of digital media, especially social media, in relation to identity conflicts, it is therefore important not to lapse into technological determinism, but to consider the use of these platforms from a cultural perspective—in other words, how users actively engage with them, how the platforms amplify pre-existing dynamics in a given society, and how they feature in people's everyday lives.

Such pre-existing dynamics in African societies also include the social inequalities and racism entrenched by the long histories of colonialism and apartheid. In this regard, South Africa continues to provide examples of how identity struggles, linked to economic and political processes and structures, are amplified in the media in general and in social media in particular.

For instance, in 2016, a White South African woman, Vicky Momberg, was the victim of a smash-and-grab robbery at a Johannesburg shopping center. When Black police officers appeared on the scene, she started insulting them. She refused help from Black police officers and emergency line operators. She was filmed by a bystander on a mobile phone as she reportedly used the "k-word"—one of the hate speech slurs in the country—forty-eight times. This video clip went viral on social media, and two years later Momberg was sentenced to an effective two years in prison for *crimen injuria* (Swailes and Adebayo 2018). This is not the first time that social media was used to record racial abuse in South Africa, although it is the first time that someone was jailed for crimen injuria alone (defined as a willful attack on someone's dignity). In another widely circulated case just the year before, two White South African men were filmed as they forced a Black farmworker into a coffin and then threatened to set it on fire (Smith-Spark and Polglase 2017). That case, which ended in a conviction of attempted murder, also resulted from a viral circulation of the recording, which received its own hashtag, #CoffinAssault (Smith-Spark and Polglase 2017).

A slightly different case that has attained notoriety for the way social media can provide a platform for the circulation of racist speech was that of the South African estate agent Penny Sparrow, who posted a racist rant on Facebook in 2016, in which she compared Black people to monkeys. This post also circulated widely on other social media platforms such as Twitter. As soon as Sparrow's post went viral, there was swift condemnation by the public and political parties. Sparrow's membership of the opposition party the Democratic Alliance (DA) was suspended, and the party laid charges against her. Sparrow was found guilty of hate speech and fined in the Equality Court (where, as pointed out earlier in this chapter in the discussion of hate speech versus extreme speech, the definition extends to speech infringing on people's dignity and not the narrower definition of incitement to violence). She was later convicted on a criminal charge of crimen injuria, for which she also received a fine (Etheridge 2016).

Yet another case in which South African social media served as a platform for racial conflict was the "white monopoly capital" trope that circulated on Twitter in 2016–2017.[3] While the cases discussed previously emerged from an initial individual transgression, this conflict was linked to broader political events in South Africa relating to Jacob Zuma, the president at the time. Zuma, who resigned in response to mounting pressure in 2018, was then mired in ongoing allegations of corruption and "state capture"—a term referring to undue influence wielded by a family, the Guptas, over the president and senior politicians. The allegations were substantiated in a report by the then public protector, Thuli Madonsela, and were lent further credibility by the leak of a substantial email cache outlining corrupt dealings between the Gupta family, Zuma, and his network of patronage (see Myburgh 2017). This led to a propaganda war, fought largely via social media.

It emerged that the Guptas had enlisted the services of the UK-based public relations firm Bell Pottinger to create a narrative of "white monopoly capital," with the designated Twitter hashtag #WMC, as a strategy to paint Zuma and his supporters as the victims of White racism supported by the mainstream media (Biznews 2017). In an attempt to shift the focus away from the damning allegations about "state capture," a host of fake Twitter accounts was created to counter the allegations against Zuma and the Guptas. Through painstaking analysis of Twitter activity, investigative journalists and online researchers (see Daily Maverick 2016; Findlay 2016) uncovered a community of tweeters, or a "troll army," consisting of about 150 fake accounts. These accounts were used to post thousands of tweets and retweets denouncing the public protector's findings of "state capture" and creating an alternative narrative of "white monopoly capital" as the real enemies of the state (Daily Maverick 2016). An analysis of where the tweets originated from (those that were subsequently retweeted thousands of times by the "twitterbots") seemed to point to media houses owned by the Guptas—the television channel ANN7 and the newspaper *The New Age*—working with an organization called Black Land First (BLF) led by the activist Andile Mngxitama.

Apart from creating a pro-Zuma and pro-Gupta narrative through the discourse of "white monopoly capital," a more vicious attack against journalists was also launched online. A series of badly Photoshopped, sexist images of Ferial Haffajee, editor-at-large of the South African *Huffington Post*, was tweeted, in which she was associated (and depicted in sexualized poses) with the billionaire businessman Johann Rupert to imply that she was a puppet of "white monopoly capital." These attacks were likely retributions for Haffajee's reports in the Sunday newspaper *City Press* about the behind-the-scenes orchestrations of the Gupta family that led to the removal of the previous minister of finance, Nhlanhla Nene (for an overview, see Haffajee 2017).

Another journalist who came under attack was the Tiso Blackstar editor-at-large Peter Bruce. After writing critical reports about the Guptas for the newspaper *Business Day* (for an overview, see Bruce 2017), Bruce was made the subject of stories on the website WMCLeaks.com, a site that promises to "reveal some exclusive leaks about the misdoings of the White Capitalists" and which has been traced back to a Gupta associate (Thamm and Le Roux 2017). The stories published on this website were based on surveillance of Bruce's whereabouts and accused him of infidelity, claimed he suffered from psychological problems, and divulged personal information about him and his family. He was also threatened on Twitter by Mngxitama that he was "going to get a heart attack" (Bruce 2017). These online threats spilled over into offline attacks when Bruce and Tim Cohen, the editor of *Business Day*, the publication Bruce writes for, were assaulted outside his home by members of the BLF movement (Goba 2017).

Eventually, however, a strong counternarrative to the "white monopoly capital" Twitter trope emerged both on social media and in the mainstream media. The professional journalists' body, the South African National Editors' Forum (SANEF), obtained an interdict against Mngxitama and BLF, preventing them from intimidating journalists. The leak of a large trove of emails, the so-called Guptaleaks (2018), led to a major collaborative investigative journalism project (see http://www.gupta-leaks.com/) that not only uncovered evidence of the extent of the Guptas' "state capture" but also linked Bell Pottinger to the #WMC campaign (Biznews 2017).

Bell Pottinger did not recover from the backlash from South Africans who decried a cynical attempt—and a foreign-based one at that—to expose the fault lines in a country still trying to overcome its painful past of social polarization and racial tension. Bell Pottinger collapsed under this public scrutiny and criticism and went into administration in September 2017.

In all the aforementioned cases it is rather clear that, although social media was not the platform upon which the racial conflict first took place, its rapid circulation suggests a strong resonance with the everyday lived experience of many South Africans. The widespread condemnation on social media of the extreme speech practiced by Sparrow, Momberg, and others may suggest a reaffirmation of the ethical norm of human dignity (a norm to which we will return in Chapter 4). The dominant narrative on South African social media has arguably become one of the rejection of racism and a growing intolerance of racism (including racially divisive tactics aimed at White people, as in the case of the Bell Pottinger campaign). As Msimang (2016) argues, the dominant narrative has shifted from the early transitional period in the 1990s, when such utterances might have been met with appeals for tolerance and understanding of White people's inability to manage the democratic transition, to one where social media is used as a form of reconstruction and reaffirmation of dignity and identity.

While popular discourses around social media tend to see it in terms of moral panic about its ability to spread hate speech, a cultural approach to this type of mediatized conflict would instead direct our attention to the surrounding social and cultural conditions and lived experiences, and the ways symbolic frameworks are inhabited. A cultural approach to media and conflict therefore moves away from questions of causality or determinacy of structure to focus on the dynamics of social interaction and signification.

Conclusion

From the discussion in this chapter it should now be clear that the relationship between media, conflict, and democratization is a complex one that can be approached from different angles. We considered three of these angles in this chapter—the critical perspective, the contestation perspective, and the cultural perspective. Democratization conflicts in Africa can be analyzed from any of these, or a combination of them, to understand what the major ethical questions are that come to the fore. From the different examples provided it emerged that democratization conflicts in Africa lend themselves to an analysis of all these various angles.

Now that we have considered various theoretical angles pertaining to conflict, media, and democracy; explored various ways of theorizing the interrelationship between these concepts; and considered some examples from the African context, we can move on to examine particular dimensions of this relationship in greater depth in the subsequent chapters. First in line is the political dimension, to which we turn in Chapter 3.

3.

The Dress of Democracy:
One Size Does Not Fit All

The link between media and democracy is often assumed to be a self-evident and universal truth. However, the mismatch between normative models derived from the Global North and African lived realities is evident in many examples where media have failed to keep governments to account, where the media served sectional interests, where the media's role in democratic societies has been disputed, or where norms imported from elsewhere did not adequately speak to the experiences, cultural frameworks, or social fabric of African contexts.

Although media scrutiny is generally considered as a positive influence in the democratization process, such celebration requires some qualification. An adversarial and hostile media could heighten the uncertainties and volatilities characterizing the transitional space, while the increasing centrality of mediatized political communication can also enable the rise of populism and a "delegative" rather than "representative" democratic culture (Voltmer 2013, 98–99). In many African countries, equating the popular will with presidential power is typical of the "big man politics" that dates back to the colonial system of indirect rule through chiefs (Houeland and Jacobs 2016). State control over the media in African countries can exacerbate a media-centered politics that provides support to such strongmen, although, like elsewhere (Voltmer 2013, 100), African opposition parties and activists also increasingly adopt spectacle, personalism, and media logic to challenge political power.[1]

Not only did the African media not conform to the ideal type designed elsewhere, but also democracy itself did not come ready-made to be fitted to African contexts. Hard-won democratic freedoms have been rolled back in recent years as new authoritarian tendencies reared their head. Democratic governance frequently takes a hybrid form, as neo-patrimonial networks continue to coexist with formal democratic institutions and procedures.

The Ethics of Engagement. Herman Wasserman, Oxford University Press (2021). © Oxford University Press.
DOI: 10.1093/oso/9780190917333.003.0003

The dress of democracy inherited from elsewhere does not always fit African media:

> When you buy a dress you don't buy it to hang in a wardrobe, you buy it to wear it, so you try on different dresses to see which one fits your bulk. If you're a bulky person and you go and buy a Barbie-like dress just because it is fashionable to be a Barbie, you won't have the opportunity of wearing that dress. The dress will not be relevant to your reality, because your reality is simply too large for the Barbie-like dress, no matter how appealing the dress might appear. It is a question of finding a dress which has room for expansion, a dress you could extend to accommodate the fullness of your being. (Nyamnjoh 2011, 20)

The Media and Democratic Regressions

While democratization in Africa has led to a much wider recognition of media freedom than before, the creeping return of authoritarianism has meant that these rights often exist in theory rather than practice. During these democratic regressions, governments tend to become increasingly intolerant of media criticism, leading to conflicts between the media and government and, eventually, the limitation or suspension of media freedoms. In these contexts, political information and debate often find expression through channels that might not immediately be recognized as the kind of factual news and public-oriented information that has come to occupy the top rung of the liberal-democratic normative media hierarchy.

One such context is Zimbabwe, where democratic struggles and the authoritarian repression of civil society and the media have led to long periods of conflict. The Zimbabwean crisis, which came to a head around 2000, had a detrimental effect on the country's formal democratic culture but also created opportunities for alternative forms of communication that illustrated how the media–democracy link may manifest in ways other than the dominant liberal-democratic normative model.

After gaining its independence from Britain in 1980, Zimbabwe incurred vast expenses as a result of its roll-out of pro-poor, state welfarist policies, which, coupled with the repayment of colonial-era debts, put the country in a precarious financial position (Mare 2016). After running up budget deficits and debts, Zimbabwe was forced to adopt structural economic adjustment programs in the 1990s, which led to massive unemployment, social unrest, and deindustrialization (Mare 2016). Politically, authoritarian tendencies inherited from the colonial period and the liberation struggle—an example of the "elite continuity" marking transitions to democracy, as referred to earlier—amplified the tensions ensuing from the unstable economic conditions (Mare 2016). This continuity extended to the retention of colonial-era laws intended to repress political competition, which significantly narrowed the democratic space. The wave of democratic reforms sweeping across Africa in the 1990s did have some liberalizing effect on the Zimbabwean public sphere in the sense that several civil society organizations sprung up during the period, but protests against deteriorating living conditions were met with repressive laws, which again constrained the democratic space. When the president at the time, Robert Mugabe, used state resources to pay gratuities to revolting war veterans, the economy went into a freefall, precipitating a political and economic crisis that was to last for a decade.

Many instances of violent conflict and political clashes occurred during the ensuing crisis. The crisis was characterized by violent land invasions, politically motivated violence, food shortages, economic stagnation, the breakdown of law and order, the rejection of a new constitution by opposition groups, and disputed presidential and parliamentary elections that were marred by violence, torture, and displacements (Mare 2016, 43; Ndlela 2005, 74). These conflicts can be considered democratization conflicts, as they are linked to failed attempts at instituting constitutional reforms and previously unsuccessful attempts at dealing with land reform after colonialism (Ndlela 2005, 74–75).

During this crisis, the state's control over the media grew, while the space for free political discussion, debate, and citizen participation shrunk. The state built up its monopoly over the media: its control over two major national daily newspapers and two major weeklies surpassed the circulation of the small, independent press, while the "public" broadcaster remained so in name only, as the state exerted monopoly control over the airwaves (Moyo 2007, 82). The state broadcaster was required to remove foreign news bulletins and prevented from playing protest songs (Mare 2016, 56). Laws such as the Access to Information and Protection Privacy Act and the Public Order and Security Act were passed, giving the government and its security apparatus further tools to control the public sphere and suppress dissenting reporting, comment, and analysis (Moyo 2007, 83). At the same time, the state-owned media were forced to practice "patriotic journalism" (Mare 2016, 55).

Within this restrictive environment, digital media—in particular blogs and social media platforms such as Facebook—provided an alternative public sphere for politically relevant information and commentary. When several newspapers were closed down and journalists arrested under the aforementioned legislation, journalists left the country en masse and started to run online newspapers as part of the diaspora (Moyo 2007, 84). These online news outlets served an important function, namely to critique the regime from outside the country and to provide Zimbabweans in the diaspora with an opportunity to stay informed of events in their home country, using correspondents operating from within Zimbabwe (Moyo 2007, 100). The crisis also attracted significant international media attention (Ndlela 2005).

Some of the most interesting developments occurred within the country, however, where the space for journalism remained severely restricted. Within this pressurized environment, alternative platforms and genres started to play an important role (even if they remained subject to politico-economic forces that limited their inclusivity, as Moyo [2011] has argued). As Willems (2010) has pointed out, mediatized resistance in the Zimbabwean crisis often took the form of rumor, humor, and gossip circulated orally and through mobile phone networks in the form of text messages and emails. Other forms of cultural expression, such as popular music, have also been noted to fulfill journalistic functions by communicating everyday life problems, circulating political messages—albeit often veiled—and addressing political, social, and economic issues in the repressive Zimbabwean context (Mano 2007). These popular media forms were especially constitutive of an emerging brand of Zimbabwean youth politics (Mare 2016, 53). Arguing that these forms of expression should be seen in terms of Ellis's (1989) well-known notion of "radio trottoir," or "pavement radio"—as the popular and unofficial account of political life in Africa—Willems (2010, 6) sees them as articulations of everyday resistance against state power.

The appearance in 2013 of a satirical Facebook account called "Baba Jukwa" is an example of such an alternative platform operating in the sphere of everyday life in Zimbabwe during the crisis. An anonymous cartoon character, Baba Jukwa ("father of Jukwa" in Shona), was featured on the page, where allegations of corruption and scandals involving politicians and state officials were posted. Predictions were made—often very accurate—of events about to unfold in Zimbabwean politics, leading to suspicions that the author was closely connected to the ruling ZANU-PF party (Tveit 2014). While ostensibly more humorous gossip than serious whistleblowing (Harding 2013), the anonymous and highly popular Facebook page called forth its readers in the language of politics, resistance, and citizenship, addressing its readers at the start of each post as "Great Zimbabweans" and ending with "Asijiki" (no retreat) (Mutsvairo and Sirks 2015, 331). Benefiting from the anonymity that the internet provides, the page attacked Mugabe and his government, called for political change, and warned users of alleged irregularities ahead of upcoming elections (Chibuwe and Ureke 2016, 1257). The page was updated several times a day to publish leaks that could embarrass the government, such as alleged assassination plots by the government, corrupt dealings, violence, brutality, and election rigging (Mutsvairo and Sirks 2015, 331). It cast ZANU-PF leaders in a comical and satirical light, and ran a naming and shaming campaign against corrupt officials (Mare 2016, 61). Not only did Baba Jukwa's Facebook page poke fun at officials and unmask malfeasance, but also it gave Zimbabwean citizens an opportunity to air their grievances directly with officials by providing their telephone numbers—and many Facebook users apparently availed themselves of the chance (Mutsvairo and Sirks 2015, 331). As a dialogic space, Facebook users could also use the digital platform to speak back to political power by leaving comments and voicing their opinions on the site (Chibuwe and Ureke 2016, 1257).

In a repressive environment, such political frivolity can have serious consequences: the editor of the state-controlled newspaper *Sunday Mail*, Edmund Kudzayi, and his brother Phillip were thought to be behind the Facebook account and were arrested in 2014 on charges of "attempting to commit an act of insurgency, banditry, sabotage or terrorism, undermining the authority or insulting the President and publishing or communicating false statements prejudicial to the state" (Chibuwe and Ureke 2016, 1248). The case was later dropped after the state withdrew charges due to a lack of evidence (Sibanda 2015). This response is characteristic of the Zimbabwean government's harsh response to political jokes made by citizens in public and its concern about circulating rumors (Willems 2010).

While observing the usual caveats about weak social ties on the internet and the limits of online activism, Mutsvairo and Sirks (2015) carefully concede that this Facebook account might have contributed to an increased level of political participation in Zimbabwe. This is not so much because of any demonstrable democratizing effect it might have had on political processes, but rather the fact that the page became a popular topic of political conversation in an otherwise highly restrictive environment.

The digital space in Zimbabwe also became a place for political contestation, as a similar figure, Amai Jukwa, appeared on Facebook. This character, however, supported ZANU-PF and seemed to serve as a counter to Baba Jukwa's allegations (Chibuwe and Ureke 2016, 1248). While Baba Jukwa could be seen to provide a counterhegemonic voice through alternative platforms and popular formats, Amai Jukwa illustrated the ways in which these new platforms could also be appropriated by the ruling class to perpetuate hegemonic narratives (Chibuwe and Ureke 2016, 1258).

These accounts also invigorated news reporting about Zimbabwean politics and upcoming elections. As an online phenomenon, they attracted the attention of local and international news outlets, but they also became trusted sources of political news in their own right—even more so than mainstream media (Chibuwe and Ureke 2016, 1249). Baba Jukwa's Facebook page, as well as the various other forms of popular expression that articulated the everyday lived experience of Zimbabweans during the period of political and economic crisis, can therefore be considered "hidden transcripts"—secretive discourses created by subordinated groups that provide a critique of power (Mare 2016, 85). Under conditions where conflicts between an increasingly intolerant and authoritarian government and the mainstream media were growing in frequency and intensity, the social media platform provided an alternative space for the journalistic functions of monitoring and the facilitation of debate—even if the format in which this occurred was different from the "objective" and factual reporting usually associated with the media's "watchdog" function.

The extent to which alternative media spaces articulating everyday life in Africa (and elsewhere) can provide viable public spheres has been the topic of much debate (for a discussion of African examples, see Wasserman 2007, 2011a). The point to note in the context of this chapter is that the media–democracy link may be established in unexpected and creative ways in African contexts marked by conflict and authoritarianism, even where the independence of the mainstream media is under threat and freedom of expression limited. Here, alternative forms of communication, not only online but also in everyday life, fulfill the function of skeptical or critical laughter that serves as a tool for the oppressed to undermine the authority of official discourses in the course of their everyday lives (Willems 2010, 11).

The Zimbabwean example illustrates the complexity of the media–democracy link in African contexts of conflict, democratization, and democratic regression. The dominant literature about media and democracy, derived from a study of established democracies in the Global North, sees a free media environment as a prerequisite for democratic debate and civic participation. Repressive environments, such as Zimbabwe during the periods of crisis, pose severe threats and dangers to journalists and critical citizens and should therefore not be romanticized. However, the examples of alternative forms of expression and channels for the circulation of political communication referred to previously illustrate how critical media fulfilling a democratic function in the public interest can, first, still be produced under nondemocratic circumstances and, second, take unexpected forms—produced on nonmainstream platforms and in genres that are not usually associated with the "serious" function of news production, but which reflect everyday lived experience. These examples confirm the point made by Hanitzsch and Vos (2016, 157) in their study of comparative journalism models globally, namely that journalism outside the Global North manifests in a wider repertoire of functions than the narrow form of political reporting often privileged in Northern scholarship of the media–democracy link, and that "everyday life is not devoid of political significance."

The previous case study of Zimbabwe illustrated how dominant understandings of the media–democracy link within a liberal-pluralist paradigm are too narrow to explain or prescribe the role of media in articulating the everyday lived experiences of Africans in authoritarian contexts.

Media's Democratic Failures

Where the dominant understanding of the link between media and democracy presumes a democratic environment as the necessary condition for media to facilitate public debate, the Zimbabwean example shows how alternative media spaces can still facilitate democratic debate under authoritarian conditions.

There are also examples of the inverse—where media freedom is not a sufficient guarantee that the media will perform its democratic functions adequately during times of conflict.

In this type of relationship, the media is provided with constitutional guarantees of freedom, but for various reasons—including historical and structural reasons—it fails, at least in some respects, to fulfill the full mandate of public service that it claims to perform in its stated normative framework.

The postapartheid South African media provides an example of this type of relationship between media and democracy. Freedom of expression, including freedom of the media, is guaranteed in the South African Constitution, and the country boasts a vibrant and robust media industry. The media have used these freedoms very well to keep political power to account, especially through investigative journalism of corruption, government malfeasance, and "state capture" by high-placed political players, including the former president, Jacob Zuma. In playing this "vertical" role of ensuring government accountability to its citizens, the South African media has played an important role of consolidating democracy in the postapartheid era. On the "horizontal" level of the deepening of democracy by facilitating greater engagement, solidarity, and cohesion across the vast social inequalities persisting in postapartheid society, however, the South African media has been less successful. The ongoing occurrence of community protests on a daily basis, despite the existence of a free, independent, and vibrant media sector, suggests that for many communities in the postapartheid context, the media is not as providing an adequate channel to voice their concerns. These communities have to resort to spectacular forms of protest to get the media's attention, in an attempt to have their grievances reach the ears of policymakers. The media's disproportionate attention to social elites compared to the majority poor suggests that formal democratic freedoms are not enough to guarantee that the media will necessarily contribute to the deepening of democracy in a substantial way that benefits all sections of the public equally. As Heller (2009) also suggests, the public sphere in South Africa is bifurcated between those who possess the means and opportunities to make their voices heard in the public sphere and know how to avail themselves of these opportunities and those whose best chance of being heard and making an impact on policymaking is by means of protest and activism. This recourse to protest as a communicative act was expressed as follows by a participant in a community protest in the township Ennerdale, in the Gauteng province, in 2017: "When voting is over, we don't exist anymore. . . . We have been protesting for the past four years, asking, making the same pleas. . . . How long are we supposed to plead? How long are they going to come here and take us for a ride? We don't love doing what we're doing" (EWN 2017).

If, according to dominant liberal-democratic theory, the link between media and democracy means that the media is an indispensable pillar of democratic debate and deliberation, and a conduit for citizens to keep government to account, why would it be necessary for protesters to resort to burning and barricading? The link between democracy—conceived of as substantive conditions that enable citizen engagement and participation in the public sphere rather than only procedural aspects such as the holding of elections—and the media is therefore not a given when media is granted freedom and independence.

An example that illustrates the problematic nature of this link is the way that the South African media responded to the massacre of mineworkers at Marikana on August 16, 2012.[2] The killing of thirty-six striking mineworkers by police at the Lonmin mine at Marikana in the North West province has been called the "bleakest moment since the end of apartheid" (Plaut 2012). Although the scope of this massacre was unprecedented in the democratic era, it was neither the first nor the last time that the state responded violently to citizen protests. During a social delivery protest in Ficksburg the previous year, Andries Tatane was beaten and shot dead by police (De Waal 2011). In 2013, four people were killed (three of them shot) in clashes between police and citizens protesting against the nonprovision of water in Mothutlung township near Brits (City Press 2014a), and a few days later, police shot and killed a man in a housing protest in Roodepoort (City Press 2014b).

In the case of Marikana, the media's privileging of rationality in the political process and the exclusion or devaluation of other modes of expression by citizens could be seen from the outset in the initial representation and dominant framings of the conflict. The footage that the world first saw of the shooting of the striking miners at Marikana was filmed literally from behind the backs of firing policemen (see the footage captured and discussed in City Press, 2012). This alignment of journalists with positions of authority when covering conflict is not unusual, but it has implications for the way the media's democratic role is conceived.

Subsequent to the shooting, academic researchers (Alexander et al. 2012) found that there was, in all likelihood, more than one site where the killing took place, and that the killing was more extensive in geographical terms than had been reported in the media up until that point. An investigation by an independent photojournalist, Greg Marinovich, confirmed these findings. Marinovich (2012) reported that "the majority of those who died . . . were killed beyond the view of cameras." Some were shot at close range or run over by police vehicles. Initially, these revelations were either scoffed at or ignored by mainstream journalists (see, e.g., Quintal 2012).

In his research, Alexander (in De Waal 2012) found that journalists paid scant attention to alternative accounts of the events and did not speak to any of the workers, focusing instead on the versions provided by mainstream sources such as politicians, police, or union leaders. Hardly any accounts of the events were sourced from people who were present at the massacre. The dominant perspectives amplified by the media were those belonging to figures of authority: police, politicians, business. Workers were used as sources for information in only 3% of the stories (Duncan 2012).

In subsequent analyses of the events at Marikana, an explanation for the motivation behind the mineworkers' defiant stance was often sought in the irrational use of "muti" (traditional medicine) by mineworkers to render them invincible, instead of an exploration of the frustrations and desperation arising from the lived conditions of these mineworkers. In media reports, the "irrational" beliefs of the mineworkers were contrasted with the official discourses of jurisprudence and medical science (see, e.g., Ledwaba 2013; Maromo 2013). Media photographs repeatedly depicted the colonial tropes of a blood-hungry horde of Black men with assegais and homemade weapons, while the voices of reason belonged to officialdom (which included the Farlam Commission's subsequent inquiry into the event; see, e.g., Times Live 2013).

The skewing of coverage in the favor of elites stems from a particular application of the monitorial approach that, while claiming to keep power to account, in fact privileges rational debate emanating from official "authoritative" sources while ignoring or neglecting the viewpoints of those who are excluded from the dominant discourse. This favoring of official perspectives illustrates one of the problems Berger (2002) identifies in the application of Western notions of "civil society" to the media in African democracies. Too often the private media are seen as part of civil society, serving as a positive counterbalance to the state, which is cast in negative terms. This, according to Berger (2002, 26, 38), not only romanticizes civil society but also underplays the problematic aspects of the private media, its orientation toward elites, the increased risk of unethical behavior as a result of commercial pressures, and the dangers of rolling back the powers of the state to such an extent that it becomes too weak to secure the safety and well-being of citizens. The media's alignment with authority during the Marikana massacre highlights the failures that such an elite orientation may lead to.

In the years after the Marikana massacre, the narrative about this important event in postapartheid South African democracy shifted toward a broader recognition of the culpability of the mining company and the police. Remaining in the "watchdog" mode of keeping government to account, the news media continued to raise questions about whether Cyril Ramaphosa, who would later succeed Jacob Zuma as president of the country, should be held accountable for his role in the events that led to the massacre.[3] Other forms of media, such as documentary films (*Miners Shot Down* by Rehad Desai and *Strike a Rock* by Aliki Saragas are especially notable), explored the views of the mineworkers and their families in greater depth and with more sympathy.

The mediatization of the Marikana massacre is a useful example to illustrate the fact that the link between media and democracy is not always self-evident if the media's role is seen as consisting of more than monitoring procedural aspects of democracy. Democratization conflicts arise not only around formal procedures such as elections but also as a result of the continued exclusions and marginalizations that mark transitional or "new" democracies. The entrenchment of media freedom and the existence or development of a vibrant media industry may not be enough to ensure that the media succeed in deepening democracy in such a way that social change is brought about or that democratic participation is broadened. The liberal-democratic emphasis on the media's monitorial role over government is often a too narrow normative guideline to ensure that other institutions of power (e.g., corporations such as Lonmin) are held accountable, or that democratic debate is broadened or deepened beyond formalistic procedures or "rational" deliberation. When understood in this broader sense, the media-democracy link can also be weak even in contexts where media freedom is guaranteed.

For the media to facilitate the participation of citizens in democratic life in the fullest sense, especially during times of conflict, the rational Habermasian mode of debate should not be the only one engaged in. Other forms of political expression that seem emotional and "unreasonable"—such as miners walking toward their death to demand a living wage—should also be taken seriously. Bickford (2011, 1026) calls on us to "think differently about what democratic political communication in a conflictual and inegalitarian context might require" and argues that "emotion and partisan thinking" should be considered "morally appropriate elements of democratic communication." Among such emotional responses may be anger (Bickford 2011, 1030), which is often dismissed as unreasonable and therefore inadmissible in political discourse as facilitated by the media.

The appeal to broaden the criteria of what may be considered appropriate contributions to political communication has as its aim not only to enrich mediatized understanding of citizenship and democracy but also to rewrite the very discursive rules upon which political communication in the public sphere takes place: "Community activists . . . are not simply trying to get a specific point heard; they are defending, or trying to legitimate, a mode of expressing and perceiving value" (Bickford 2011, 1031).

These clashes can be considered democratization conflicts, as they relate to the ongoing contestations around what the dividends of democracy should be for citizens and communities in a context of persisting and severe socioeconomic inequality. By protesting for a living wage, community activists (and, in the case of Marikana, striking mineworkers) were giving content to what the right to human dignity, as contained in the Constitution's Bill of Rights (Republic of South Africa 1996), means in substantive terms for the poor. They could also lay claim to the democratic right to peaceful assembly and demonstration, as enshrined in the Constitution.

At stake, therefore, is the distinction between the formal democratic rights that citizens bear as members of a formal constitutional democracy and their ability to practice those rights in practical terms in their everyday lives (Heller 2009, 134). The ongoing protests in South Africa—of which Marikana is one, even though it was in the first instance aimed at the forces of capital rather than against local government—and the state's crushing of such forms of dissent occur in this chasm between citizens' formal rights and the opportunities available for them to practice their citizenship through input in policy formation. The protests at Marikana can be seen as an "act of citizenship" (Isin and Nielsen 2008) that highlighted this gap between the status and practice of citizenship and asserted a belief in democracy that has not yet reached its fulfillment. While the protests achieved in the first instance the intended outcome of securing a better wage agreement, it could be argued that the frustration of the mineworkers also arose from the experience of not being recognized and heard as citizens. The expression of anger in itself is therefore an act of citizenship in that it claims the democratic right to be listened to. Strikes, disruptions to business as usual, and incidents of violence or destruction of property could in this context be considered to serve as forms of communication in a desperate attempt to be heard. This suggests the importance of an ethical response to democratization conflicts that is oriented toward "listening" and receptivity on the part of journalists in ways that will affirm the dignity and voice of marginalized citizens. This proposed "ethics of listening" is one of the key arguments running through this book but will form the center of our discussion of normative frameworks in Chapter 5.

What role did the South African media see for itself during these democratization conflicts? Since democracy arrived in the country in 1994, the media's role in the new social and political environment has been vigorously contested. The conflicts that emerged between journalists, media organizations, and the government could therefore be seen as democratization conflicts in and of themselves, as they were aimed at setting the parameters for the role of the media during and after the democratic transition. The possible answers to what the ideal role of the South African media should be have mostly been limited to two contrasting normative frameworks: that of watchdog journalism in the framework of liberal democracy and that of development journalism. Public debate about the media in South Africa is still characterized by this tension between, on the one hand, a broadly collaborative and supportive position for the media in the new South African democracy and, on the other, a more critical, monitorial one (for an exposition of these positions, see Christians et al. 2009). The problem with the dominance of these two approaches in normative debates in postapartheid South Africa is that they often crystallize into a dichotomy between supporters and critics of the media and government, respectively. The result is that little room is left for alternative positions that allow for more imaginative ways to envisage the relationship between media and government while retaining the possibility of critique for both of these powerful institutions.

The consensus among mainstream media in South Africa has been to follow a liberal-democratic "watchdog" approach. There have been many instances where this watchdog role has made an important contribution to the sustainability of postapartheid democracy (e.g., in the "Guptaleaks" saga referred to in Chapter 2). However, where this monitorial role has been conceived of too narrowly as dictating an "objective" or "impartial" stance, it has, paradoxically, limited the media's ability to keep the powerful to account and to speak on behalf of a wider South African public that extends beyond the media's immediate audience or market. This is because a narrow notion of impartiality may discourage journalists from actively seeking out and listening to other voices, proposing solutions for conflicts, or advocating for a particular cause in the interest of social justice. Exceptions to this stance can be noted from time to time, when circumstances prompted the media to collaborate more with government and balance a critical, watchdog stance with a more supportive one. One such case was the drought crisis in Cape Town already referred to, where the media supported government's appeals to citizens to save water. Even while the media kept playing their watchdog role by scrutinizing official strategies and infrastructure projects, they passed on official communication from local government about water restrictions and regulations and encouraged members of the public to comply with these. Another, more recent example of where the media found a compromise between their monitorial and collaborative roles was during the Covid-19 crisis,[4] when the media not only provided daily updates on infections and deaths but also amplified government messaging about precautions and hygiene to prevent transmission of the virus while also holding the government accountable for its managing of the outbreak.

When the South African government announced a nationwide lockdown to be enforced by the military and the police, the media assisted government's efforts by communicating the regulations that would apply and explained how the lockdown would work. They continued to play their monitorial function by reporting on incidents of police or military brutality and failures in government's communication systems (e.g., when press conferences were delayed or postponed or information was unclear) or logistics, and asked critical questions about the impact of the lockdown on the economy.

These examples illustrate that the role of "watchdog" is increasingly seen by South African journalists as not wholly incompatible with a more "developmental" or collaborative role (De Beer et al. 2016). By and large, however, during the usual course of events, the South African media adopted an adversarial stance toward the postapartheid government and held an almost automatic, knee-jerk contempt for any type of journalism that could be seen as supportive of the government. When calls for more "patriotic" journalism were made (e.g., by former presidents Thabo Mbeki and Jacob Zuma), these were rightly dismissed as unhelpful attempts to promote "sunshine" journalism. The media's preference for a sustained critical stance has on many occasions been successful in holding the new democratic government to account. However, such scrutiny has not always led to concomitant action on the part of those in power to root out corruption or address governance failures. Instead of increased accountability and transparency on the part of the government, it often failed to use media scrutiny as an impetus for improvement. Worse, it often reacted with hostility and counterattacks that sought to delegitimize the media's democratic role.

Casting the media primarily as an adversary to the government has also, ironically, on occasion, had the effect of undermining its power to act as a watchdog. If the media is perceived as promoting sectional interests or neglecting the plight of marginalized citizens, its adversarial position can exacerbate existing social tensions and polarizations, undermine trust in the media, and erode its social legitimacy. This was seen in the way the South African media was accused of (in a deliberately crafted political campaign) being owned by and promoting the interests of "white monopoly capital" (as discussed in the previous chapter), thereby undermining the media's legitimacy.

As we can see from the previous discussion, the media–democracy link is not self-evident in African contexts. This is partly because we cannot assume that the democratization process itself is a homogenous process that is rolled out in the same way across different contexts, or that the process itself is a linear one. The media's role in democratization conflicts, therefore, is likely to differ according to the nature of the particular democracy itself.

Different Democracies

In a teleological view of democratization, the process is seen as starting off from authoritarianism and moving through various stages, until a mature democracy is established. In this view (summarized by Voltmer 2013, 73–74), the process starts with liberalization, when the authoritarian regime starts opening up, either gradually or abruptly. This stage may include the relaxation of state control, ownership, or censorship of the media. The next stage—often a tumultuous one marked by conflicts and contestations—is that of transition, when the demise of the old regime leads into the construction and development of new institutions. When a new constitution has been negotiated and elections held, the process of consolidation starts, in which the new institutions "put down roots" (Voltmer 2013, 75) and the democratic culture is deepened.

The arrival of a "third wave of democracy" (Huntington 1991) in Africa in the 1990s, sometimes referred to as a "second independence" (Joseph 1997, 364), brought widespread political changes, which also included the opening up of tightly controlled media. This wasn't a uniform process, however, nor did it display a simple teleological chronology, as modernization theorists would suggest.[5]

Although African societies were not as media saturated as other parts of the world going through similar democratization processes, political communication on the African continent has "leapfrogged" into a media-centered politics (Voltmer 2013, 51, 98).

As elsewhere in postauthoritarian societies around the world, the transition from authoritarianism to democracy in Africa did not follow a smooth path but often resulted in hybrid regimes, where democratic institutions and procedures combined with continued authoritarian tendencies in government (Vladisavljević 2015), neo-patrimonial networks (Stremlau and Iazzolino 2017), and a continuity of elites in powerful positions (Sparks 2009).

Various "transition trajectories" (Cheeseman 2015, 93) can therefore be noted in African states, some of which were initiated before the end of the Cold War and the "third wave." These include transitions "from above" (where the ruling party initiated reform, as in the case of Senegal and Tanzania), transitions "from below" (where ruling parties democratized because of domestic and international pressure), and "externally triggered transitions" (where donors intervened to break the stalemate in negotiations between the ruling party and the opposition and demanded elections, as occurred in Angola, the Democratic Republic of the Congo [DRC], Liberia, and Sierra Leone). External involvement in African conflicts and democratization processes, however, has its limits and often ended up adding to the complexity of conflicts or exacerbating them. In contrast, "negotiated transitions" occurred where the deadlock between the ruling party and opposition was resolved by both sides making compromises (Cheeseman 2015, 93–107). Such negotiations sometimes resulted in the "Africanization" of democratic systems by incorporating local traditions of governance and establishing systems through which clans or ethnic groups may gain political representation. These hybrid forms, originating from within local contexts, proved to be more effective than the importation of external frameworks and processes (Cheeseman 2015, 228).

The reintroduction of multiparty democracy in Africa, however, also suffered setbacks right from the start. As Cheeseman (2015, 1) points out, the return of party politics in African democracies in the 1990s coincided with the resumption of the civil war in Angola (in 1993) and the genocide in Rwanda (in 1994). Such violent episodes lead Cheeseman (2015, 143, 167) to question "the wisdom of introducing elections in deeply divided African societies," as they may exacerbate pre-existing instabilities. Voltmer

(2013, 190) echoes this sentiment by pointing to the "unsettling truth" that elections and uncensored media—both markers of liberal democracy—can "frequently deepen antagonisms, even to the point of the recurrence of physical violence, because electoral competition inevitably increases the visibility of differences and divisions."

Democratization and Conflict in Africa

Several of the transitions from authoritarianism to democracy in Africa, and the subsequent regressions from democracy, have been marked by violent conflicts. The determinants for conflict vary—weak institutions and a high level of neo-patrimonial social organization could contribute to conflict, as can unstable economic factors (Cheeseman, Collord, and Reyntjens 2018, 32).

Foreign governments remained involved in the promotion of democracy in African countries after the introduction of multiparty elections in the 1990s. Western powers set up a billion-dollar "democratization industry" (Cheeseman 2015, 115; Ottaway 1997, 5). This included directing aid toward the funding of elections, the development of democratic institutions, and the building of civil society (Cheeseman 2015, 115). The focus fell on peacebuilding efforts to end civil strife and conflict. These strategies often saw electoral politics as the hallmark of successful democracy, and peacebuilding efforts therefore often revolved around setting up and successfully running elections while monitoring the fairness of those elections (Cheeseman 2015, 117). The involvement of external players, however, also contributed to the deterioration of democracy, as Cold War antagonists backed their allies, and confrontations between different sides in African conflicts became proxy battles for global players (Joseph 1997, 364). These proxy battles hampered peacebuilding, as was the case in Angola when the United States (and South Africa) supported the UNITA rebel movement (seen as "anti-Communist"), while the Soviet bloc supported the MPLA government (Cheeseman 2015, 118). Given these broader global geopolitical interests that have played out in African democratization processes, the presence of international donors and political actors has often increased the complexity of conflicts instead of resolving them.

Ultimately, the prospects for sustainable democracy and peaceful transitions are determined by local factors rather than international facilitation (Cheeseman 2015, 119). Among these local factors influencing the end of authoritarian rule is the resistance offered by local journalists, intellectuals, lawyers, trade unionists, and activists—a resistance often met with violent repression, even if these groups frequently had to enter into compromises with governments to survive (Cheeseman 2015, 69).

It is often hoped that democratization will bring about the lessening of ethnic conflict (Z. K. Smith 2000, 22), which may temporarily increase during the liberalization period as pent-up ethnic tensions surface but subside once disputes may be resolved by functional democratic institutions (Z. K. Smith 2000, 23–24). Ethnic differences do not always lead to conflict—alliances and coalitions are often formed among ethnic groups during elections, and political candidates also rely on other campaign promises that go beyond identity politics (Cheeseman 2015, 189).

Not all conflict is inspired by ethnic tensions, however, and economic pressures exerted by external actors, such as the structural adjustment programs (SAPs) of the International Monetary Fund (IMF), have also been seen to contribute to ethnic tensions (Adekanye 1995). For this reason, it can be argued that the best way to reduce violent conflict and civil war in Africa is to institute democratic reforms that can address high levels of poverty, failed political institutions, and dependence on natural resources (Elbadawi and Sambanis, 2000).

The Positive Side of Conflict

Many of the conflicts that have marked the transition to democracy in Africa have been violent and destructive, and their detrimental and painful effects should not be underplayed or minimized. The assumption that democratization could occur without any level of conflict at all is naïve, however. Resistance to the redistribution of political power is always high (Ottaway 1997, 14), and conflict is a key feature of democracy as a political system. Democracy, therefore, is a system designed not to avoid conflicts or suppress them to create a semblance of consensus, but to manage them in nonviolent ways (Ottaway 1997, 14).

Counterintuitive as it might sound, conflict can also bring about positive changes by acting as "an agent for reform, adaptation and development" (Hamelink 2016, 12). Conflicts arising from the democratizing process could, when managed correctly, help deepen social, political, and economic relations between various stakeholders. In this sense, conflict is an integral part of democracy:

> Without conflict, societies could not be democratically organized. The essence of politics is conflict. Political practice is about the distribution and execution of power and inevitably involves opposite positions. Therefore, disagreement and tension are part of the political process. Expressing those frictions is more productive for democracy than seeking consensus, as consensus politics always tends to exclude people. (Hamelink 2016, 12)

To be sure, conflicts can pose challenges for democracy. They can threaten social stability, polarize democratic debate, undermine democratic institutions, and endanger outspoken critics of those in power. However, provided they are not violent and destructive, conflicts can also be productive:

> They [are] often the harbingers of that same democracy and they can play an essential part in revitalizing moribund "democracies" and extending and deepening democracy within civil society. It is in and through mediatized conflicts, the array of views and voices that surround them and the public spaces that they manage to secure to define and defend their claims and aims, that the state of democracy in today's societies becomes revealed and, in important respects, constituted and open to evaluation. (Cottle 2006, 3)

Such conflicts can also provide entry points to rethink the media's ethical responsibilities in a democracy. A prominent exponent of this view of democratic conflict is Chantal Mouffe (2005, 9). For Mouffe, conflict and tension are inherent features of liberal democracy. "Agonistic confrontation" between conflicting interpretations of core democratic values is therefore inevitable. Such conflicting interpretations may include different understandings of the media's ethical responsibilities, the limits to its freedom, and its role in deepening democratic culture. A central conflict in democracies in particular is the balance between individual liberties and the democratic conception of equality. Conflict in itself should therefore not be seen as exogenous to democracy and, hence, possible to eradicate entirely, but as an inherent part of democratic life. The question is: How should such conflict be dealt with for it to remain a constructive rather than a destructive force? And what role is there for the media to play in this process?

Mouffe (2005) offers a helpful distinction between two forms of antagonism that could make the difference between violent, destructive conflict and more productive and constructive forms. She distinguishes between "antagonism proper," which is between enemies who do not share a common "symbolic space," and "agonism," which "involves a relation not between enemies but 'adversaries.'" Adversaries can be defined as "'friendly enemies,' that is, persons who are friends because they share a common symbolic space but also enemies because they want to organize this common symbolic space in a different way" (Mouffe 2005, 13).

Because all agents in democratic politics are always already positioned in relations of difference, and because difference is always inscribed in power relations, a democratic society should not be romanticized as one where everyone lives together in perfect social harmony. Rather, democratic pluralism "implies the permanence of conflict and antagonism" (Mouffe 2005, 33). The acknowledgment that consensus is conceptually impossible within a pluralistic society does not jeopardize the democratic ideal, but rather the opposite: it guarantees that the democratic process, built on the acknowledgment of pluralism, difference, and contestation, is kept alive (Mouffe 2005, 33).

For conflict to attain a democratic, agonistic character, it needs to be engaged with from within an ethically reflexive, value-driven conception of politics: "Such a project recognizes that the specificity of modern pluralist democracy—even a well-ordered one—does not reside in the absence of domination and of violence but in the establishment of a set of institutions through which they can be limited and contested" (Mouffe 2005, 22). For this reason Mouffe (2005, 30) takes issue with Rawls. In her view, Rawls's idea of a well-ordered, rationally-deliberative society does not allow for struggle among adversaries about different interpretations of liberal-democratic principles. Especially missing from Rawls's rationalist conception of the political sphere is passion, power struggles, repression, and violence (Mouffe 2005, 31). Conflict is a part of politics in the real world. Even when suppressed, "(i)t does come back, and with a vengeance" (Mouffe 2005, 31).

Challenges to this conception of liberal democracy have been developed with a view to recover its moral dimension and legitimacy among disaffected publics. An example is the approach of deliberative democracy (Mouffe 2005, 83), in which the media has a central role to play in facilitating impartial and equal dialogue and citizen participation in democratic processes aimed at reaching a rational and legitimate consensus. For Mouffe, however, a "deliberative" or "communicative" model of democracy, as conceived by Rawls and Habermas, is still premised on rationality, which ignores "a central element which is the crucial role played by passions and affects in securing allegiance to democratic values" (2005, 95). The result is a view of democratic citizenship that privileges individuals and individual liberty above society, as rational subjects "abstracted from social and power relations, language, culture and the whole set of practices that make agency possible" (Mouffe 2005, 95). This allowance for outrage and emotion alongside rational deliberation is an important point to bear in mind when considering African democracies, where the repertoires of political debate often include a range of expressions and formats including dance, song, theater, jokes, satire, and street protest. These repertoires draw from a political history of anticolonial resistance, as well as from networks of orality and conviviality in African societies that resist easy incorporation into Western models of rational deliberation.

When citizens are not allowed to participate in political life in ways that acknowledge their location in communities and cultural formations, it can have potentially dangerous consequences. The rise of extremism in response to the disavowance of cultural, religious, and other identities in democratic life may lead to unproductive and destructive conflict:

> Extreme forms of individualism have become widespread which threaten the very social fabric. On the other side, deprived of the possibility of identifying with valuable conceptions of citizenship, many people are increasingly searching for other forms of collective identification, which can very often put into jeopardy the civic bond that should unite a democratic political association. The growth of various religious, moral and ethnic fundamentalisms is, in my view, the direct consequence of the democratic deficit which characterizes most liberal-democratic societies. (Mouffe 2005, 96)

Instead of deliberation, Mouffe (2005) argues, democratic practices should form the bedrock of citizenry and civic life. As I will argue in Chapter 5, for the media these democratic practices should not only include the dissemination of knowledge for "rational" decision-making but also extend to the acknowledgment of affect and identity in public discourse. A normative stance of "listening" to affective expressions, as well as an active attempt to include lesser-heard voices in media narratives, can contribute to an agonistic democratic culture that can help overcome social polarization in transitional contexts. Such a stance will not necessarily eliminate conflict—in fact, it might even increase clashes of opinion—but it could ensure that such conflicts are between "adversaries" sharing a symbolic space, rather than "enemies" competing for access to it.

The key point to take away from Mouffe's (2005) conception of democracy in the context of our current discussion of the link between media, democracy, and conflict is that conflict is not merely an unwanted by-product of democratization and transition, but will always remain central to democracy and social life in general. Mouffe goes a step further to see conflict playing a constructive, "integrative role" in modern democracy, if conflict is recognized and legitimized rather than suppressed:

> A well-functioning democracy calls for a confrontation between democratic political positions, and this requires a real debate about possible alternatives. Consensus is indeed necessary but it must be accompanied by dissent. . . . Consensus is needed on the institutions which are constitutive of democracy. But there will always be disagreement concerning the way social justice should be implemented in these institutions. In a pluralist democracy such a disagreement should be considered as legitimate and indeed welcome. (2005, 113)

A superficial insistence on social cohesion and a desire for the absence of conflict, as may be the case in some versions of communitarianism and reconciliatory politics, may exacerbate authoritarian tendencies and social conservativism. In an attempt to quell conflict and create the semblance of consensus, existing imbalances of power may be entrenched as challenges to dominance are suppressed. Only when adversarial positions are made explicit and political frontiers are made clear can power relations be reconfigured and social progress be achieved—but this will necessarily involve contestation (Mouffe 2005, 121). This is not to say that the media should stoke or amplify tensions—which can easily happen when media insist on a seemingly value-free, objective position in relation to conflict and pit two opponents against each other. Rather, as we will note in the following chapters, when the media adopts a moral stance of care and listening, it can intervene in conflicts in ways that can imagine new outcomes, overturn existing hierarchies, and amplify the agency of those contestants in the agonistic game who have historically been marginalized or whose voices have been suppressed. A media that contributes to agonistic sparring is therefore a media that listens, engages, and seeks social justice rather than one that stands on the sidelines with arms crossed while watching conflicts unfold. When the media makes tensions and disagreements explicit, it should be in order to address them more constructively instead of self-servingly using reporting of such conflicts to gain audience share.

Agonistic contestation, Mouffe (2005, 137) argues, may remain open-ended and impossible to resolve completely—instead, we should think of pluralist democracy as always in the making, always "to come." This is not considered to be a negative characteristic of agonistic democracy. The open-endedness of democratic contestation means that it remains dynamic, adaptable, and resilient. Such a conception of democracy also extends to the way citizenship is conceived of. If democratic culture is always being constructed through open-ended, agonistic engagements between citizens, it follows that citizenship itself should be an active, dynamic category rather than merely a static, formalistic one—constituted through everyday acts rather than merely enshrined in laws:

> Often it is stated that what is important about citizenship is not only that it is a legal status but that it involves practices—social, political, cultural and symbolic. In other words, formal citizenship is differentiated from substantive citizenship and the latter is seen as the condition of the possibility of the former. Yet, whether the focus is on status or practice, it remains on the doer rather than the deed. To investigate citizenship in a way that is irreducible to either status or practice, while still valuing this distinction, requires a focus on those acts when, regardless of status and substance, subjects constitute themselves as citizens or, better still, as those to whom the right to have rights is due. But the focus shifts from subjects as such to acts (or deeds) that produce such subjects. The difference, we suggest, is crucial. (Isin and Nielsen 2008, 2)

Like democracy in Mouffe's (2005) view, this conception of citizenship is one in which acts constitute status—democratic citizenship is only *constituted* inasmuch as it is *enacted*. Participation in democratic culture, with the agonistic conflicts that such participation presupposes, is important precisely for this reason. Herein lies a further challenge for the media, namely to facilitate such participation and action in a multitude of ways, including rational deliberation but also emotive expression, contestation, and robust engagement.

As Hsu (2008) argued with reference to the Tiananmen Square protests,[6] acts of citizenship point to the gap between the actual conditions of life and the potentialities of justice and democracy. These "emotional-volitional acts" are aimed at inscribing democracy into what Derrida referred to as the gap between law (coinciding with the formal status of citizenship) and justice (an ethical imperative that exceeds the law). This democracy is always still to come, never fully realized, continually deferred, and therefore needs to be claimed and reclaimed on an ongoing basis: "Democracies are always to come in the sense that we cannot be satisfied with what claims to be just or democratic. 'To come' especially indicates infinite imperfectability or even impossibility. Justice and democracy have to be questioned, deconstructed and criticized in an open-ended process" (Hsu 2008, 255).

To sum up: In a democracy marked by pluralism and difference (as is the case in most, if not all, African societies), but which remains open-ended and dynamic, conflict is inevitable and inherent. The question is whether this conflict is handled in a way that causes divisions between citizens who see themselves as enemies or whether this difference at the core of pluralistic democracy will be incorporated into an agonistic democratic model. Here the role of the media is of crucial importance, and of ethical import. The media, this book argues, is a vital institution through which democratic contestation can be not only managed but also encouraged, steered, and reflected upon in ethical ways.

It is important to note, however, that difference and pluralism are not directed away from the political sphere to an ethical domain seen as somehow separate from public life and political contestation. The ethical and the political are fundamentally entwined and at the core of pluralistic, agonistic democracy. In such a context, conflict is more likely to be productive rather than destructive:

> Politics aims at the creation of unity in a context of conflict and diversity; it is always concerned with the creation of an "us" by the determination of a "them." The novelty of democratic politics is not the overcoming of the us/them opposition—which is an impossibility—but the different way in which it is established. The crucial issue is to establish this us/them discrimination in a way that is compatible with pluralist democracy. Envisaged from the point of view of "agonistic pluralism," the aim of democratic politics is to construct the "them" in such a way that it is no longer perceived

as an enemy to be destroyed, but an "adversary," that is, somebody whose ideas we combat. (Mouffe 2005, 101–2)

The questions that lie at the heart of the development of an agonistic de- mocracy are therefore ethical ones: How can difference—of identity, power, and resources—be engaged with in ways that are constitutive of democratic culture? What are the ethical values that should guide a media that sees its democratic role as facilitative of constructive agonism? From the discussion thus far, it is clear that the Habermasian prerequisite of "rationality" alone is not adequate to ensure an inclusive, participatory democratic culture in contexts marked by inequality, difference, and historical legacies of dom- ination and subjugation. Values such as human dignity, equality, respect, and a commitment to the fulfilment of citizens' capabilities—understood within a relational rather than an individualistic framework—would be more appropriate to guide the mediatization of conflict in such settings. We will return to the ways in which this agonistic relationship can be facilitated by the media when we discuss the normative framework of "listening" in Chapter 5.

It is important at this point to distinguish between the type of agonistic, productive conflict that Mouffe (2005) and others see as an inherent feature of democratic culture and the type of violent clashes that have marked many democratic regressions in African countries. These clashes have often been a result not of democratic agonism, but of its opposite, namely authoritarian attempts to close down the agonistic space for debate and criticism, and a re- version to essentialist ethnic identities instead of the sustaining of dynamic difference. The many transitional conflicts between warring factions that Cheeseman et al. (2018, 35) refer to are therefore not based on inclusive and participatory political contests, but construct opponents as enemies. These conflicts display a disregard for the needs of citizens and the sustaining of state institutions. Consequently, prolonged periods of conflict in African states, such as in Somalia or the DRC, "have done little to promote demo- cratic norms and values" (Cheeseman et al. 2018, 35). Violent conflicts of this kind can contribute to authoritarianism, the militarization of the political sphere, less cohesion among political elites, and the weakening of political institutions (Cheeseman et al. 2018, 57). Violent conflicts that arise from au- thoritarianism and the exclusion or elimination of political opponents there- fore have to be clearly distinguished from democratic agonism. The former is aimed at the silencing of antagonists; contest and criticism are suppressed, and the ensuing conflict is destructive. In contrast, the latter does not see political adversaries as antagonists but as participants in an inclusive culture, where contest and conflict are inevitable but productive. The key is that in an agonistic engagement, the opponents are not bent on destroying each other or the symbolic space (such as the media) they occupy, but aim to reorganize that space according to their own convictions.

Destructive conflicts, as described earlier, still characterize the setbacks to democratic processes occurring around the continent. These range from violent clashes around elections in Kenya, the repression of the opposition in Zimbabwe, disruptions to proceedings in the South African parliament during the Zuma presidency, and renewed conflicts and democratic regression in Mali and South Sudan (Cheeseman 2015, 2; Chuma, Bosch, and Wasserman 2017). Indeed, "democratic breakdowns . . . continue to be a prominent feature of multiparty politics" in Africa (Cheeseman 2015, 1).

These setbacks have in some cases been reversed through the election of new political leaders, in countries such as South Africa, Ethiopia, Liberia, and Sierra Leone, in recent years (2017–2019). However, the disregard for constitutional periods of tenure remains a problem in many African countries, for instance, the Congo, the DRC, and Uganda, where leaders seem to be "addicted to power" (Maphunye 2018). Having said that, several examples have been noted in recent years of African politicians being constrained by constitutional rules, indicating that democratic institutions on the continent are making a difference to political cultures, even if not all of them are performing equally well (Cheeseman 2018). These instances of political leaders who subject themselves—willingly or not—to constitutional limits and electoral processes are not always visible in popular media discourses. As Martin (2018) argues, the global media often reverts to stereotypes about ethnic clashes when reporting on African elections, as was the case in Sierra Leone in 2018. These stereotypes around democratization processes, or the lack of thereof, in Africa, feed into power relations about how Africa is represented in global media discourses, as a continent rife with dictators, coups, and civil war.

While regular transfers of power are not a panacea for governance and socioeconomic problems such as systems of patronage and ethnic tensions, they contribute to a culture of accountability (Maphunye 2018). The introduction of multiparty democracy is therefore by no means a safeguard against conflict, as conflicts do erupt as a result of competition between political parties. Sometimes these conflicts relate to pre-existing ethnic polarization and networks of patronage that predated colonialism, were reinforced through colonial rule, and presented an obstacle to democratization processes on the continent (Cheeseman 2015, 16).

The backsliding of democracy in many parts of the continent has also had a negative impact on the media, ranging from the imprisonment and harassment of journalists to threats to freedom of expression and the erosion of media pluralism (Wasserman and Benequista 2017, 1). However, despite the often shrinking space for free and independent media in these countries, there are also many examples of journalists who continue to challenge political authoritarianism and corruption, as well as alternative media platforms that provide information and commentary (some examples will be provided later in this chapter). These instances—of authoritarian lapses despite the existence of pluralistic media and, conversely, the continuation of journalistic practices despite democratic regressions—raise the question of how media and democratization in Africa are linked.

The Tenuous Link between Media and Democratization

The link between media and democracy[7] is habitually assumed to be self-evident, with popular claims that the media is a central "pillar" of democracy or a "watchdog" over the "public interest" frequently passing without scrutiny or criticism. The media can play an important role in the democratization process: they often exert pressure on authoritarian governments and, in so doing, help precipitate their collapse; they report on and interpret the dramatic fall of the old regime and the transition to a new one. However, as Voltmer (2013, 23) reminds us, the media "are not democratic by nature," and they "serve dictatorships as happily as they flourish in democracies."

Whether, and how, the media serves democracy is not an inherent quality of the media itself, but is instead determined by ethical norms, regulatory frameworks, and institutional structures and how well the media performs its democratic role. Consequently, the role of the media in upholding or deepening democracy has been contested in established and new democracies alike (Voltmer 2013, 23–24). Familiar questions regarding the extent to which structures such as ownership, markets, technology, and regulation determine the ability of media to play a democratic role, or whether journalists and media users have the agency to shape the way that media facilitate or deepen democratic participation, culture, and debate, also apply to transitional contexts.

Voltmer (2013, 56–57) identifies different schools of thought in scholarship on democratization processes. The first, rooted in modernization theory, emphasizes structural factors—such as economic development, capital markets, a strong middle class, resource decentralization, and individual liberties—as prerequisites for successful democratic transition. Critiques of this approach include that it is too deterministic and rigid, not allowing for the complex interactions and contestations characterizing transitional contexts. The second school of thought emphasizes agency and the role of political actors, whose actions can steer transitions into particular directions, often leading to unpredictable outcomes.

Instead of seeing these two dimensions as separate, a view of transitional processes that understands structure and agency to be in interaction is a more productive approach. Combining structure and agency in analyses of democratic transitions also allows for recognition of the different ways in which media impact these processes. While the inclusive or exclusive structures of media technologies and industries are important influences on democratic participation, media platforms and technologies are also adopted and adapted for democratic purposes by their users in interaction with particular social conditions. Similarly, the choices made by media practitioners also add a dimension of flexibility and unpredictability to the role media may play in democratization (Voltmer 2013, 59).

The media's role in democratization processes can be summarized as (Voltmer 2013, 71)

- linking distant individuals and groups,
- accelerating social and political processes,
- constructing social reality,
- setting agendas for public debate and policymaking, and
- providing a sense-making narrative by interpreting and analyzing events.

Once democratization has occurred, the media can also play an important role in fostering a democratic culture and establishing or transforming democratic institutions, by demanding transparency and encouraging citizen participation (Voltmer 2013, 96).

Democracy itself, as a political system and public culture, is often treated as homogenous and universal. As pointed out in Chapter 1, democratization on the African continent should be seen in terms of cyclical and multilinear processes rather than a teleological progression. The links between media and democratic processes also vary. While there are many examples on the continent of vibrant media institutions that hold political power to account and social media platforms that have extended capacities of voice to citizens, freedom of expression is also often tenuous and the sustainability of media organizations precarious.

The moves toward greater democracy on the continent have, on the whole, rejuvenated the media. As democratization brought the end of military regimes and dictatorships in postcolonial Africa, it also brought greater press freedom, citizen participation, and media freedoms (Wasserman and Benequista 2017, 1). Democratic reversals on the continent have, however, been widespread in recent years, with a corresponding decline in media freedom (Wasserman and Benequista 2017, 1).

Despite the ebb and flow of democratic culture in Africa, and the waxing and waning of media freedom, a variety of media practices and journalistic forms continue to burgeon on the continent. These include online and mobile media, which have shown strong growth in recent years and continue to do so, as well as older forms of print and broadcast media, which remain relevant as trusted sources of information for the majority of Africans. Alongside these media platforms, more informal, small-scale forms of communication have functioned as important channels of expression in everyday life across African countries. These draw from a wide symbolic repertoire that may include oral communication, popular theater, dancing, communal singing, jokes, storytelling, and gossip (Berger 2002, 29; Bosch, Wasserman, and Chuma 2018). These alternative forms of communication can be seen to have sustained a participatory culture, especially where more formal media platforms have been out of reach of rural Africans or have come under political pressure.

The relationship between media and democracy in African contexts can therefore be seen to take a variety of forms. In this regard, African examples illustrate the multiple and creative ways in which users appropriate and adopt media for democratic life, and how the links between media and democracy differ across geographic contexts globally (Zelizer 2017, 63).

However, a closer consideration of how media report on conflicts in transitional democracies in general, and in African countries specifically, reveals that not only the nature of these links but also their normative value should be subjected to scrutiny. In other words, the way media play a role in democratization conflicts differs depending on context, but moreover, this role is not always a positive one. Despite claims to the contrary, media often contribute to the escalation of conflicts during democratization processes rather than their de-escalation or resolution. And although the wave of democratization in Africa brought about the burgeoning of independent media, the media frequently managed to deepen rather than overcome social polarizations, or to obstruct the deepening or consolidation of new democratic institutions (Voltmer 2013, 72). Often, superficial conversation and partial perspectives are made to stand in for substantial deliberation and wide, inclusive democratic participation. These failures of the media usually come about as a result of inequalities in access to the media, the media's bias toward elite perspectives, and attempts by governments to exert control over the media when it becomes too critical (Chuma, Wasserman, et al. 2017).

Examining the media's role during periods of heightened tension and conflict can illuminate the fissures in the assumed link between journalism and democracy. The tenuousness of this link not only is evident in transitional democracies, however, but also can be noted in more advanced democracies in the Global North, as Zelizer (2017, 37) has noted with regard to the coverage of the refugee crisis, ethical scandals, and the use of the media by the Islamic State (ISIS). It is, however, in contexts of political transition that questions about the link between media and democracy are heard most clearly.

It is widely accepted that the media plays an important role in shaping the "rules of the game" in contemporary democratic politics, to the extent that strategic media management and public relation campaigns are deemed indispensable for political success (Voltmer 2013, 3). Whether this *empirical* centrality and influence of the media is also *normatively* a democratic good has been the topic of some debate.

The idea that the media is of central importance to democracy is usually based on a liberal-democratic conception of the media as a watchdog that protects the individual liberties and rights of citizens while encouraging rational deliberation in the public sphere (Christians et al. 2009). Such democracies can be seen as mostly procedural and competitive, with regular elections as a criterion for success (often used when evaluating democratization processes in Africa, and still a normative ideal rather than a reality in many parts of the world), or as participatory and deliberative, with involvement by citizens and members of civil society being emphasized (Strömbäck 2005).

These optimistic views of the media's role in democracy have been subject to reassessment as a critical literature emerged that pointed out the various negative effects the media may have, even on established democratic cultures in the Global North. The impact of "media-centered" politics on the "quality and viability of democracy" also applies—arguably more so—to new democracies, as these democracies might be more vulnerable to the vagaries and unpredictability of global media markets driven by the profit motive (Voltmer 2013, 4). The centrality of the media in shaping politics has been seen to contribute to political cynicism, to a preference for spectacle and strategy over substance, and to a tendency of politicians opting to follow a media strategy that emphasizes visibility and popularity rather than substantive policy positions (Strömbäck 2005).

However, beneficial effects of media coverage—such as increased civic engagement and political knowledge, with a resultant influence on changing political orientations—have also been noted in established and new democracies (Voltmer 2013, 111). In transitional societies in Africa in particular, studies have suggested that the media can help enhance citizens' understanding of democratic principles and rules, especially during periods of transition; however, this effect is probably stronger among educated, urban populations (Voltmer 2013, 112).

It would seem, therefore, that the links between mediatized politics and the deepening of democratic culture are not self-evident, automatic, or generalizable, and are often simplified or exaggerated. The extent to which media may influence political culture depends on a variety of factors, ranging from the level of media saturation, to the type of media in question, to the specific social and political dynamics of the context (Voltmer 2013, 12). For these reasons, the inevitability of a link between media and democracy has in recent years been subjected to much critique (see, e.g., the special issue of *Journalism*, volume 14, issue 4, devoted to the theme of "De-coupling Journalism and Democracy"). The increasingly precarious economic environment for journalism globally has, at least in some cases, made commercial survival a more pressing consideration for many media practitioners than the media's contribution to democratic life (Gronvall 2014).

The criticism that there is a mismatch between the stated ideals of journalism as a democratic practice and the way journalists actually perform these ideals is valid. However, this criticism does not yet address the question as to which standards of democracy are being applied when measuring the media's performance (Strömbäck 2005). This bias toward journalistic roles in Western democracies has also skewed journalism scholarship to the extent that it has often failed to account for the way journalism functions in relation to politics and citizenship in nondemocratic and non-Western countries (Hanitzsch and Vos 2016). The liberal-pluralist assumption of political competition facilitated by a dense media environment simply has not applied historically to most African countries (Berger 2002, 23). Journalists in non-Western and/or transitional democracies may also choose to adopt roles that are more suited to a developmental context or be more committed to preserving harmony and social cohesion in their communities than is the case in Western normative frameworks premised on individualism (Hanitzsch and Vos 2016). Even when alternative normative frameworks for the media's role in African countries, such as developmental journalism or facilitating citizen participation in between formal elections, have been explored, it has often been done by borrowing concepts such as "civil society" or "public sphere" from contexts very different to the African ones where they were applied (Berger 2002, 24).

Moreover, Western scholarship has constructed a normative hierarchy that positions the "public-spirited verifier of factual information as the superego of the news industry," relegating other roles—such as relaxation, escape, entertainment, and conviviality—to the margins (Hanitzsch and Vos 2016, 150). This privileging of journalism's political role creates a gap between normative ideals and actual practice in Western societies, especially given the broad shift in contemporary media's focus—in (post)modern consumer societies particularly—away from public affairs to the domain of "everyday life" (although everyday life and political life are increasingly intertwined) (Hanitzsch and Vos 2016, 156). It also ignores the fact that most journalism in the world is practiced in societies that cannot be defined as democratic. Central to the problem of the media–democracy link, therefore, is the erroneous assumption of global universality. As Josephi (2013, 476) argues: "using a political system as the main descriptor of journalism proves too limiting a frame in which to view it. Historical and recent examples will be used to make evident that journalistic professional knowledge and values can exist within and alongside a variety of political forms, and under differing sets of political pressures and expectations."

Various models of democracy exist around the world, with different expectations regarding what type of media practices would be ideally suited for the context (Strömbäck 2005). Depending on the particular type of democracy, different normative expectations may be set for the media's role within such a democracy. George (2013, 491) argues that, although democratic values are widely accepted around the globe today, democracy may manifest differently and deviate from the ideal type along a spectrum. Expecting that democracies everywhere should conform to the same liberal model—or be considered inferior—is an "ethnocentric" assumption (George 2013, 492). Yet, while acknowledging different iterations of democracy, George suggests that normative frameworks for journalism globally should retain democratic values at their core, to prevent cultural relativism from becoming a smokescreen for authoritarian rulers claiming exceptionalism. However, particular principles and practices—including the role and practices of media—should be allowed to differ across different democratic regimes (George 2013, 492).

A preference for procedural democracy may set the minimal expectation that the media acts as a watchdog to ensure that electoral roles and procedures are not compromised and to allow a free "marketplace of ideas" to flourish. A competitive model would, in addition, expect the media to provide trustworthy information to enable voters to exercise informed choices. In participatory and deliberative models of democracy, the media's role in facilitating collective decision-making, by linking citizens together and helping them to find solutions to common problems, would be more important (Strömbäck 2005).

We will return to some of these normative questions in Chapter 5. Of relevance for our current discussion on the link between media and democracy is the realization that, since there is no single model of democracy, there is also no clear or universal link between the media and democracy. As Stremlau and Iazzolino (2017, 5) argue, media systems reflect local norms and values, and the relationship between politics and media is informed by "local ideas and structures of power that define the degree of independence of the latter from the former and, more broadly, the way they influence one another."

A simplistic link between media and democracy, in which democracies with free and independent media are simply contrasted with countries where this is not the case, is no longer adequate to explain the variety of media practices within democracies or the different degrees of freedom of expression found within different countries formally defined as "democratic." Such a simplistic view sees the relationship between media and politics in established Western democracies as universally normative, instead of viewing media systems contextually in terms of their own logics (Stremlau and Iazzolino 2017, 6). It further relegates to irrelevance a large part of the world where different journalisms are practiced, even under conditions that do not comply with a narrow definition of media freedom and democracy (Zelizer 2017, 70). Instead, the ways in which media and political authority interact are "highly contextual and cannot be reduced to a simple dichotomy as to whether the media are subordinated to the power, thus acting as an instruments of propaganda, or are instead in a position to hold it accountable and play a public service role" (Stremlau and Iazzolino 2017, 6).

In countries that have undergone major transitions, especially where high socioeconomic inequalities persist, the question of whether the media contributes to or damages democracy is even more complex. In societies emerging from a political transition and where conflict is either still present or latent in people's memory, media are often aligned with—or are seen to be aligned with—a particular section of society. In such a context, attempts to create an agonistic "marketplace of ideas" may add to tensions and exacerbate conflicts, leading to a preference for a more cooperative stance toward government:

> The volatility of the transitional situation might raise the question as to how conducive an adversarial press is for the consolidation of the new regime. In some situations a more cooperative relationship can provide the newly elected government with much-needed breathing space to manage the complexities of transition without the pressure of an excess of public criticism. (Voltmer 2013, 34)

The danger, of course, is that governments can appeal to the media's support or cooperation to deflect criticism or underplay new authoritarian tendencies or failures on the part of the new government.

Because the media's "watchdog" role is mostly defined in relation to state or political power, its vigilance over economic power in new democracies is often neglected. This economic power resides not only in the new elites or the elites inherited from the authoritarian dispensation but also in the commercialized media itself. As was noted in Chapter 2 when discussing the political economy approach to understanding the media's role in conflict, these societies often display severe asymmetries of access to media agendas, which undermine the ability of marginalized social and political actors to participate in deliberative or competitive models of democracy.

As Stremlau and Iazzolino (2017, 7) have pointed out with regard to the transition in post-Soviet Russia, by focusing only on the liberalization of the media and its links with procedural aspects of democratic politics, one risks losing sight of the way that economic elites can capture the formally democratic state and the media, leading to an oligarchic media–politic nexus. To some extent, such an elite capture can be seen in postapartheid South Africa, where, despite its diversity in terms of outlets and platforms, most mainstream media remain oriented toward an economic and social elite. That country has also seen an increased overlap between political and economic influence in some media outlets. One example of this has been the newspaper *The New Age* and its sister television channel ANN7 (both now discontinued), whose former owners, the Gupta family, were linked to former president Jacob Zuma and alleged to have been involved in "state capture" (a corrupt relationship with Zuma and his allies). For the most part, however, the relationship between the postapartheid government and the media has been fraught with conflict ever since the arrival of formal democracy (Wasserman and De Beer 2005). This conflictual relationship is typical of the "fierce contestations" and "media wars" that have also characterized other new democracies, where there are disagreements over political access to media agendas, media regulation, and norms and practices for the media in the transitional democracy (Voltmer 2013, 4).

The prevalence of neo-patrimonial networks of patronage in transitional societies, including many in Africa, is a further factor to take into account. Ethno-patrimonialism remains a "dominant feature of African politics" (Voltmer 2013, 187), and ethnic and regional identities consequently underpin many democratization conflicts, for instance, in Cameroon and Kenya. The dominance of patronage networks also has an impact on media practices. When patron–client networks are compounded by poor socioeconomic conditions, the chances of corruption in journalism may rise steeply. One example is the use of bribes (widely referred to as "brown envelope journalism" in Africa, or by particular terms in specific countries, such as "gombo" in Cameroon; see Ndangam 2006) (Voltmer 2013, 212).

The coexistence of informal networks of power based on personal connections and a clientelist relationship with the more formal institutions of democracy introduced during transition lead Stremlau and Iazzolino (2017, 13–14) to suggest that governance in such societies should be considered as "a patchwork, or the outcome of an ongoing negotiation among heterogeneous actors, engaged in communicating with each other and with their own constituencies—or, in other words, a hybrid." A hybrid conception of governance would also allow for a wider and more flexible understanding of the media–democracy link than would merely binary terms such as "free" versus "unfree."

It is therefore unsuitable to merely apply democratic theory developed in more stable, established, and homogenous democracies to the development of democracy in Africa after colonialism, and its subsequent waxing and waning as a result of internal and external factors and players. At the same time, comparative approaches leading to hybrid formulations are preferable to isolationist and solipsistic approaches that view Africa only as exceptional. As Joseph remarks:

> Developments in Africa oblige us to approach seemingly settled issues anew and to adopt a critical approach regarding such fundamentals as the meaning of democracy and democratization. . . . To be avoided is the passive application to Africa of externally devised frameworks, as well as the analysis of African politics solely within Africa-derived paradigms. (1997, 364)

While the global geopolitical proxy battles that played themselves out in Africa often exacerbated conflicts and hampered peacebuilding efforts, they represented fundamentally different paradigms of democracy. At stake was the contest between capitalism and Western democracy, on the one hand, and Communism and social democracy on the other. As such, African democratization processes provided an opportunity to reflect on the very meaning of democracy (Joseph 1997, 365). They demonstrated that the outcome of democratization processes, the possibility for conflict to erupt, the outcome of elections, and the sustainability of democratic institutions depend on the political and economic landscape within which these processes are introduced; therefore, context-specific models need to be developed to understand them (Cheeseman 2015, 176). The conflicts erupting as part of the democratization process in Africa, as well as the democratic regressions setting in, prompt a reconsideration of the "dominant way of characterizing democracy according to a set of electoralist, institutionalist, and proceduralist criteria" (Joseph 1997, 365). The way these processes unfolded in Africa demonstrates that the tensions between the normative ideals of liberal democracy and the particular forms of governance emerging in African societies should not be collapsed; rather, this tension should provide occasion for an assessment of democratic values that extends beyond the minimalist requirement of elections (Joseph 1997, 365).

The link between liberal democracy and capitalism has also been a matter of reflection and debate. While capitalism and democracy are often considered to create mutually favorable conditions, the relationship between them can also create exclusions that undermine democratic rule (Voltmer 2013, 162). Although big business has often supported dictatorships, the "third wave" democratization processes in Africa and elsewhere always involved market-oriented economic reforms. This was despite the unsuitability of the wholesale importation of these reforms to these contexts, where the eradication of inequality has been empirically proven to be more important in deepening democratization than market reforms:

> Economic transitions in the wake of the recent wave of democratization have taken place during the rise of neoliberalism to an almost undisputed global doctrine. The results, though, are not wealth and happiness for all. While for some (individuals, groups, countries) the liberalization of markets has brought about significant gains of wealth, for others it simply led to disaster and a downward spiral of poverty. (Voltmer 2013, 163)

The liberal assumption that democracy is always best served by a free market can pose problems in transitional societies that still reel under the major socioeconomic disparities created by colonialism (and apartheid, in the case of South Africa). Conflicts arise as a result of contesting economic models for redressing the inequalities inherited from the past. An example of such an economic conflict is the policy proposed in 2018 by South Africa's ruling party, the African National Congress (ANC), to amend the Constitution to enable land expropriation without compensation, in an attempt to redress inequities related to land ownership after colonialism and apartheid. The default approach to this policy by most mainstream media in the country has been to consider the impact of this policy on the property markets in which their elite audiences participate, rather than its impact on the poor (whether this may be positive—in terms of historic redress—or negative as a result of its effect on the overall economy, exchange rates, and so forth).

The importance of developing hybrid models to understand democratization conflicts in Africa also extends to the media. The role that the media may be able to play in the transition to, and deepening of, African democracy is not only determined by its adoption of global normative value frameworks but also influenced by its position in relation to domestic factors. African media may, for instance, be embedded in networks of social relations such as race, ethnicity, or community, and these networks may position them in particular ways toward the various transitional actors—or create the perception that they are positioned thus, and therefore less trustworthy (Chuma, Wasserman, et al. 2017). In such unequal and stratified societies, the voices being amplified by the media may be those of actors who already have the most power to influence media and political agendas, rather than those on the fringes who need to be drawn into the political process (Voltmer 2006, 3). Merely viewing the media as providing a neutral space for stakeholders to compete politically could therefore result in the media contributing to the further marginalization of historically oppressed, weaker, or vulnerable sections of society.

Not only has the media an active role to play in the transition of societies from authoritarianism to democracy, but also the media itself is required to transform to better reflect new democratic ideals (Stremlau and Iazzolino 2017, 6). Where the media is slow to transform or resists change, it often displays an "elite continuity" (Sparks 2009)—an orientation, political economy, or organizational culture that continues to bear traces of its predecessor and that may result in the emergence of new hegemonies and threats to press freedom. Although substantive normative debates about the role the media should play in new democracies are important to ensure trust in the media and agreement about its rights and freedoms, such debates may also delay the transformation of these institutions. While such debates continue, older behavior patterns and norms and the organizational culture inherited from previous regimes may persist (Voltmer and Wasserman 2014). In these cases the persistent socioeconomic and political inequalities are all the more likely to be reflected in media access and participation.

Limiting the media's role to that of a monitor of procedural aspects of democracy is also inadequate in transitional and conflictual situations, where the media could contribute more actively to peacebuilding and the rebuilding of social ties. Transitional democracies are "frequently faced with fragile identities, deep social divisions and unfinished nation-building" (Voltmer 2006, 5). This is especially true in many societies in Africa, where racial and ethnic identities have been key elements of political organization and have shaped the way the media have conceived of and catered to its audience in relation to its broader definition of the public interest (Rodny-Gumede 2017, 17).

In these situations, limiting the media's role to that of an objective observer may result in its complicity in the entrenchment or perpetuation of such divisions. While watchdog journalism has its place when exposing the corruption and creeping authoritarianism of African elites that often accompany the democratic regressions on the continent, an antagonistic, watchdog-styled media in these contexts could also deepen divisions in society if the media is perceived to be taking sides or favoring particular viewpoints. This has been the case in South Africa, where tensions between the media and the government have been high in the postapartheid era. The postapartheid government has accused the media of being "untransformed" and "racist" for continuing to view the social reality from a "white" perspective (Rodny-Gumede 2017, 17).

Even when the deliberative and participatory model of democracy is held up as an ideal for transitional societies, the media might have to play a more interventionist role to facilitate participation of such marginalized groups. Normative models such as peace journalism or democratic listening—to which we will return in Chapter 5—may therefore offer more appropriate frameworks within which to consider the media–democracy link in these contexts.

Conclusion

Given the variety of political contexts around the world within which media operate, it has become clear that the relationship between media and democracy is all but self-evident, universal, or homogenous. The added complexity of the media's role in transitional democracies and the conflictual and polarized nature of many of these societies in Africa make critical scrutiny of this link unavoidable when considering the mediatization of conflict on the continent. When the normative dimension of this link is considered, a hybrid or "domesticated" approach becomes all the more important. Not only is the application of fixed normative frameworks developed in established Western democracies to conflictual and transitional democracies in Africa inappropriate and unfeasible, but also it may reflect a Northern-centric and imperialistic outlook that tends to construct African media and politics in terms of failure and lack. At the same time, vigilance is needed to ensure that insistence on the domestication of the media–politics relationship does not amount to merely a "justification of the persistence of authoritarian practices" (Voltmer 2013, 5).

As this chapter has pointed out, the relationship between media, conflict, and democratization is a multileveled one that manifests differently across various transitional contexts. Various factors in African societies complicate our understanding of this relationship even further. These include the prevalence of the politics of identity and ethnicity, linked to a history of colonialism; persisting social and economic inequalities in the postcolonial era, including an elite continuity in media organizations, which impact media access and representativity; and a recurring or creeping authoritarianism during democratic regressions and lapses. These factors illustrate the importance of allowing for differentiated and hybrid approaches to the relationship between democracy and the media that may deviate from the dominant normative models as derived from established democracies in the North. There is no consistent pattern of democratization across Africa, nor is there only one type of democracy.

At the beginning of this chapter, two ways in which the media–conflict–democracy link manifests in Africa were highlighted. The first can be found in conflict contexts where the media still manages to serve a democratic culture despite pressures on media freedom—even if the types and modes of communication used for this purpose do not conform to the dominant definitions of political news and debate, as found in liberal democracies in the North. The second type is where democratic transitions have secured a free and safe space for media to operate in, but where the liberal-democratic normative framework adopted by the media has proven to be an inadequate, or at least only partially appropriate, response to the broader and more substantial demands articulated through democratization conflicts.

In both of the aforementioned conflict case studies, it appeared that the link between media and democracy in Africa is not always as self-evident as liberal-democratic orthodoxy may suggest. The example of "hidden transcripts" in social media from Zimbabwe illustrated that journalism can flourish despite the absence of ideal democratic conditions. In that context, journalism may not always take the typical form of rational, fact-based, dispassionate reporting; instead, satire, gossip, jokes, and other forms of cultural expression could also serve to reinvigorate the public sphere and sustain a democratic culture in the face of creeping authoritarianism or democratic regression.

The South African example of the mediatization of the Marikana massacre (read together with ongoing community protests in this country, referred to in Chapter 2) suggests that even in a democracy where media freedom is constitutionally entrenched, the liberal-democratic model of monitorial journalism, premised on the primacy of an adversarial relationship to government, is too narrow a normative guideline in democratization conflicts. This view of the media–democracy link constructs politics as an elite conversation and marginalizes emotive expressions of anger, frustration, and outrage. The result is an emphasis on monitorial journalism at the expense of other functions, such as facilitating dialogue, restoring dignity to the historically disadvantaged, and amplifying the voices of those on the social and economic margins of the new democracy. While the media in such a conception may be "free," it does not necessarily deepen democracy in the best way possible. Therefore, the liberal-democratic understanding of the link between media and democracy may in fact serve to promote conflicts, as violent protest action becomes "the only language authorities understand" (G. Smith 2018).

These two examples also illustrate the fact that the export of the liberal-pluralist form of democracy to Africa is not helpful if all it does is "hold up a watchdog model and measure Africa's historic deficit" (Berger 2002, 22) during times of conflict. The "democratic obsession" (George 2013, 500) with vertical media–state relationships is insufficient to conceptualize a role for the media in democratization conflicts. If the need for media to connect citizens horizontally is increasingly important in established democracies in the North, as George (2013) suggests, the need for a deepening of democracy in transitional, unequal, and polarized African societies is acute.

Conceiving of the link between media and democracy not only in vertical but also in horizontal terms would, however, require a reorientation toward citizens as coproducers of meaning at the center of mediatized processes. Instead of merely acting on its own as a monitor of the government, the media would seek out instances where citizens are already holding government to account and acting as agents in political processes, even if such processes might traditionally not be viewed as political participation in the formal sense. Acknowledging, developing, and listening to the ways in which citizens communicate through alternative media or outside the formal media in other communication networks during times of conflict could contribute to a more productive way of engaging with conflict. Listening to opposing voices and allowing them to speak out on a variety of platforms may not necessarily lead to the prevention or resolution of conflicts but could turn them into agonistic engagements that eventually deepen democratic cultures rather than impoverish or erode them.

These are not only political questions but also more broadly normative ones pertaining to what should be considered journalists' ethical responsibilities and professional identities in African democratizing conflicts. This is what we turn to in the following chapter.

4

Media Ethics, Professionalism, Codes, and Accountability

Introduction

We have so far discussed the links between media, conflict, and democratic transitions, noting that these links are not always self-evident, nor do they look the same in all democratic settings. African democracies have shown that the democratic process is not monolithic—periods of liberalization have been followed by relapses to authoritarianism, during which the new-found freedoms of media also came under pressure. We also saw that in those instances where the media did manage to remain free from government interference, it did not always succeed in consolidating or deepening democracy across the different divides in African societies, which are frequently characterized by cultural and ethnic polarizations and tensions or by huge socioeconomic inequalities. How then should the media navigate an ethical course between these fragile democratic structures and social and economic divides?

One of the key arguments this book is making is that such an ethical course can only be properly charted if it is done collaboratively, departing from actual lived experience and contextual conditions. Given the wide disparities in media access and the low levels of trust in media in African countries where there is a history of state control of information or elite capture of mainstream media, understanding ethical mediatization of conflicts only in terms of codes guiding professionals is not imaginative or flexible enough. For media to engage ethically with democratization conflicts in these contexts, it needs to conceive of media ethics in ways that involve citizens more broadly and cut across social divides.

This chapter will examine this question of the relationship between media ethics, codes, and accountability to society in the light of these contextual challenges. It departs from the assumption that a domesticated, socially informed understanding of the relationship between media ethics and

The Ethics of Engagement. Herman Wasserman, Oxford University Press (2021). © Oxford University Press.
DOI: 10.1093/oso/9780190917333.003.0004

African democracies needs to be found. At the same time, vigilance should be exercised when appeals to "indigenous" values are made. These appeals to authenticity can often provide a smokescreen for relapses to authoritarianism, including exerting pressure on or attacking the media. Instead, the question posed in this chapter is how normative frameworks for the media as well as regulatory processes can be responsive to African lived experiences, local histories and social conditions, and evolving and varying types of media use. It is therefore not only the notion of democracy itself that is "built on normative paradoxes that require constant reinterpretation and readjustment in response to changing circumstances" (Voltmer 2013, 18) but also the professional values and ethical norms of the media.

Before addressing those conceptual challenges in more depth, it is useful to first consider how ethics function in actual communities of media practice. Two examples from South Africa may be illustrative of the limits of "professional" codes of ethics within democratizing societies and attempts to widen the remit of professional codes of ethics to become more participatory, inclusive, and open-ended. These examples also show some of the flaws and pitfalls of such a process.

The Press Council of South Africa

Since the advent of democracy in South Africa in 1994, and even earlier during the period of negotiated transition, there has been fierce contestation over the ideal role of the media in the new society, as has been discussed previously.

One of the key developments during this period was the establishment of self-regulatory mechanisms, namely the Press Council of South Africa and the Broadcasting Complaints Commission of South Africa, to adjudicate public complaints about breaches of the newly constructed media ethics codes. This self-regulatory system was especially significant given the historical experience of state control over the media during the apartheid era. Both these bodies drew on international ethical codes but adapted them for the local context.

On several occasions during the first decades of democracy, the South African Press Council was criticized for not enforcing stronger sanctions where its code had been breached. This criticism coincided with broader threats to the self-regulatory system from the increasingly intolerant ruling party during the Zuma presidency (2009–2018). One of these threats was a call to establish a statutory Media Appeals Tribunal (MAT) that could impose stricter penalties on errant media.

In an attempt to re-establish its legitimacy, the Press Council of South Africa in 2010 embarked on a consultative process to revisit its self-regulatory system and code after being criticized for not being strict enough with media organizations that contravened the ethical code. This process was an attempt to create greater transparency about the Press Council's self-regulatory work, largely in an attempt to ward off the threat of statutory regulation by the ruling party, which had at its national conference in 2007 proposed establishing a statutory MAT because they viewed the self-regulatory system as biased toward the media (Malila 2014, 14). An MAT, which could foreseeably impose stricter sanctions on journalists, was widely seen as a cause for concern and a potentially negative influence on the free flow of information and freedom of speech (Reid 2014, 60).

The public consultations around the country prompted the Press Council to revise its press code, constitution, and complaints procedure. The revision process did not end there. A Press Freedom Commission (PFC) was established in 2011 by two bodies representing the media, Print Media South Africa (PMSA) and the South African National Editors' Forum (SANEF). The PFC was chaired by a former chief justice, Pius Langa, to further investigate the self-regulatory system. The PFC recommended revisions to the system, including greater participation by members of the public. These changes were adopted by the Press Council—even though the majority of the submissions to the PFC seemed to prefer independent regulation rather than the coregulatory system that was eventually adopted and in which the public had greater representation (Reid 2014, 59; Reid 2017, 92).

These efforts to restructure the self-regulatory system in South Africa in an attempt to ward off statutory interventions can be seen as a first step toward a more collaborative and open approach to the renegotiation and development of ethical norms. Consultative processes such as this one can help to open the professional system up to the cultural dynamics of the context, in order to reinvigorate and reinterpret the core ethical foundations upon which the system rests. Engagement between professional journalists and the public may help the former to respond better to changing expectations of the media's role in a changing society.

However, despite the broadening of the Press Council's appeal structure, which now included significant representation by members of the public (i.e., nonjournalists), this exercise was one of reform rather than a complete overhaul of the system. Although the public now has stronger representation in the complaints procedures, the system itself ultimately still serves to uphold "professional" standards and thereby works to maintain the boundaries between journalists and the public. This was not the first time that South African journalism bodies engaged in a process of repairing and renegotiating the journalistic paradigm after apartheid (Berger 2008; Wasserman 2006). What the Press Council hearings did was to get more public input into its systems and procedures. In the end, however, the system exists to maintain the integrity and standing of journalistic professionalism. Although the process was a step in the right direction, a more radical opening up of journalism to the public is needed for it to become truly participatory. For journalism to respond to the ethical challenges of democratizing conflicts and to contribute to agonistic contestation across the whole, broad social spectrum, media ethics would need to be conceived of as not only something that concerns professionals but also an ongoing critical reflection on all aspects of media production, circulation, and consumption in which the public is involved on a daily basis. This is not to say that such radical rethinking of media ethics would make bodies like the Press Council redundant. Rather, recognizing that mediation of conflicts involves a range of actors, ways should be found to extend ethical reflection and participation beyond the limits of "professional" bodies.

The SABC's Consultative Process

Another example of a participatory approach to media ethics is the consultative meetings held by the public broadcaster in South Africa, the SABC, to gain input into their revised editorial policy. The importance of public broadcasting in countries undergoing democratization is evident from the history of state ownership, control, and interference in broadcasting in many African countries. The transition from a state broadcaster to a public broadcaster has also been an important aspect of the democratization of the South African media, given the draconian measures applied by the apartheid regime to control broadcasting content.

In the postapartheid era, however, the SABC has come under renewed criticism. After several years of major mismanagement, financial crises, and managerial and political interference in editorial processes, the broadcaster lost a great deal of public trust and relevance. The chief operating officer at the height of the SABC's troubles, Hlaudi Motsoeneng, had gained notoriety for his authoritarian style, which seemed to favor the ruling party, the African National Congress (ANC). One of the manifestations of this interference was Motsoeneng's decree that forbade coverage by the broadcaster of violent protests; several journalists who criticized his editorial position were suspended (Makinana 2016). By forbidding journalists to report on democratization conflicts, Motsoeneng was forcing the broadcaster to renege on its most important ethical duty, namely to inform the public about matters pertaining to the ongoing consolidation of democracy. These protests can be seen as a characteristic of the agonistic democratic contestation that Mouffe described. To refuse to air them was to deny participants in this agonistic contest the right to recognition and dignity.

Motsoeneng was dismissed in June 2016 after a disciplinary hearing. In what can be seen as an attempt to restore confidence in the SABC, the corporation in the following year embarked on public consultations to gain input into the revision of the SABC's editorial policies. According to the SABC's statement at the time (SABC 2017), the consultations were intended to ensure compliance with the self-regulatory policies of the Broadcasting Complaints Commission of South Africa, the Advertising Standards Authority of South Africa, the South African Broadcasting Corporation's licence conditions, and the provisions of the country's Broadcasting Act. Its policies also had to comply with the Press Code of the Press Council under which the SABC's digital platforms fall.

The SABC's invitation to the public to participate in editorial policy review meetings can therefore be seen as an attempt to restore the public credibility of the broadcaster after the departure of this figure who caused so much damage to its reputation—including through his mishandling of the reporting of conflict—and to increase transparency in the SABC's editorial processes. The interim chairperson of the SABC board, Khanyisale Kweyama, stated at the start of the editorial policy review process that the public hearings were an attempt to ensure that the content provided by the broadcaster was "in line not only with legislative and regulatory requirements, but also with public sentiment" (SABC 2017). This greater involvement by the public in shaping the content of core ethical norms and their application may be seen as being in line with the ideal of an open and participatory ethics. The call on the public to help review the broadcaster's policies can be seen as an attempt to reclaim the publicness of the public broadcaster and recognize its role in deepening a democratic culture of agonism and contestation.

Media Ethics in Situations of Conflict

The previous example attests to the view that the media not only reports on conflicts as they play out in democratizing societies but also is in and of itself a player in the unfolding drama of democratization. The recognition that the public has a stake in media policymaking, and that those policies have been themselves contested, indicates that the media is not merely a spectator but a participant in the agonistic jostling of democratization. How it plays this role, how it positions itself in the contestation, who it involves in the conversations and debates it facilitates and who gets left out—all these are important ethical questions for the media to consider.

It is therefore understandable that the media is often seen as playing a key role in how conflicts will develop and play out, and the mediatization of conflict therefore raises many ethical questions that have to be answered within the specificity of the political, cultural, and historical contexts in which they arise. Despite the widely held orthodoxy that the media is a fundamentally democratic institution, the media has often been accused of contributing to the fomenting of tensions or even inciting violent conflict—with the African case of the Rwandan genocide being the prime example.

The other side of the coin is that the media, when conducting itself ethically, also has the potential to de-escalate conflicts and contribute to peacebuilding. This hope is expressed in the preamble of UNESCO's constitution: "Since wars begin in the minds of men, it is in the minds of men that the defenses of peace must be constructed," thereby giving expression to "a profound belief: that communication can promote tolerance and provide the foundation for a politics that makes it possible to change peacefully (without violence and social turmoil) the rules we live by" (Magder 2003, 30).

In the context of such idealism, it is important to emphasize that the ethical dimension of media and conflict should not be seen as somehow separate from politics. If we consider media ethics not as a rule-based notion of morality but as the constant reflection on values and on the processes through which these values are constructed within particular contexts, then the ethical and the political are intertwined, and rational deliberation in politics cannot take place in a rational sphere devoid of power relations (Mouffe 2005, 134). Mouffe (2005, 134), therefore, reminds us that an ethical approach to conflict (and its mediatization) should not be based on the naïve and unrealistic proposition that conflict can be eliminated or avoided completely. All human interaction involves adversarial relations and conflicts, and therefore an ethical approach to the mediatization of democratic conflicts, for Mouffe, does not seek to *eliminate* conflict, but rather to *change its character*—to "transform the potential antagonism existing in human relations into an agonism" (2005, 235).

When we consider the ethical dimension of mediatizing conflict, we are also asking questions about the nature of the conflict inherent in pluralist democracies. When considering the ethics of pluralistic democracy, we do not uphold an illusion that conflict can be eradicated or that ethical considerations of the media's relation to conflict can somehow proceed without taking the political into account. Instead, we have to "come to terms with the never-ending interrogation of the political by the ethical" (Mouffe 2005, 140).

When we consider the intertwined role of ethics and politics in Africa, it is soon evident that, while the media can play an important role in ensuring the stability of African democracies, it can also be part of the problem. As is the case in other transitional societies marked by heightened social polarization, historical tensions, and socioeconomic inequality, the media can potentially aggravate tensions and conflicts in African democratization processes, as it tends to privilege the voices of those who already have access to mediatized communication and who are therefore in a position to set the media's agenda (Voltmer 2006). Some of these tensions may arise from group identity (such as religious and ethnic identity) and contestations around notions of citizenship that have been found to be key drivers of conflict in young democracies in Africa and elsewhere (for a comparison between South Africa, Kenya, Serbia, and Egypt, see Pointer et al. 2016). The media may be seen to be biased toward a particular social group, and its reporting on conflict may therefore feed into and amplify these tensions rather than de-escalate the conflicts.

Given the aforementioned limitations of the media's role in deepening African democracies, it is therefore important that assessments of the role of African media in democracy go beyond procedural aspects of democracy to ask more substantive questions about the ethical dimensions of the media's engagement with conflict. Besides the important question of not doing harm by exacerbating tensions and divisions, the ethical responsibilities of the media in democratization also include truth-telling (e.g., imparting information regarding elections and playing a monitorial role over governments) and reinforcing the political and social dignity of citizens. The latter can be achieved by enabling conversations across difference, highlighting marginalized voices, offering agency to subaltern citizens, and articulating the everyday needs and concerns of all citizens on an ongoing basis and not only at times of heightened political activity.

We have seen in the discussion so far in this book that the conflicts arising from democratization in Africa have often been violent in nature, but not always. Some of the conflicts arising from these transitional processes pertain to intense conflicts of opinion or issues of ethnic or cultural identity positions. These conflicts may not always result in physical violence but often manifest in instances of extreme speech, the infringement of human dignity, and the social ostracizing of adversaries. These types of conflicts could be referred to as "representational conflicts," as they have to do with the ways in which mediatized subjects are constructed within discourse and can also have serious ethical implications. In transitional or postauthoritarian societies, social polarizations can create fertile ground for representational violence in the form of offensive or extreme speech that could, in the long run, inflict damage comparable to physical injury (Voltmer 2013, 40). The difficulty—especially when it comes to regulating the media—of preventing such forms of speech lies in where to draw the line between hurtful and offensive speech that should be outlawed and the fostering of a free and open exchange, which demands a certain level of tolerance for criticism (Voltmer 2013, 40). When is speech robust and agonistic, and when does it cross the line from acceptable, healthy contestation into a form of violence?

Representational Violence

Although it might not manifest in physical force or bloodshed, the representational process in itself may have a dimension that could be described as violent. While robust, agonistic debate is considered a healthy, indispensable part of democratic culture, we have to consider the possibility that some contestations are intent not on gaining the upper hand in a shared democratic symbolic space so much as they aim to destroy an opponent and eliminate them from that space altogether.

In societies that have transitioned from authoritarian rule to democracy, the newly opened political and social sphere allows for a range of competing interests to be voiced and different actors to enter the arena. Although the space where this jostling takes place might be new and allow for greater freedom of expression, the participants bring with them long-standing cultural differences, ethnic identities, material inequalities, and political tensions that may now erupt in conflict that increasingly plays out across media platforms and is often difficult to contain. The tension between the new individual liberties guaranteed by the liberal-democratic dispensation and loyalty to a new shared, democratic society can at times prove challenging. In these contexts, the media may struggle to define the ethical boundaries of acceptable speech and also have to consider how power relations determine the nature of the exchanges. The central ethical questions for the media then relate to how to ensure that democratic contestation remains agonistic rather than adversarial, and how such contestation could be as broad, participatory, and inclusive as possible.

These questions about power, democratic discourse, and ethics are relevant not only within new democracies but also across global mediated spaces. This is especially relevant when considering the global asymmetries in discursive power wielded by the media. The global imbalances in media access and resources result in an unequal distribution of the power of representation. Despite the rise of new media technologies that have made it possible for the inhabitants of the Global South to create contraflows and speak back to dominant global discourses, older colonial divisions between the metropolitan subjects and the marginal objects of global media discourses still resonate. From the point of view of representational ethics, it is also important to bear in mind that the division between center and margin not only is true on a global level but also exists within localities, between the powerful and the weak, the rich and the poor, the connected and the disconnected.

In her well-known essay "Can the Subaltern Speak?," Gayatri Spivak coined the term "epistemic violence" to refer to the "remotely orchestrated, far-flung, and heterogeneous project to constitute the colonial subject as Other" (1988, 280–1). In Spivak's conception, discursive representations of those on the margins—"men and women among the illiterate peasantry, the tribals, the lowest strata of the urban subproletariat"

(1988, 283)—often silence these subjects further or deny them any form of subjectivity or agency beyond their already overdetermined, assigned position in colonial discourses. This stereotyping is often found in global media discourses about conflicts in Africa, where violent conflict is reduced to a trope that serves to construct Africa as inferior, chaotic, and in need of saving.

A related concept, used by Robert Nixon (2011) to describe those who are impacted by environmental catastrophes—and by the global policies that mitigate the effects of these catastrophes on the North while amplifying them in the South—is that of "slow violence."[1] This term is also very useful in attempting to understand the way in which conflicts in Africa related to democratization and social change often impact most adversely the poor and the socially marginalized. The effect of these conflicts on their lives is often as destructive as violent conflict might have been, but it is drawn out over a longer period, less visible to the media's eye, and therefore often hidden from public scrutiny and intervention.

Nixon (2011, 2–3) describes "slow violence" as follows:

[A] violence that occurs gradually and out of sight, a violence of delayed destruction that is dispersed across time and space, an attritional violence that is typically not viewed as violence at all. Violence is customarily conceived as an event or action that is immediate in time, explosive and spectacular in space, and as erupting into instant sensational visibility. We need, I believe, to engage a different kind of violence, a violence that is neither spectacular nor instantaneous, but rather incremental and accretive, its calamitous repercussions playing out across a range of temporal scales. In so doing, we also need to engage the representational, narrative, and strategic challenges posed by the relative invisibility of slow violence. . . . Such a rethinking requires that we complicate conventional assumptions about violence as a highly visible act that is newsworthy because it is event focused, time bound, and body bound. . . . A major challenge is representational: how to devise arresting stories, images, and symbols adequate to the pervasive but elusive violence of delayed effects.

This form of representational violence is often exerted discursively within the media as a result of ingrained news values that focus on spectacular instances of conflict but neglect ones that unfold over a longer period on the margins of the media's field of vision, and it characterizes many democratization conflicts in Africa. When we therefore consider the ethical implications of the mediatization of democratization conflicts, our attention should extend beyond violent conflicts in the conventional sense—thereby risking a scholarly replication of journalistic attention to spectacle—to forms of discursive violence that may remain present in democratization processes and transitions after formal transitions have been completed.

It should also be borne in mind that the victims of epistemic violence are not only those on the receiving end of global media stereotypes but also those on the margins of African societies marked by high levels of inequality that tend to be overlooked, ignored, or stereotyped by media oriented toward elite interests. Comparative studies (see, e.g., Pointer et al. 2016) have highlighted the media's failure in many transitional contexts to articulate the voices of the socially marginalized and the poor.

The ethical question for the media that emerges from Nixon's conception is how to render this "slow violence" in media discourses in such a way that turns the "long emergencies of slow violence into stories dramatic enough to rouse public sentiment and warrant political intervention" (2011, 3).

Normative Frameworks

How, then, should media meet the ethical challenges that arise in the mediatization of conflicts, regardless of the form or level of violence present in these conflicts? Normative frameworks are often not specifically developed to deal with conflict, or are codified in too vague or generalizing ways to provide guidance to journalists in conflict situations. Codes that view ethical duties primarily in terms of professional duties and obligations may also fail to sufficiently account for the increasingly relational and participatory nature of contemporary media.

Although the focus of this book falls on democratization conflicts in Africa, their mediatization usually has a global dimension. Because of the global nature of contemporary media, the ethical principles guiding the mediatization of these conflicts therefore have to resonate globally. The point of departure for the evaluation of the various normative frameworks dealing with the mediatization of conflict will therefore be the considerable work done in recent years on the question of "global media ethics"—in particular, the three "protonorms" of human dignity, nonviolence, and truth-telling.

The Empirical and the Normative

Before embarking on this exploration, a note regarding the relationship between empirical and normative analyses of media ethics is necessary. Thus far in this book reference has been made to various empirical examples of how conflicts manifest during democratization processes, and how media have represented them. Normative assertions of what the media ought to do are often mixed with empirical studies of what they are actually doing (Voltmer 2013, 26). It is important to note, however, that the empirical and the normative belong to different categories of analysis. Although empirical studies can show us how conflicts are mediatized in practice and what the links between media, conflict, and democratization look like in actual contexts, these two categories—namely "is" (empiricism) and "ought" (normativity)—could be combined or compared but should not be confused. This does not mean that the one should supersede the other or that they should be thought of in isolation. The empirical and the normative can serve as important counterbalances to each other.

When, for instance, we questioned the link between media and democracy earlier, we noted that, when we consider the empirical context within which journalism is practiced around the world, the assumptions that journalism supports democracy and that journalism depends on democracy to function often do not hold true. This then led us to reconsider the assumption of a causal link between media and democracy. However, this analysis based on empirical observations does not negate any normative ideals we may have for the way media *should* ideally function and contribute to a democratic culture, nor does it negate the view that a participatory, inclusive democracy is ideally the best system within which media could practice.

Similarly, when we consider normative frameworks for the mediatization of conflict in this chapter, we are not doing so based on incontrovertible empirical evidence of their existence and feasibility. Rather, we are exploring and evaluating these frameworks in terms of their theoretical robustness and their likely productivity or limitations in the contexts under study. While it remains important to apply normative frameworks to empirical situations, this should be done not in an attempt to "prove" or "falsify" normative frameworks, but to enrich them by exploring how key ethical concepts are interpreted in specific contexts.

This is especially important given the historical dominance of Western theorization in media ethics. Critiques of attempts to construct a global media ethics (see, e.g., Rao and Wasserman 2007) have pointed to the problematic assumption that ethical frameworks developed in the Global North can be easily applied to lived realities in the Global South (although it should be noted that there is no single ethical framework in the North, nor a single lived reality in the South). While there may be agreement on key ethical principles, these principles may be interpreted in specific ways and be informed by local cultural values that resist their easy incorporation into such Northern frameworks (Rao and Wasserman 2007, 34). For instance, while the existence of free and independent media is widely accepted as an important determinant of the sustainability and depth of African democracies, it has become clear that Western normative ideals of "objectivity" within an individualist, liberal-democratic framework are not always feasible or desirable in African settings, where belonging and conviviality are deeply entrenched in the societies within which media operate (Nyamnjoh 2005). The very assumption that Northern frameworks are inherently universal, and the use of examples of practices in the South to support and validate Northern theories, could arguably be considered to be an example of epistemic violence in itself.

Therefore, the ongoing attempts to develop media ethical frameworks that are relevant for a globalized media environment should be conducted in a dialectical fashion, namely by exploring how local interpretations and applications of key ethical principles can deepen and broaden such principles (Wasserman 2011b). Universal values, therefore, should not be imperialistically imposed on contexts but should be shaped in relation to everyday experience, from the bottom up.

These interpretations and applications can be established empirically, by asking journalists how they interpret certain key values such as truthtelling, human dignity, or nonviolence. Through such an empirical study it might emerge that normative frameworks that were previously thought to be in tension, or even diametrically opposed, are being negotiated in ways that render them more compatible in practice than thought of in theory. For instance, empirical studies could show that the normative roles of "watchdog" and "developmental" journalism are not as diametrically opposed as previously assumed (De Beer et al. 2016). This finding could then further inform the development of normative theory in the African context by suggesting ways in which norms could evolve that encapsulate both these positions. Alternatively, an empirical study (Lodamo and Skjerdal 2009) of the socioeconomic conditions under which journalists in African countries work can help explain the practice of accepting "brown envelopes" as bribes and help improve working conditions rather than rejecting the norm itself.

The point of empirical studies of media ethical practices is therefore not to "prove" or "falsify" normative theories (which themselves are socially constructed, contextually rooted, and therefore contested), but to contribute to their development so that they can be better suited to specific contexts. We therefore see an interplay between normative theory and empirical descriptions.

Journalistic Role Performance

A third dimension to the complex question of the relationship between the normative and the empirical is the question of journalistic role performance. This pertains to the way journalists actually perform the roles and put into practice the norms they say they subscribe to, their different responses to ethical dilemmas, and the general journalism culture within which they operate. Within the general journalistic culture in a given setting, certain professional ideologies can be found, made up of sets of values, orientations, and predispositions (Hanitzsch 2007, 370). While the performance of professional roles and occupational ideologies can be empirically tested, this does not yet necessarily tell us whether the norms journalists subscribe to are actually the most appropriate ones for their context or what alternative norms may be more suitable.

Both comparative empirical and normative studies therefore require a combined analysis of generalized norms and values that may have universal resonance cross-culturally (the etic dimension) as well as in the particular perspectives of the participants in a given media culture (the emic dimension) (Hanitzsch 2007, 370).

The multiple, complex, and deep ethical questions raised in relation to the mediatization of conflict are particularly pressing when these conflicts turn violent. These questions include the influence of mediatized violence on behavior, representational issues, and spectatorship and compassion.

The Influence of Mediatized Violence on Behavior

Violence in the media, and its potential influence on audiences, has been a topic of long-standing debate in media ethics, as well as in "effects" studies. Media—especially entertainment media such as films and video games, as well as popular music—have frequently been blamed as being a direct cause of violent behavior. Michael Moore's 2002 documentary film *Bowling for Columbine* has become a well-known example of how the causal link between such media formats and violent behavior can be debunked, yet the moral panic about violent media content and its effects, especially on youth, frequently raises its head. However, as Boyle (2005) discusses at length, the "media blaming" becomes a common-sense explanation to link violent acts with individual media texts, while often ignoring broader social influences on behavior from perpetrators' surrounding culture (which includes media influences).

Although the effects of entertainment media on behavior might not be as pertinent to the mediatization of conflicts in Africa, some aspects of this debate do have relevance for questions around extreme speech and the incitement of violence. The extreme speech messages broadcast by Radio Télévision Libre des Mille Collines (RTLM) during the Rwandan genocide is often cited as an example of media "effects" on behavior in conditions of ethnic tension in Africa. However, as Straus (2007) has argued, this example raises familiar questions about the extent to which media messaging has a direct, causal effect on behavior. He argues that such effects should be considered "conditional," as the messages only take on significance when considered against the broader social context of violence.

Representational Issues

In the mediatization of conflicts such as war, terror attacks, or violent political clashes, which usually involves graphic depictions and descriptions of death or injury, representational issues come into play. Ethical dilemmas of this kind frequently arise out of a tension between truth-telling, the preservation of human dignity, and the imperative not to do harm. While most media ethical codes uphold truth-telling as a central precept, this imperative is usually balanced with the constraining values of protecting the dignity of those involved and limiting the harm that representations of violence may do to those involved, to their relatives and loved ones, and to audiences (especially children) who might be subjected to graphic images of violence.

Commercial pressures and orthodox news values (the old adage of "If it bleeds, it leads") make it difficult for journalists and other media practitioners to make decisions independently and according to their own ethical convictions. When faced with the question of whether to depict images of violence or how much of this violence should be shown, how it should be represented, and in what context, the ethical imperative of "maximizing harm" is therefore often difficult to balance with those of "minimizing harm" and "acting independently" (Black, Steele, and Barney 1995).

Spectatorship and Compassion

The issue of spectatorship and compassion represents a central question arising from the tension between journalists' attempts to balance the imperative of truth-telling with that of not doing harm and acting independently, namely how to bear witness to conflicts in an ethical way. The value of "objectivity" has come to dominate journalists' ethical frameworks and professional ideology over many years, despite the fact that it is often poorly defined and not always a desirable or realistic approach. A holistic and pragmatic approach to objectivity (Ward 2018) therefore has to be developed that moves beyond mere notions of facticity and neutrality to a more compassionate stance premised on human dignity.

The question, however, is what constitutes the "proper distance" (Silverstone 2007) from which violent conflicts should be observed. Journalists have to steer an ethical path between standing too close or too far from the conflicts they report on. If they stand too close to the conflict, they could become voyeurs, focusing on the spectacular aspects of conflicts and dishing them up for audiences who consume images and descriptions of violence as if these were entertainment, a pornography of blood and battle. A related danger of standing too close to a conflict is that perspective may be lost and that attention to the impact of the conflict and its intensity may result in journalists picking a particular side or neglecting to show the other side of the disagreement. Here, the ethical value of "acting independently" can be a useful counterbalance to the type of truth-telling that shows granular detail at the expense of wider context. On the other hand, standing too far away from a conflict—merely observing "neutrally" without committing to a particular position on the basis of ethical reflection, and not proposing solutions or interventions—could turn journalists and their audiences into mere spectators of suffering (Chouliaraki 2006), which is also an ethically untenable position.

Besides the ethical questions raised by the portrayal of pain, these representations also have a political dimension: the portrayal of suffering can make the difference as to whether someone is considered a victim or a martyr, and the political currency that may result from either designation (Seaton 2003, 49–50). "Bearing witness," if not done from an honest position of self-reflexivity, could also be used as a claim by journalists seeking to affirm their authority over the narrative, deciding on "what counts as public knowledge" and "rationalising suffering by processing it according to journalistic principles which are also economic and industrial" (Markham 2011, 101–2).

Ethical Norms across Cultural Difference

Where do we start from when evaluating the media's roles and responsibilities with regard to these moral problems? What are the central values that apply cross-culturally and can be used to guide the media in a variety of political and social contexts where conflicts arise? Given that democratization processes play out in contexts that vary greatly, and that the media's ability to contribute to the de-escalation of conflict in these contexts is shaped by a variety of historical, cultural, social, and economic forces, how can a universal framework for ethical conduct be constructed?

These questions relate to the difficult problem of ethical universals and particulars, which has received a great deal of attention in recent years (see, e.g., Christians et al. 2008; Ward and Wasserman 2010; Wasserman 2018a). Given that the mediatization of democratization conflicts in Africa often includes a cross-cultural dimension, similar questions about the applicability of ethical norms across cultural difference also arise. The insights from scholarship into global media ethics about universal values and cultural particulars are therefore useful to consider in this context.

Democratization conflicts in Africa are often characterized by inter-ethnic strife, and the mediatization of these conflicts is made more difficult by the fact that the media itself often mirrors the ethnic polarization of society. In Kenya, for instance, journalists have indicated (Wasserman and Maweu 2014b) that they often experience a tension between their belonging to a particular ethnic group and their commitment to journalistic impartiality. Ethnicity in that context frequently serves as a "filter" that influences the ethical decisions journalists make. In another African country, South Africa, there have been long-standing debates and conflicts over whether journalists should follow normative frameworks inherited from their professional counterparts in the Global North or whether "African" values such as the communitarian philosophy of *ubuntu* are more appropriate (see the discussion of these debates in Wasserman 2018a).

Added to this cultural complexity that characterizes media within African countries is the fact that the mediatization of these conflicts is often done by media that are based outside of the context in which the conflicts occur. This cultural distance between the subjects and objects of mediatization further raises questions with regard to how journalists are shaped by their own cultural backgrounds and belonging, and how their social positioning shapes their ethical values.

A Universal Protonorm as Point of Departure

Given the aforementioned cross-cultural complexities, the insights from scholarship into global media ethics can provide a useful starting point from which normative frameworks for dealing with conflict in a variety of settings can then be evaluated. Based on empirical case studies across cultures, Christians and Nordenstreng (2004) identified the "protonorm" of sacredness of life having cross-cultural reference and universal validity. As a subset of this central norm, three linked principles—human dignity, truth-telling, and nonviolence—can be used to guide ethical norms across cultures and contexts (Christians and Nordenstreng 2004). We can use these three principles to categorize the key ethical issues pertaining to mediatized conflict.

Human Dignity

This ethical principle is enshrined in international human rights law (Hamelink 2016, 6) and in democratic constitutions (e.g., Republic of South Africa 1996). In the African context the issue of human rights often revolves around historical remnants of ethnic and racial discourses of colonialism and apartheid.

The media's role in restoring people's dignity has also come to the fore globally with the rise in identity politics in recent years. The recognition of equal rights and respect for difference has been thrust to the fore of the public symbolic realm, in which the media is a key player. Here again the ethical and the political cannot be separated: "Questions of recognition . . . are not trivial matters; they are simultaneously ontological and political and go to the core of social being and claims to democracy" (Cottle 2006, 170). As Cottle (2006, 171) also indicates, the politics of recognition and the politics of redistribution are not always distinct, and power struggles for the latter often include claims to the former.

From an ethical perspective, we can add that human dignity—especially in African contexts marked by high levels of inequality and poverty—cannot merely be restored through the symbolic means at the disposal of the media but should extend to structural and material determinants as well. In this regard, a more activist role for the media can therefore be foreseen, as it couples symbolic respect for difference with demands for political intervention into the material aspects of people's lives. We will return to the question of how a more active, interventionist role for the media has been envisaged in different normative frameworks.

Human dignity can easily be eroded due to the pressures under which journalists report on conflicts in the contemporary media. The 24/7 news cycle privileges spectacle above complexity and technological explanations above social and political ones. By turning wars and conflicts into "infotainment" (Thussu 2003, 127), those involved in conflicts may be portrayed in one-dimensional, binary terms as perpetrators or victims, and their experiences paraded on screens and pages for the consumption of others. Even when this is done with an ostensible motivation to provide a "voice to the voiceless" (a notion we will return to in the next chapter when discussing the ethical approach of "listening"), it is often done at great speed, with superficial attention to the suffering of others, or with the simplistic and self-congratulatory stance of having shone a light on conflict. Seldom is time taken to pay close attention to the full humanity of everyone involved, and very rarely do objects of news coverage become the subjects of their own narratives.

This is not to say that reporting on suffering, violence, and atrocities necessarily has to be superficial and callous. The human dignity of the victims of violence, conflict, or degrading epistemic violence is more likely to be restored when journalists reflect on their own positioning and their responses to what they see. Such a reflective stance transforms journalists from detached observers, who unquestioningly submit themselves to the vagaries of the 24/7 news cycle, into witnesses who acknowledge their own emotional responses and recognize their own humanity in the faces of those they report on. Done from this ethical position, the act of bearing witness itself could bring about in audiences the awareness of the "degradation of all humanity," in the words of the reporter Fergal Keane (Tumber and Prentoulis 2003, 222). Bearing witness to atrocities in such a way—through an honest, humanizing narrative that contributes to the understanding of conflicts and the way people experience them—can pave the way for audiences to respond and interact with human suffering (Cottle 2006, 186). Witnessing and recognizing the suffering of others in a way that recognizes their inherent dignity as subjects rather than objects in an instrumentalist news narrative can therefore in itself be an ethical act (Seaton 2003, 50).

Truth-Telling

The notion of truth-telling as an ethical imperative is often in tension with other ethical values, such as the duty to respect privacy and to care for others, as has already been touched on earlier in this chapter. Nevertheless, truth-telling is a central value for the media. The question does arise: what is truth-telling in service to? The commonplace defense frequently offered by journalists when asked why something ostensibly controversial or shocking was reported on despite its potential to offend goes something like: "It was a good story" or "The public has a right to know" or "We hold up a mirror to reality." This type of response suggests that truth-telling is an end in itself and requires no further justification. Although the truth has inherent value as a cross-cutting ethical norm, its position as a principle linked to the overarching protonorm of sacredness of life means that it is not a moral absolute but has to be understood in relation to human dignity and nonmalfeasance. Truth-telling as a moral value, in other words, exists in service of the protonorm of sacredness of life. As a justification for mediating conflict, truth-telling therefore cannot operate on its own. Truth is in the service of life—this means that it should ultimately promote human dignity and avoid undue harm.

As an ethical value, truth-telling is complicated further when linked with notions such as objectivity, neutrality, and impartiality. These notions are especially central to conventional understandings of the media's monitorial role. In the conventional liberal-democratic "watchdog" mode, objectivity—murky as the concept may be—occupies a more central position than is the case in normative frameworks that may emphasize the media's duty of care or see a more interventionist role for the media to contribute to social change. (For a discussion of objectivity and its relevance for contemporary global media, see Ward 2018.)

A central problem with regard to truth-telling as an ethical concept is that reporting always implies selection: choices are made as to which conflicts are covered, which are considered more important than others, and which dimensions of and actors in a conflict receive more attention than others (Hamelink 2016, 32). The mediated "truth," therefore, is not self-evident. It is the result of a production of news that takes place according to an ingrained "media logic" that tends to highlight individual events rather than long-term processes and trends, emphasize sensational and dramatic events, and de-contextualize and dehistoricize conflict incidents (Hamelink 2016, 32).

Such selectivity on the part of the media can lead to conflict also being directed at the media itself, as dominant media narratives are challenged or rejected. The media may be criticized for not portraying the truth fully enough, or in a version that lacks complexity or texture. The media's location within relations of power—social, political, and economic—means that its version of the truth is always partial and subject to contestation.

This problem is compounded by the global media's commercial interests, which orient the media toward profitable audiences and advertising markets. Media's orientation toward markets can cause ethical dilemmas when journalists are faced with conflicts of interest (e.g., to tell truths that may be damaging to advertisers or the economic elites making up their audiences) or when particular perspectives on or solutions to conflicts are omitted or downplayed because they may threaten elite economic power or control.

Public service and community media are, ideally speaking, meant to provide a counterbalance to the commercial media's orientation toward elite audiences. However, in African contexts public service media are often owned and controlled by the state, and therefore ideologically compromised and unable to provide a balanced picture during political conflicts. This legacy of state interference in the media in predemocratic settings—which, in the case of many African countries, continues into the democratic era—has led to the dominance of the marketization of the media as the only viable option for media democratization, despite its many problems (Voltmer 2013, 169).

The ethical imperative of truth-telling, already under pressure due to the inherent selectivity of media routines and practices, is further complicated by the nature of language and representation. Journalistic narratives frame conflicts in particular ways, and these frames have implications for the way audiences are likely to relate or respond to particular conflicts, and the legitimacy or urgency they will attach to them. For instance, presenting a conflict as an "insurgence," "liberation struggle," "terrorism," "civil war," or "clash of opinion" can make a significant difference to public perception of an issue.

Often, journalistic frames are provided by external definers such as politicians, spin doctors, or "perception managers" (Hamelink 2016, 34), raising further questions around media independence and accountability. As Wright (2018) shows, foreign reporting from Africa has increasingly become a collaborative effort between journalists and nongovernmental organizations (NGOs), as news organizations cut back on foreign correspondent costs and NGOs have broadened their reach into journalism. Palmer (2019) has highlighted the important role that "fixers" play in providing journalists with information and contacts that shape their reporting.

Because of these collaborative efforts, and the reliance of journalists on information provided to them by outside organizations and networks, "truth-telling" as an ethical obligation becomes more difficult for journalists, as they cannot claim to have independent control over the information procured and produced. As the chances increase of reporting being slanted or influenced by the agendas set by actors other than journalists, so does the complexity of journalists' ethical obligation toward the truth. The other side of the coin, however, is that such collaboration can also provide journalists with a fuller, richer, and more complex picture of conflicts than they might have been able to achieve without the social, cultural, and contextual insights they receive from their collaborators.

While the media's selective representation and framing of conflicts and the omission of certain perspectives and voices present an ethical dilemma—as it always presents a partial version of the truth—the opposite situation also could pertain, raising different ethical problems. This ethical dilemma relates to the depiction of the horror and suffering associated with violent conflicts. Even in the case of conflicts that are representational in nature—for instance, conflicts on social media expressing racism, misogyny, and xenophobia—the assault on people's dignity, privacy, and emotional well-being can cause severe harm.

As mentioned earlier in this chapter, this tension between the ethical values of truth-telling and human dignity raises the issue of the problem of voyeurism. In these circumstances, the ethical question that arises is how much of the truth should be represented in the media so as not to amplify the pain already inflicted, or how suffering could be reported on in such a way that it does not merely serve an entertainment function for spectating audiences. While the ethical protonorm of truth-telling can serve a vital democratic function to raise public consciousness, sympathy, or outrage, it should not be at the expense of the dignity and privacy of victims of conflict.

An argument in favor of showing suffering in all its horror is that such depictions may serve to remind audiences of the inhumanity of human-kind, in the hope that this realization may prevent a repeat of the conflict. Audiences exposed to such depictions may come to acknowledge that even modern, high-tech wars are never "clean" or without pain inflicted upon in-nocent people and children (Hamelink 2016, 35).

Arguments against the depiction of the horrors of conflict include that the mediatization of suffering could in effect double the suffering of victims: after having suffered violence, degradation, or pain, they are again humiliated or retraumatized by having images of their suffering broadcast back at them. A further argument against a no-holds-barred depiction of violent conflicts is that it might inure and desensitize audiences to images of violence, with the result that these images eventually lose their power to shock. Or, while depictions still have the ability to create shock and outrage, they may result in an escalation of violence, as people are motivated to engage in acts of revenge (Hamelink 2016, 35; Sontag 2002). We see, therefore, that the protonorm of truth-telling is not absolute but has to be balanced against the norms of human dignity and nonviolence.

The ethical question with regard to depicting the truth of suffering as a result of conflict therefore becomes one of avoiding a "spectatorship of suf-fering" (Chouliaraki 2006). This is especially a prevalent issue in the reporting of African conflicts, where images of war, conflict, and violence have formed part of the repertoire of colonial discourse that constructed Africa pessimisti-cally as a geopolitical "Other," a place marked by savagery and darkness.

We have already mentioned the work of Roger Silverstone (2007, 47), whose notion of "proper distance" as an ethical value implies that journalists have to develop the practical wisdom of knowing how far to stand from a conflict when reporting on it. Collapsing the distance between journalist and subject completely, as in "embedded journalism," leads to a relationship that is too close for journalists to remain vigilant over abuse of power. On the other hand, portraying a subject as a distant Other who cannot be understood but can only be pitied is a stance that is too far removed.

A further, more conceptual challenge for the media when striving toward greater truth-telling is how exactly "truth" is defined. It should be clear that mere facticity is not precisely equal to truthfulness. Recent debates about "fake news" have made it clear that issues of fabrication and facticity only partly explain the way these reports resonate with audiences. A larger cynicism and distrust in the mainstream media, or a lack of recognition and resonance between people's daily lived experience and the way reality is constructed in the media, may be at the root of the distinctions audiences draw between what they consider to be "real" and "fake" news (Nielsen and Graves 2017). The rise of misinformation in African contexts (Wasserman 2017) also suggests that audiences respond to information that resonates with their experiences, beliefs, fears, and political orientation.

The ethical question for the media thus becomes how to engage in "truth-telling" in ways that are about more than merely the dissemination of facts, but that creates meaning and relevance in people's lives. Rethinking media reporting as storytelling that includes different levels of communication—such as reason, rhetoric, images, emotions, and narratives—can be one way of striving to provide a fuller version of the truth that can facilitate understanding during conflicts, by revealing people's experiences, their values, and how they make sense of their being in the world (Cottle 2006, 172, 173). If journalists see their ethical responsibility toward the truth not in a positivistic sense as relating only to "objective" rationality and facticity but also to interpretation and storytelling, they could contribute to social cohesion and community-building (Zelizer 2017, 177). Such an approach to truth-telling, as contextual, meaningful, and rich rather than merely "factual," is closely related to the framework of "listening" to be discussed in the next chapter.

Nonviolence

The third principle linked to the overarching, cross-cultural protonorm of sacredness of life is that of nonviolence, or doing no harm (Christians and Nordenstreng 2004; Hamelink 2016, 7).

This norm could be interpreted passively—in situations of conflict, the media may see their ethical responsibility as simply avoiding doing further harm. A more constructive way to look at it is to consider what the media can actively do to solve, defuse, or de-escalate conflicts. Such an interventionist role, however, may be considered as being at odds with the liberal-democratic normative framework that envisions a more impartial role for journalists. This framework remains the dominant orthodoxy in many parts of the Global North and has been exported via journalism training programs, exchanges, and education to Africa and Latin America (see Paterson, Gadzekpo, and Wasserman 2018). Various normative frameworks, such as peace journalism and public journalism, have suggested alternative approaches that would enable journalists to contribute more actively to the solution of conflicts. However, these alternatives, to which we will return later in this chapter, have in turn also been subject to critique.

The ethical principle of nonviolence can be understood in the context of conflict to guide the media to not only avoid exacerbating conflict but also commit to its de-escalation and to facilitating democratic outcomes. This principle should not be confused with a kind of naïve idealism that foresees the possibility or even the desirability of a democratic life without any contestation. As we have noted already, disagreements, when managed properly and not allowed to turn into animosity, may in fact be productive and constituent of the kind of agonistic democracy that Mouffe (2005, 114) has in mind. While there may be agreement about democratic ethical values such as liberty and equality, the profound disagreements that may arise around their meaning, the way they should be implemented, and how power relations should be reconfigured to adhere to these values should be accepted as precisely "the stuff of democratic politics" (Mouffe 2005, 114). Especially on a global scale, Mouffe (2005, 135) emphasizes, alterity and otherness are "irreducible," and conflicts and contestations are therefore to be expected.

When we therefore consider nonviolence as a central value against which normative frameworks should be evaluated, it is implied that during such contestations respect for the sacredness of life remains paramount. If nonviolence is at the core of the way media engages with democratization conflicts, it would seek to report on such conflicts in such a way as to avoid the symbolic annihilation (Tuchman 1978) of contestants in the conflict. Instead, conflict reporting would focus on finding ways to confirm people's human dignity and offer solutions to help de-escalate the conflict. The commitment to nonviolence also implies a relational stance toward others, rather than the impassionate and detached observer role so often proclaimed as journalistic gospel. The Levinasian notion that it is in the face of the Other that one recognizes the Self asks of the media to recognize participants in conflict and victims of violence as human beings, subjects in real encounters rather than objects or figurants in a story. Where feasible, the media could facilitate face-to-face encounters, dialogues where human dignity can be reaffirmed and the possibility of violence can be diminished when faced with another human being. When peace becomes the normative goal, the media's ethical duty is reconfigured as one of care (Christians and Nordenstreng 2004, 23). The principle of nonviolence asks of the media to pay particular attention to the weak and the vulnerable and to highlight ways in which resources could be shared so as to prevent conflict and heal those affected by it (Christians and Nordenstreng 2004, 23), instead of adding to the burden of violence by uncritical and uncaring reporting.

Ethics, Codes, and Professionalism

The ethical principles discussed are foundational commitments that recognize a common humanity across cultures and orient the media toward finding ethical values that transcend parochial interests. The adherence to the protonorm of sacredness of life, and the ethical principles of dignity, truth, and nonviolence therefore go beyond the subscription to professional media ethical codes. These values, or some iteration of them, do inform most media ethical codes, even if they do so implicitly. How codes operate in contexts of conflict, and how ethics relates to the notion of professionalism, is worth considering.

Morality and ethics are often seen by journalists as a matter of "common sense or professionalism" (Markham 2011, 105) rather than a philosophical position or an ongoing reflective practice. Journalists' perceived ability to instinctively distinguish between right and wrong can sometimes lead to a disavowal of ethical reflection as being too complicated, self-righteous, or abstract and therefore unsuitable for the demands of fast-paced, pragmatic practice. Such a disavowal then can become a moral claim in itself, with the aim of constructing the journalist as a pragmatic professional actor who is naturally morally orientated (Markham 2011, 105).

Ethical codes may or may not be seen as pragmatic enough to support these claims. Some journalists claim a type of Aristotelian wisdom that does not require codes in order to know how to "do the right thing" (Markham 2011, 105). Codes do, however, occupy a central place in journalistic discourses that make claims to professionalism. UNESCO, for instance, links ethical codes to media legislation and regulatory bodies as dimensions of "professional journalistic standards and ethics" that act as accountability mechanisms across different countries (UNESCO, n.d.)

While ethical codes can provide useful normative outlines for journalistic practice, they are often not considered adequate to assist in the complex and dynamic contexts within which ethical dilemmas arise. One of the reasons for this inadequacy is that they tend to be very vague and general, and therefore fail to provide the kind of specific ethical direction that journalists often seek in particular instances of moral conflict. Another problem is that these codes, at least as they have been developed in the Global North—and adopted and only slightly adapted for context by African journalists—tend to be based on liberal-democratic frameworks that do not allow for much deviation from orthodox positions. Consequently, negotiating new or alternative ethical positions such as care, listening, or intervention (e.g., in the form of peace journalism) is difficult to accomplish within the circumscribed framework.

A further issue is that ethical codes operate within a conception of journalism as a "profession." The professionalism approach to journalism has been subject to extensive critique (some of which we will touch on later). Criticism of this approach often centers around the problem of the division that is set up between journalists and their audiences when journalists identify as "professionals." This division can further broaden the gulf between the subjects and objects of mediatization, which can be substantial in conditions of high inequality, such as that which characterizes many African societies. The rise of misinformation and "fake news" has again emphasized the importance of authoritative, accurate, and trustworthy news channels that media users may turn to when feeling overwhelmed by the avalanche of false information. There is no disputing that properly researched, fact-checked information is vitally important. In times of violent conflict, trustworthy information can make the difference between life and death.[2] Limiting media ethics to professional codes, however, might not be the most appropriate way of ensuring a stronger commitment to ethical production and consumption practices.

Christians and Nordenstreng (2004, 17) approach the question of codes and professionalism from three angles. Codes can be considered in a positive light, as a means of educating journalists as professionals and raising awareness of ethics. This approach, which Christians and Nordenstreng (2004, 17) call "naïve," is still a widespread one in "so-called developing and post-Communist countries." As such, the critique of codes and professionalism that Christians and Nordenstreng offer is relevant for the discussion of conflict in transitional democracies, which this book focuses on. One of their points of criticism is that codes often serve as "mere rhetorical devices, as deliberate window dressing and camouflage, or at best as manifestations of hypocrisy" (Christians and Nordenstreng 2004, 18).

However, Christians and Nordenstreng also offer an analytical perspective that views codes as part of a broader system of regulation that may not provide a good way of regulating the media within a democratic society:

Medias [*sic*] in the contemporary world have become so vital that there are indeed good grounds to take them as a fourth branch of government—not just rhetorically but even in political theory and legal and ethical practice. This means that the codes are designed not just for the selfish purpose of safeguarding the journalists' fortress but also for an idealistic purpose of serving the public interest. (Christians and Nordenstreng 2004, 18)

From this perspective, ethical codes can serve a constructive function in transitional societies and new democracies, as they provide the public with an opportunity to demand transparency and accountability from journalists and to insist that they conduct themselves in accordance with journalistic values. Codes can also help journalists reflect on their own values and practices. However, if journalists do not also make an effort to include citizen perspectives in their ethical deliberation, such professional self-reflection often becomes parochial and solipsistic. The changes in the structure of the Press Council of South Africa discussed earlier, aimed at allowing greater citizen participation, is an example of such an effort at reorienting regulatory processes toward greater audience participation. However, it also attracted criticism, either for undermining journalistic authority or for not going far enough in involving the public.

The Notion of Objectivity

The conventional approach of linking ethics to journalistic professionalism has proved to be problematic and limiting. In this conception of journalistic values and roles, ethics is usually codified and seen as a hallmark of a profession. Primary among these values, at least in the way they developed in the liberal-pluralist democratic tradition in the Global North, has been the notion of "objectivity." Often conflated with related terms such as "impartiality," "balance," and "neutrality," objectivity has been key to defining journalism ever since it was conceived of as a profession (Tumber and Prentoulis 2003, 215, 216).

Factual, investigative journalism can play a crucial role during transitions to democracy, to uncover corruption and suppressed information and to break "through the fog of propaganda," even if this is not done in a detached, "objective" manner (Voltmer 2013, 81). When journalism's role during conflict is critiqued, or evaluated against its stated normative claims, these values are then also often appealed to. Journalists would typically defend their interpretation of events as merely reflecting "reality," assuming a "hierarchy of truth which the journalist is given to be uniquely authorised to discern" (Markham 2011, 96). When one side of the conflict is aggrieved by what is perceived or experienced as media bias toward their opponents, the media is routinely accused of not being "objective"—therefore unfair or untrustworthy and, by implication, unprofessional.

The notion of objectivity has been subjected to extensive critiques that will not be repeated here (for substantial discussions on the history and contemporary applicability of this concept, see Ward 2005, 2018). Suffice to say that the mediatization of conflict within democratization contexts occurs within social and cultural contexts that influence the process of representation. Voltmer's (2013, 65) succinct summary of news as the product of agents within structures is helpful in this regard:

> Even though the media are dependent on the input they obtain from their sources—political leaders, experts and, increasingly, material provided by ordinary citizens—this does not mean that they simply transmit the messages of others. Rather, news is a cultural product that provides an interpretation of social reality through the "grammar" of journalism, i.e., the norms, routines and aesthetic judgements news people apply when

processing their raw material and transforming it into a text that is widely recognized as news.

This process results in the construction of a "media reality," which, in turn, can set agendas for political and social processes, make meaning of events by interpreting and framing them, and as a consequence have an influence on the development or outcome of conflicts (Voltmer 2013, 66).

The Notion of Professionalism

Due to the many claims made for professionalism as a signifying framework for journalists, it is important to examine the usefulness of this overarching conceptual context. Especially during times of conflict, and within contexts of societies undergoing democratic transformation, the ethical demands that are made of journalists are often couched within the discourse of professionalism, as are their own self-definition of their roles and responsibilities. The framework therefore demands scrutiny.

There are good reasons that the notion of professionalism has held some appeal in fragile African democracies marked by conflict. Especially under the influence of Western media assistance organizations, professionalism, coupled with self-regulation, is often seen as a bulwark against state intervention and pressure. The claim to a professional morality is in itself a way to establish authority and is therefore strategic when journalists vie for status and influence (Markham 2011, 98). In other words, moral authority can be used as symbolic capital to deflect criticism in a way that serves journalism's own interests in the marketplace (Markham 2011, 99).

In its attempts at constructing itself as accountable and transparent, the media in the African context could also have its own, market-oriented interests at heart. While such attempts to attain status and influence might be hedonistic in certain contexts, in fragile democracies journalists' very self-preservation may hinge on such claims. It is therefore with some anxiety that one criticizes the notion of professionalism (and its support by international agencies) in African contexts marked by fragile press freedom, democratic regressions, and cyclical authoritarian tendencies, and where threats to journalists have been on the rise in recent years (Paterson et al. 2018).

It is very important to note that a critique of professionalism should not be seen as an attack on media freedom or opposition to journalism that relies on good training, ethical reflection, or in-depth investigative work (Paterson et al. 2018). Instead, it is precisely because of the importance of journalism in African communities—in contexts where democratization processes are fragile; journalistic norms are still being negotiated and contested in relation to changing circumstances and sociopolitical needs; and societies are polarized, unequal, and engaged in various forms of conflict—that we have to ask whether professionalization is the optimal conceptual framework within which to consider the ethical responsibilities of the media.

Several points of criticism regarding the notion of journalism as a profession have been offered in the literature. The idea of professional journalism has been seen as "antithetical to democratic communication" from a wide range of theoretical and analytical perspectives and have been subject to Marxist, communitarian, and Foucauldian critiques (Waisbord 2013, 106). First, journalism is often practiced without much regard for the usual "trappings of professionalism" (Zelizer 2017, 178), such as training, education, and licensing. Journalism lacks a specific set of required knowledge requirements and formal rules and procedures, although it claims professional autonomy, especially when reporting on conflict situations (Tumber and Prentoulis 2003, 217). Formal training and education are often seen as insufficient without the osmosis that happens during exposure to the "real world" of journalism practice (Zelizer 2017, 178), and ethical codes are frequently disregarded, given lip service, or seen as constraining. In conditions of conflict and war, this process of osmosis and absorption of occupational demands is especially prevalent among journalists, who then develop strong bonds in hazardous and stressful conditions and identify more closely with their practice and "profession" (Tumber and Prentoulis 2003, 219).

Second, conceiving of journalism within the frame of professionalism has tended to espouse an orientation among practitioners toward distance, neutrality, balance, objectivity, and expertise as the basis for their social authority, coupled with autonomy from undue political or economic interference (Markham 2011, 96; Zelizer 2017, 176). This orientation has often led to a wide gap between journalists and their publics, which in turn has tended to breed a cynical view of journalism as an institution. Paradoxically, insisting on the status of professionals to ensure ethical practice can therefore have the unintended consequence of eroding the relationship of trust between journalists and communities if the former is seen as aloof and removed from the lived experience of the latter. This critique is of particular importance in contexts of inequality, social polarization, and ethnic tension, such as those marking democratization conflicts in Africa. As pointed out earlier, this cynicism has been shown to lie at the root of the rise of so-called fake news, as people turn to news that resonates with their experience and tend to view "real" and "fake" as points on a spectrum rather than binary opposites.

In African contexts of high socioeconomic inequality, the orientation of journalism toward professionalism has also been shown to favor elite perspectives on the news, experienced by audiences as a lack of relevance to and resonance with their daily lives (for findings from South Africa in this regard, see Malila et al. 2013). As mentioned earlier, an ethical conception of truth-telling that includes storytelling and collaborative constructions of social reality could contribute to social cohesion and community-building (Zelizer 2017, 177). Such collaboration between journalists, publics, and citizens-as-participants in the media sphere can be especially important during times of conflict, when social polarization and fragmentation are more acute, and particularly in transitional societies where divisions and tensions do not lie far below the surface. This type of collaboration would, however, hinge on journalists accepting that they have to relinquish claims to control over the narrative and seek truth collaboratively. Such a stance would require a different normative framework to those premised on journalistic independence and objectivity, and would envisage a more relational orientation for journalists. One framework that could contribute to such a conception of journalistic ethics in times of conflict is that of "listening," to which we will return in the next chapter.

Furthermore, within a framework of "professionalism," journalists' ethical responsibilities are often expressed by means of ethical codes. While codes can have the positive effect of signaling journalists' commitment to accountability and providing audiences with points of reference in demanding such accountability, without further contextual interpretation codes can be vague and generalizing. They can also be too static to account for the dynamic nature of changing norms and practices in contexts of transition and rapid social and technological change. Even when journalists reflect on codes or revisit accountability procedures (e.g., the efficacy of self-regulatory bodies), these discussions of ethics among journalists themselves "tend to be conservative insofar as they implicitly reinforce more than they submit to scrutiny";

in addition, "ethical debates tend toward dogmatism because they remain blind to the existence, and possible normative merit, of an 'outside' of ethics" (Markham 2011, 95). Theories of journalistic professionalism tend to be self-reinforcing and solipsistic, as they are "reproduced by mutual performance and projection as such by individuals" (Markham 2011, 95).

Deciding on the appropriate ethics code for a given community of practice is complicated by a "blending of time, space, institutional cultures and technology" (Zelizer 2017, 88). The globalization of the media has also complicated the question of which ethical framework is appropriate in globalized, multicultural settings and whether ethical frameworks can be applied universally (Christians et al. 2008). Prescribing ethical standards for journalism around the world, given the wide variety of circumstances within which journalism is practiced, is therefore well-nigh impossible (Zelizer 2017, 94). Using the notions of professionalism derived from Western contexts to guide and evaluate journalistic performance in postauthoritarian contexts marked by democratization conflicts will often mean that journalism in these contexts is considered as lacking or underperforming, unless local conditions, needs, and expectations are taken into account.

Professionalism and Codes of Ethics in Transitional Contexts

Despite the wide range of journalisms that have emerged alongside hybrid forms of democracy in postauthoritarian contexts, reflecting "the huge diversity of the political, economic and social realities in the new democracies of the 'third wave'" (Voltmer 2013, 198), the normative models that have had the strongest influence worldwide have been derived from Western democratic contexts. However, the historical contexts, social conditions, and cultural values in African societies undergoing transitions from colonialism to postcolonialism and from authoritarianism to democracy have differed very strongly from those in Western democracies. Some alternative normative models have been developed to suit these contexts better. Among these, "development journalism" has been a particularly strong contender, although also a controversial one due to its association with a subservient and collaborative journalism in authoritarian postcolonial settings (Obijiofor and Hanusch 2011, 26).

Other attempts to indigenize media ethics by drawing on African cultural histories and value frameworks have been made (for a summary, see

Wasserman 2014). However, these are not without the potential to create further problems, such as cultural essentialism and the reinforcement of social hierarchies, the stifling of free speech, and exclusions based on group membership. Not only do the norms defining what constitutes "good journalism" differ across cultures and societies, but also these criteria change over time and are modified when applied in different settings (Voltmer 2013, 2013). During periods of political transition, social values change, ideological hegemonies shift, and new commercial demands impact on how journalists and audiences may conceive of the ideal journalistic roles (Voltmer 2013, 199).

A rigid application of "professional" standards and ethical codes imported from more established democracies would therefore not do justice to the particular demands of journalism in these transitional settings. This is not to say that a lower bar should be set for journalism in these contexts. It does, however, point to the importance of developing ethical guidelines in response to local conditions, challenges, histories, and norms.

Ethical codes, by and large, are "an invention of the industrialized democracies of the West and Global North." As such, certain key assumptions— such as a free and independent press, journalism as an objective watchdog, the public's right to information, and notions such as objectivity, neutrality, facticity, and independence—form the basis of such codes. Generally there is little, if any, critical reflection on their applicability in countries such as those in Africa, where "soft authoritarianism, transitional governance, government-owned media, odd mixes of colonialism and post-colonialism, blends of secular and religious authorities, self-censorship and government interference are prevalent" (Zelizer 2017, 94). Understanding the ethical duties of the media in relation to conflict and democratization in Africa within the narrow structures of professional codes of ethics may therefore be too limiting to meet the demands of these contexts. Hybrid ethical frameworks, which arise from contextual responsiveness while acknowledging journalists' aspiration to and membership of a global journalistic community, therefore have a better chance of success (Voltmer 2013, 99).

Norms versus Practice

A further question that arises is how well journalists perform the roles set out in the professional codes and guidelines of practice in the first place. Codes of ethics linked to professionalism are often not very effective. They do not have a good track record of eradicating unethical behavior—not only in Africa but also globally (Zelizer 2017, 93). Furthermore, evidence has shown that there is a gap between the ideal norms that journalists profess and their actual practices, in conflict situations and in general (Hoxha and Hanitzsch 2018, 47).

The challenge for media scholarship is therefore to develop ethical frameworks that are responsive to local cultural, political, and material conditions in their normative imagination, but also realistic in their assessment of the descriptive, empirical conditions within which journalism is practiced. This cognizance of the practical, lived conditions of journalism practice in Africa is important to avoid the imposition of ethical standards on a context where journalism practice exceeds the conventional norms of journalism as these have been understood elsewhere (Zelizer 2017, 98). During times of conflict and heightened tensions, especially when these are linked to political transitions and processes of democratization, moral frameworks and journalistic value systems are subject to flux. In these conditions, journalistic paradigms are defended, contested, and renegotiated, as has been seen in journalistic "boundary work" in South Africa during the postapartheid period (Berger 2008; Wasserman 2006).

The rise of technological possibilities that put the production of media texts within the reach of members of the public who do not identify as "professional journalists" has led to changes in journalism practices. It is therefore important to bear in mind that, given these changes, ethical norms will increasingly be negotiated and contested between "conventional and nonconventional journalists, as well as non-journalists, in the available maze of digital spaces" (Zelizer 2017, 99). For this reason, journalism ethics should be conceived of as open, dynamic, and fluctuating—in other words, difficult to pin down in codes decided upon by "professionals" (Ward and Wasserman 2015). In the context of media reporting of conflict, this would include other role players, such as activists, NGOs, and members of civil society, who also communicate within this conflictual space (Wright 2018) and may have their own, often divergent, conceptions of what would be considered ethical communicative practices in conflict situations.

It is therefore clear that a consideration of the ethics of the mediatization of democratization conflicts in Africa requires a broader, more fluid, and more inclusive conception of journalism ethics than professional codes can provide.

Journalism Ethics as a Culture

Instead of thinking about media ethics as codified and linked to institutionalized notions of "professionalism," we could also think about it as part of media culture. This would entail thinking about ethics as it forms part of journalists', media practitioners', and media consumers' shared web of meanings and interpretative horizons. In other words, what ethical values exist within the "horizon of understanding" of the various members of the interpretive community of media practitioners and consumers? And how may these values shape their interpretation of an event and their response to it?

Viewed from a phenomenological perspective, which assumes that meanings are attached to events because they exist within the "knowledge structures and interpretive frameworks" of the observer (Hirsch 2013, 130), media ethics should not be seen as a reified, static deontology that should be codified, but rather as a cultural orientation that shapes the interactions and meaning-making practices within an interpretive community. Because the interpretive framework of members of this community is linked to their own experiences, a study of media ethics and attempts to construct ethical frameworks for the media should be rooted in the lived experiences of people rather than ethical abstractions. Indeed, an "individual's interpretive structures do not exist in some abstract metaphysical plane; instead, they are inextricably linked to the embodied experience of being in the world" (Hirsch 2013, 131).

Instead of seeing media ethics, codified, as a hallmark of journalistic "professionalism," it might therefore be more useful to try and understand the surrounding culture within which journalists and publics make sense of events, decide on their actions, and rationalize these decisions in terms of their own perceived role and standing in a given context. Of course, these interpretations and actions have ethical dimensions, and interpretations of events and responses to them certainly have ethical consequences. Viewing ethics from a cultural rather than a professional perspective is therefore in no way an attempt to escape ethical responsibility and accountability. On the contrary, knowing how ethical values are formed, how events are interpreted, and how responses are formulated in relation to the everyday experiences and interactions of journalists and publics provides us with a way to more meaningfully and successfully engage with ethical questions. As Zelizer (2017, 202) explains with reference to the media's role in the Iraq War, seeing journalism culture as underpinning the reporting of war and conflict and the ethical decisions involved provides us with a way to better engage journalism about the omission of certain voices:

> Because the culture of journalism references action taken in accordance with conventional understandings that guide journalists to act in collective ways, the prism necessarily reflects the resources journalists draw upon to coordinate their activities. By recognizing that journalism's record of the war took shape as much through improvisation, adaptation, trial and error and informal discussion as through more frequently discussed journalistic cues, journalism as culture helps explain how shifts on the ground forced the continual retweaking of journalistic practice, an inevitable state of affairs in wartime.

A key component of seeing journalism as culture is to examine its inhabitants—in other words, those who are considered to be included in the interpretive community of media and journalism (Zelizer 2017, 202). Garman (2005, 199) argues that, in the South African context, journalists should see themselves as part of interpretive communities to help refocus "journalism's place in a wider world of culture and dissemination of social meanings," and that journalism education should focus on such a broader conception of journalism and not only on "professional" skills. In the South African context, marked by severe social inequalities inherited from apartheid, it may be argued that facilitating dialogue with and between communities—which may require a journalism that is more closely integrated with the public—is an ethical responsibility in itself.

If media practices are analyzed as part of a wider culture, rather than narrowly linked to media "professionalism," with its strategic rituals (Tuchman 1972) of "objectivity," "neutrality," and "distance," an ethical framework can be developed that is responsive to specific contexts and cultural imaginaries and that is relational. Such a framework would remain sensitive to the different ways in which events such as conflicts are interpreted by various participants of the interpretive community and would therefore see the resolution of such conflicts as intricately bound up with the lived experiences and material conditions in which these interpretations take place.

A journalism that sees its ethical role as one characterized by distance, neutrality, and rationality—the tropes of modernity that have marked dominant notions of journalism ethics (Christians et al. 2008, 147)—is especially limited in conditions of conflict. Conflicts "are never merely about objective conditions but instead involve subjective feelings" (Hamelink 2016, 20). A journalism that privileges rationality, eschews affective responses, and underestimates emotions such as outrage, anger, fear, and distress is therefore bound to be inadequate as a conduit for dialogue or a facilitator for peace. Indeed, "because conflicts have both substantive and emotional components, the balance between cognitive capacity and emotional sensitivity is crucial to prevent escalation" (Hamelink 2016, 20).

The shift from an ethics of professionalism based on rationality and objectivity to one in which ethics is developed within culture and in response to everyday life is especially important to consider in conditions of high inequality and social polarization such as those existing in Africa, where interpretations of events and appropriate ethical responses to them may differ greatly. From this point of view the questions of who belongs and who has the right to speak are in themselves ethical questions. An orientation toward journalism as a profession can result in (even unintended) elitist conceptions of media practice that can have a detrimental effect on the quality of democracy in polarized, "bifurcated" public spheres (Heller 2009). Heller argues that, in these contexts, there exist different public spheres for those who can access media agendas and policymaking processes, and for those who remain marginalized from these spaces. When journalism is viewed as a "profession," the danger exists that practices, genres, and formats that deviate from the hegemonic mainstream will be delegitimized or viewed as inferior, as has been the case with tabloid journalism (Wasserman 2010b) or photojournalism (Zelizer 2017, 203), not to mention other, "citizen" members of the broader interpretive community that participate in the production and consumption of meaning in the mediatized public sphere.

Seeing media practices from a cultural perspective therefore assumes a more dynamic, flexible definition instead of imposing boundaries and rules to decide who belongs and who doesn't (Zelizer 2017, 203). This also implies a wider and more democratic conception of who can contribute to the construction of ethical frameworks and participate in ethical decision-making. If journalistic ethics remains internal to the journalistic field, as the preserve of "professionals," it enables the "reproduction of hierarchy" rather than imbuing the public with moral authority (Markham 2011, 105–6), thereby undermining claims by the media to represent the public interest. A more "open ethics" (Ward and Wasserman 2015) would see ethics not as a closed, static code that belongs in the domain of journalistic professionals but as a dynamic value system that keeps evolving as it responds to contributions from all members of the interpretive community that makes up the media landscape—this includes not only formal media practitioners but also members of the public, who should now be seen as active "users" and coproducers of content and meaning.

Such a view of ethics—as open, dynamic, participatory—requires attention to be paid to African publics as users with agency, who engage with media texts and platforms to actively make meaning and also increasingly coproduce media content as a result of greater access to media technologies (Willems and Mano 2017, 4). In other words, instead of limiting the responsibility of reflection over the media's ethical duties during times of conflict and crisis to "professionals" guided by codes, a cultural approach to the media would investigate the ways in which media production is linked to the everyday life of African publics, who share the duty of ethical reflection and responsibility.

Once ethics is opened up in this way, to become a participatory field to which the broader interpretive community can contribute, ethical norms are also likely to be more responsive to the particularities of specific contexts. This might mean that a tension could arise between normative ideals for the media, drawn up by regulatory bodies and professional associations, and those values emerging from the lived experience of publics who also participate in the interpretive community by consuming and coproducing media messages and meanings—unless the former is willing to embrace the latter.

Approaching journalism from a cultural perspective therefore means that journalism practices and ethical values should be constructed, renegotiated, and interpreted from the bottom up (Zelizer 2017, 211). An inclusive and participatory approach to the development of ethics would be particularly appropriate for new democracies in Africa, where a variety of ethical frameworks, derived from the Global North as well as from indigenous value systems, compete for dominance (Wasserman 2011b, 794). Knowing how various publics in these contexts interpret ethical principles such as dignity, nonviolence, and truth-telling would make for a richer and more textured understanding of how they function in actually existing mediatized public spheres. A dialectic between normative protonorms and the empirical, everyday reality of media as it is practiced and consumed—*lived*—in specific contexts can therefore be very productive.

Media Accountability in Africa

As mentioned earlier, adopting a cultural approach to media practices in Africa as concerns the coverage of conflict, instead of relying on the framework of "professionalism," implies greater involvement of the public in the construction of ethical values for the media. Such a participatory approach has implications for the way in which media's accountability and transparency are understood.

Media accountability can be defined as "any non-State means of making media responsible to the public" (Bertrand 2000). The related notion of "transparency" is a narrower one and refers to the ways in which media institutions may make their editorial processes known to the public. In a global context, where trust in the media has been eroded in recent years, the ability for publics to hold media accountable is increasingly seen as important in the interest of the media's democratic role (Fengler 2012, 175).

The systems of press councils and self-regulation referred to previously form part of these accountability measures, as do practices such as the use of public editors or ombudsmen, inviting suggestions and comments from readers or audiences, editorial explanations for controversial decisions, and even newsroom tours (Zelizer 2017, 254). Some of these practices include activities associated with the "civic" or "public" journalism movement in the United States, such as public meetings, forums, and talk shows, held in an attempt to reconnect with cynical or distant audiences. At the heart of this value is the commitment to openness, to showing the public how reporting was done in an attempt to create greater credibility and trust in the media (Zelizer 2017, 254).

As Zelizer (2017, 257) notes, the adoption of greater transparency in journalism worldwide seems to reflect the recognition that nonjournalists—members of the public who participate in the wider interpretive community—may be better positioned to constructively critique the media from the sidelines than those who are immersed in mainstream media practices. Journalists are, however, often very sensitive to criticism and tend to be dismissive or defensive when such critique is offered. Public input may be construed as interference in editorial independence. Transparency in the form of public criticism therefore does not always have the required effect (Zelizer 2017, 259).

Several formal means of trying to ensure the accountability of mainstream media in Africa have been established since the wave of democratization that occurred in the 1990s. There has been an "upsurge" of media councils in southern

Africa in recent years, for instance, in South Africa, Tanzania, Botswana, Malawi, Zambia, and Namibia (Kruger 2009). Not all these media councils have been benign, as Kruger (2009, 7) points out. For instance, in Botswana a statutory media council operates alongside a self-regulatory one, and statutory councils have also been taking root in Uganda, Rwanda, Nigeria, and Kenya.

Tettey (2006, 235) also points to instances of "assigned accountability" on the continent, where insult laws, criminalizing criticism of government officials, are still in place in various countries (e.g., in Swaziland). Journalists are still imprisoned in African countries under this form of libel legislation, despite condemnation by the World Association of Newspapers (WAN) in the form of the "Table Mountain Declaration," issued in 2007, which called for the abolition of insult laws (Voltmer 2013, 145).

In another postconflict African country, Rwanda, the government of President Paul Kagame decided on a type of "benevolent censorship" (Voltmer 2013, 192) that outlawed any reference to ethnicity in an attempt to defuse lingering tensions between Hutus and Tutsis that might be fomented through ethnic stereotyping. While ostensibly aimed at avoiding conflict and ensuring that journalism serves peacebuilding, this ruling has strengthened the positions of those in power and has led to the closure of several Rwandan newspapers and the imprisonment of journalists in that country (Voltmer 2013, 193).

With the rise of new digital technologies that facilitate greater participation by audiences, new, more informal ways of keeping media to account have been emerging, for instance, media criticism or media bloggers that use online platforms for this purpose (Fengler 2012, 180).

Now that the discussion in this chapter has made clear that the model of professionalism is inadequate to conceive of ethics in a productive enough way to guide journalists when reporting on democratization conflicts in Africa, a further question arises: what measures can African media take to promote transparency and an open, participatory ethics and build peace? The starting point would be to reconsider the normative frameworks and ethical ideals underpinning their practices. This is what Chapter 5 will explore.

Conclusion

This chapter has argued that when media ethics is considered from the point of view of "professionalism" and ethical values are codified, media ethics runs the risk of becoming a static set of guidelines that is not dynamic enough for the changing, fluid contexts within which democratization conflicts occur in Africa. Furthermore, seeing journalists as "professionals" can result in the widening of the gap between journalists who report on conflicts for mainstream institutions and wider publics who increasingly also mediatize conflicts through, for instance, eyewitness accounts on mobile phones or through social media. It was pointed out that in contexts of high inequality and social polarization, relegating the responsibility for ethical reflection on conflict mediatization to a small group of "professionals" may widen the gap between elites and other members of society.

A cultural approach to media ethics, rather than a professionalized one, was proposed as more appropriate. Such an approach recognizes that "journalistic conventions, routines and practices are dynamic and contingent on situational and historical circumstance" and that a productive, viable media ethics therefore requires "a view of journalism that is porous, relative, less judgmental and more flexible" than static, professional approaches (Zelizer 2017, 211). Such a dynamic and collaborative stance on ethics is particularly apposite in democratizing or transitional African contexts where the social and political roles and responsibilities of journalism are still being (re)negotiated as a result of ongoing social and political conflicts, shifts, and transitions.

While it was acknowledged in our discussion in this chapter that media ethical codes can provide useful starting points for ethical discussions and sketch the broad contours of ethical conduct, the chapter pointed to the importance of viewing ethics in a more open-ended, collaborative way. Acknowledging the importance of public involvement and the cocreation of ethical frameworks does not imply absolving journalists of the responsibilities attached to their role as moral agents. Despite the increasingly open and participatory nature of the media landscape, also in Africa, the biggest share of symbolic power in this space still belongs to journalists:

> Journalists impart preference statements about what is good and bad, moral and amoral and appropriate and inappropriate in the world, and their preference statements implicitly or explicitly shape the news. Journalists' positioning as the creators and conveyors of views about how the world works is linked with the positioning of their audiences, who make sense of the news in ways that reflect their own identity politics and that of institutions that grant them access and/or protection. (Zelizer 2017, 208)

In Africa, political restrictions on journalism, inequalities of access to the media, and the prevalence of "nanomedia" such as oral networks and visual expressions (Bosch, Wasserman, and Chuma 2018) might erode the power of journalists to set the public agenda. However, their responsibilities to reflect on their role and influence should not be diminished but rather reconceived as a collaborative endeavor with the publics that they serve.

Another way of making media ethical reflection more open, participatory, and collaborative could be through more informal networks. In these informal networks, reflection on and discussion of the ethical duties of the media can take the form of serious media critique. However, publics can also avail themselves of satire and humor, aspects that have characterized "sidewalk radio" (Ellis 1989) in Africa for a considerable time. These informal networks in Africa have proven useful in widening participation in the mediatized public sphere, especially where media have been under the control of the state or in the hands of elites, or where local media narratives are overshadowed by global constructions and stereotypes.

The growth of access to online media in Africa has also provided media publics with ways to become more involved in the production of media and to critique unethical behavior by journalists. An example of this was the #SomeoneTellCNN campaign, driven by Kenyans on the social media platform Twitter since 2012, in response to reports on the US cable network CNN that reaffirmed stereotypes of Kenya as a violent country prone to terror attacks (Bunce 2014; Nyabola 2017; Tully and Ekdale 2014). The hashtag became a site for "playful engagement" (Tully and Ekdale 2014, 73), where Kenyans could hold the global media accountable for perpetuating stereotypes about Africa through misrepresentation in its reports on a terrorist attack in Nairobi. However, it is important to note that the use of social media in humorous and playful ways to keep media accountable also builds on the long-standing and extensive use of satire, gossip, and rumor in informal oral networks to hold power to account in African contexts where the mainstream media is compromised or mistrusted (Ellis 1989).

While these playful ways of holding media to account have often been celebrated, there is also a darker side to the use of social media to critique the mainstream news media in African democracies. Attacks on the media by those who have been the targets of media exposés have also occurred on social media, often using the language of media accountability. An example of this was when, with the help of the British public relations company Bell Pottinger, defenders of South Africa's former president Jacob Zuma used fake

Twitter accounts, also known as "twitterbots," to deflect criticism of Zuma as being corrupt, as already discussed in Chapter 2.

Digital and social media can therefore be seen to form a space of contestation in African democratization conflicts. Nevertheless, the use of social media platforms to demand greater accountability and transparency of the African media may be considered a form of "open ethics," as it facilitates the participation of a greater number of members of the audience in shaping media ethics.

The question is whether these attempts at transparency followed the cultural approach to journalism, with media practices that were immersed in the everyday experiences of the public and that created opportunities for participation, dialogue, and interpretation of ethical values by media users. In other words, were media users positioned as audiences (albeit with an opportunity to provide input into the way "professionals" regulate themselves)? Or was a more immersive approach followed? In the latter approach, media users would be seen as cocreators of normative frameworks and equal members of the wider interpretive community, with the power to reinterpret ethical values and normative frameworks from their own vantage point, located in everyday experiences. For such a collaborative, immersive approach to be successful, it would need to be built on a coherent normative framework that rethinks the role of journalists in relation to citizens, beyond that of professionals serving audiences.

We will address issues and debates about the most appropriate normative frameworks for media in African contexts undergoing democratization processes and accompanying conflicts in the next chapter. There, we will draw on these insights on collaborative approaches to ethical decision-making when we explore the notion of an "ethics of listening" in relation to a range of other ethical frameworks.

5

The Ethics of Engagement: Listening for Peace

Introduction

When we ask the question, how should the media act ethically during times of conflict?, we assume that the media have responsibilities to democratic societies that extend beyond their mere functioning as commercial industries, digital platforms, or public institutions. When we use the language of values and ethics, we are speaking "responsibly and prescriptively about how we should do global communication, especially in a world full of fear" (Magder 2003, 29).

This means that while descriptive studies are a good place to start assessing what role the media have been playing during democratic transitions, how journalists view their roles or how they have enacted them, or how much audiences trust the media, these questions should form the point from which we start to think normatively to envisage ways in which the media can improve. In other words, descriptive studies should tell us what the media are doing so that we can ask the normative question: how can they do it better?

We have already established that when media ethics is conceived of within the framework of "professionalism," it limits the ways in which we can imagine new roles for the media to play in democratizing societies. Although professionalism can, to some extent, provide a bulwark against intimidation and threats to media independence in hybrid or authoritarian African contexts, it also raises several problems. The definition of "professionals" does not apply fully to journalists, and even if such a denominator is used, it could widen the gap between journalists—as an elite group in society—and their publics. This is especially a problem in unequal, fragmented, and polarized societies such as those in African democracies undergoing transitions and conflicts. Furthermore, distilling what should be an ongoing process of ethical reflection into static media ethical codes alone is not adequate to deal

The Ethics of Engagement. Herman Wasserman, Oxford University Press (2021). © Oxford University Press.
DOI: 10.1093/oso/9780190917333.003.0005

with the complex moral problems emerging from African democratization conflicts. Codes are often too vague and general or are inherited from established liberal-democratic contexts, with the result that they are not always as responsive to particular local conditions as they should be.

The ethical protonorm of sacredness of life, consisting of the related ethical values of truth, human dignity, and nonviolence, can guide media toward a starting point for thinking about media ethics in ways that cut across cultural and ethnic differences, as it is rooted in ontological respect for human beings and oriented toward peace and truth. Although these norms still need to be made more specific and contextual by interpreting them from the ground up, within particular contexts, they offer a way for media to think about their responsibility toward society in a way that emphasizes relationship rather than professional distance. When the media considers its primary responsibility to be that of affirming life, and upholds this ethical imperative by seeking truth, upholding dignity, and striving for peace and nonviolence, it would orient itself toward people's everyday lives and experiences.

If we accept that the protonorm of sacredness of life is a suitable guiding principle for the democratic media in contexts of conflict, we can proceed to develop a normative framework built around this central ethical principle. Such a framework, it will be argued, is best summed up as an "ethics of listening." Rooted in the respect for all human life; committed to dignity, equality, and justice; and based on the fundamental understanding of the media's role to tell the truth, an ethics of listening encompasses the various dimensions of the ethical protonorm with a clear call to action. Listening, in this sense, is active rather than passive—it calls for a conscious reorientation of the media toward voices that are suppressed or marginalized, asks for the media to engage in relationships rather than detachment, and has as the ultimate aim the de-escalation and reorienting of conflict toward peace. Oriented as it is toward dialogue and interaction, an ethics of listening is appropriate for an agonistic democracy that promotes rigorous debate and contestation without lapsing into either authoritarian suppression or violent anarchy.

Like other similar normative frameworks such as peace journalism, the ethics of listening contains an element of intervention. Instead of assuming a passive role for the media as merely an observer or a "mirror" of events, these frameworks impose an ethical duty on the media to contribute to building peace, de-escalating violence, or finding solutions.

These normative frameworks also present a challenge—they require the media to re-examine its taken-for-granted roles and to reimagine its position in democratic society. Because such a reimagining is daunting, the first response from journalists and other media practitioners may be to dismiss them as impractical or idealistic. Besides acknowledging that normative theory to some extent is always idealistic, as it prescribes ways for the media to aspire to higher standards—and proposes a vision for a better world—these frameworks should start out from the premise that such visions should be rooted in an understanding of specific local conditions. So, while an ethics of listening might sound idealistic, it should not have to be unrealistic or impractical. An ethics of listening, however, can be characterized as alternative or even radical, in the sense that it charts a different course for the media than the conventional "watchdog" or monitorial role. To better understand the need to develop alternative frameworks such as listening, it is useful to reflect on normative theory in itself and the ways in which certain normative theories have become dominant.

Normative Theory, Media Practice, and Northern Dominance

The point of departure in this chapter is that normative ethics provides a framework that guides the media in seeking the most ethically justifiable approach for their actions, while constantly reflecting on this framework itself. At issue in normative theory is "not only what *is* the role of journalism in society but above all what this role *should* be" (Christians et al. 2009, vii).

Frequently, there is a gap between dominant normative theory, as it has underpinned media training and media development efforts in Africa and elsewhere in the Global South, and media practice in actual democratizing contexts. This gap has led to a growing realization that Western norms and assumptions about the role of the media in democracies cannot be exported to the rest of the world unproblematically. Such exportation has also been subject to postcolonial critique (e.g., Rao and Wasserman 2007), as it suggests an epistemological imperialism resonant with colonial discourses of universality. Nevertheless, journalism globally continues to be "measured against what ought to be rather than what is" (Josephi 2005, 576). While Josephi's point about the theory–practice gap could be misunderstood as an argument against normative models per se, it should rather be seen as an argument against *inappropriate* normative models exported to contexts to which they are not suited yet where they continue to wield influence. Among these normative frameworks that have been applied across global contexts is Siebert, Peterson, and Schramm's (1956) book *Four Theories of the Press*, which offered a framework rooted in Cold War geopolitics and classical liberalism and reflected the "simplicity of the binary of libertarianism and authoritarianism" (Josephi 2005, 577). Despite being widely critiqued by scholars, the book remains an influential point of reference against which many subsequent attempts to construct normative and empirical models for global media systems have been played off. Among these subsequent explorations of global media frameworks have been Hallin and Mancini's influential studies of global media systems (2004 and 2012), which can be seen as an attempt to construct universally relevant models for media based on a number of empirical cases from selected countries. A more inclusive empirical study of journalistic role perceptions, practices, and professional identities is the study by Hanitzsch et al. (2019) emerging from the ongoing "Worlds of Journalism" project. Although impressive in its scope, its aim is to provide an empirically rich description of journalism around the world rather than construct normative theoretical models. As far as normative theory-building is concerned, *Normative Theories of the Media* by Christians et al. (2009) has so far been the best attempt to move beyond *Four Theories*, although it limits its scope to media in democratic societies.

The fact that normative theory tended to take Western democracies as their foundational norm and devalued everything deviating from it as inferior does not make normative theory as such irrelevant. Indeed, the assessment of the media can never be value-free (Josephi 2005, 581). Empirical studies on their own are not sufficient to build normative theory, as deriving norms ("should") from empirical facts about journalistic performance ("is") can result in a category error. In contrast with sociological theory, which describes the factual roles and conduct of media in society, normative theory is related to the cultural values held by participants in media discourses (Christians et al. 2009, ix). Normative theory "attempts to explain why a certain organization of public discourse leads to better collective decisions and eventually to an improved quality of life" (Christians et al. 2009, ix).

Like all theories, normative theory is not developed in a vacuum. Whether explicit or not, normative theory is informed by social and cultural values and assumptions. Historically, media ethics has been informed by the conditions in the Global North, and there has been increasing demands for scholarship (e.g., Ward and Wasserman 2010) that can extend normative theory to become more responsive to a range of conditions and contexts around the world. As Willems (2014, 7) points out, the Global South tends to be theorized from a vantage point in the Global North, from where it "represents the negative imprint of, or features the active intervention of the Global North." Willems (2014, 7) consequently argues for an approach to "media cultures" rather than "media systems," as this would acknowledge the way media is consumed and practiced within people's lived experience. Included in this perspective would be the understanding that the South is not homogenous, but contains a variety of lived experiences and also contested meanings.

For normative theory to be valid, adequate, and appropriate in these settings, it has to take cognizance of the actual lived experience, cultural values, and structural conditions within which it is being applied. Normative theories should therefore remain open and flexible and be developed from the ground up. This is not an argument for cultural relativism, as the protonorm of sacredness of life would still remain the starting point from which ethical guidelines are formulated across different contexts. However, the meanings attached to these norms, their interpretation in relation to particular socioeconomic conditions, and their application within specific structural configurations would differ according to context.

Ethical frameworks that are imposed from above and assumed to have universal value are not only bound to fail but also in themselves based on an imperialistic assumption that values developed in the Global North can be immutably applied around the world (even while the North itself presents all but a homogenous normative picture). Rather, ethical frameworks should be arrived at through a study of ethical concepts as they exist, circulate, and develop within specific historical contexts, against the background of everyday lived experiences and practices, and through an open-ended, critical dialogue among all participants in mediated practices. This would entail, therefore, an ethnographic, cultural approach to media ethics rather than an abstract, essentialist one.

The assumption in this chapter is therefore that ethical frameworks are best developed through a dynamic dialectic between normative concepts and reflective practice: an ongoing process that combines ethical concepts and theories with an analysis of their appropriation, adaptation, and application in actual, specific contexts. This approach shows similarities with grounded theory research, where theory is developed on an ongoing basis during qualitative encounters in the field, with the object of developing and modifying existing theory (Strauss and Corbin 1994).

The normative frameworks dominating the field of journalism and media studies are still mostly informed by perspectives emanating from the Global North and informed by Enlightenment values such as modernity, rationality, universalism, and progress (Zelizer 2017, 148). We have already seen that the normative link between the media and liberal democracy is often assumed to be universal, despite the fact that liberal democracy is only one form of political organization among many and often does not suit African realities neatly.

Normative differences demonstrated by media in contexts outside of the Global North routinely lead to a reduction of the complexity of such contexts. These variant contexts are then reduced to "simplified versions of who they are" (Zelizer 2017, 148) and studied as deviancies rather than iterations of different ethical frameworks that should be taken seriously and used to inform central theoretical conceptions in the field. As Steele (2018, 136) has pointed out with regard to Islamic journalistic ethics in Southeast Asia, journalists outside the North often uphold similar basic ethical norms as their counterparts do (e.g., truth-telling, accuracy, balance, and independence), but they may articulate these principles differently. Attempts to construct ethical frameworks that draw on value systems found in African cultures (see Wasserman 2014) similarly find points of overlap between African and Western principles, although in some cases crucial differences can be noted, especially around the relative importance of individual and community rights and identities.

In recent years, an increasing amount of scholarship in this area has critiqued the assumed normative universality of Northern media ethical norms and explored the possibility of a global media ethics (e.g., Christians et al. 2008; Rao and Wasserman 2007). Steering a path between cultural relativism and universal values would require developing global media ethics from the ground up, so that universal values obtain specific meaning in particular contexts (Wasserman 2011b).

It is not only different, contesting, and shifting normative frameworks that make it difficult for journalists and other media practitioners to find, agree on, and implement ethical guidelines in transitional contexts marked by conflict; media practitioners often have to juggle a variety of competing imperatives, including commercial pressures, time pressures, audience demands, and occupational ideologies. Within these "multiple vagaries of action" with which journalists "must wrestle" (Zelizer 2017, 85), ethical dilemmas often arise for which the appropriate standard of practice is not always clear or evident. In Africa, the contextual pressures on journalists—such as low or inconsistent pay, precarious working conditions, and poor economic conditions—often make adherence to professional ethics, as defined in established democracies and wealthier countries, difficult. For these reasons, corrupt practices such as "brown envelope journalism" (Skjerdal 2010) may take hold more easily.

If "the issues of 'what is' and 'what should be' repeatedly collide" in contexts of the Global North as a result of changing dimensions of practice, temporality, geography, institutional culture, and technology (Zelizer 2017, 89), this is arguably even more the case in African settings, where these factors are amplified by social inequalities, political instability, ethnic and cultural differences, economic pressures, and, frequently, a large distance between the normative expectations inherited from professional codes devised in the North and the empirical realities on the ground. Conditions such as intimidation and imprisonment of journalists and state ownership, control, or influence over the media, combined with material factors such as low literacy rates, high socioeconomic inequality, poverty, and transitional or unstable governmental structures, mitigate against the possibility of applying norms derived from societies in the Global North (Zelizer 2017, 146). Indeed, the history of trying to implement liberal democracy in Africa "attests to this clash of values and attempts to ignore African cultural realities" in a way "akin to the behavior of a Lilliputian undertaker who would rather trim a corpse than expand his/her coffin to accommodate a man-mountain, or a carpenter whose only tool is a huge hammer and to whom every problem is a nail" (Nyamnjoh 2005, 1).

This unsuitability of a Northern model for the socioeconomic, political, and cultural realities of African societies has often been mistaken for a failure on the part of African countries and their media to live up to the standards of the Global North. Instead, this gap between Northern norms and African practices could have been harnessed to expand conceptual understandings of the variety of possible relationships between media and democracy. The opportunity to use African experiences for the enrichment and domestication of theories of liberal democracy should not be confused, however, with the opportunistic attempts by authoritarian African rulers to appeal to cultural relativism to hide wrongdoing. There are many examples of the use of such "nebulous claims of African specificities to orchestrate high-handedness and intolerance" (Nyamnjoh 2005, 26). One should be careful, therefore, not to equate a critique of the assumed universality of Northern ethical guidelines with a culturally relativist stance of "anything goes." However, the construction of normative frameworks should occur in relation to contextual specifics and the needs of local publics.

What is important, therefore, is to recognize the "situated nature of communication in non-western environments" and the existence of "multiple journalisms." These varied journalisms could be used to "rethink existing theories from anew, rather than positioning scholars in enclaves across from those who think differently, and could facilitate an updating of the notions that communication originally put in place as part of its own disciplinary ground" (Zelizer 2017, 147). The role of media during conflicts can provide a useful lens to examine the ways in which African media conceptualize, domesticate, and practice ethical values, and how such conceptualizations and practices might differ from, complement, or deepen the normative expectations of media as understood in the Global North.

The Ethics of Engagement

One area where strong differences of opinion about the media's ethical responsibilities have existed—both between dominant Northern and non-Northern ethical frameworks and within the dominant Northern normative discourses themselves—is the extent to which media should intervene or engage actively during times of conflict.

The dominant, conventional ethical frameworks that see a primarily monitorial role for the media have emphasized media independence, "objectivity," and balance. The way these values have usually been interpreted in conflict contexts has tended to limit the media's role to that of observer, and has precluded further and more active engagement between the media and participants in the conflict or other affected parties. A different way to think about the media's ethical responsibility in conflict is to see it play a more active role toward peacemaking. In asking what journalism is *for*, the answer from this point of view would be not to only provide information but also "more aggressively meld community and public citizenship" (Zelizer 2017, 117).

This notion of a journalism actively contributing to peace is not entirely wishful thinking without empirical grounding. Journalists in transitional countries have already indicated that they find ways in their practices to balance Western "professional" values of detachment and objectivity with ones that are more appropriate to their context (Hanitzsch et al. 2019). For instance, journalists in the Western Balkans—often accused of fueling conflict and fomenting ethical hatred—have developed an approach to their work that could be defined as "transitional journalism," which includes support for national development, advocating for social change, and educating the audience (Andresen, Hoxha, and Godole 2017, 626). Ethnic and nationalist loyalties among journalists have been found to persist after armed conflicts, raising a tension with the professional notion of independence (Andresen et al. 2017, 626). This is a similar tension to the one in Kenyan newsrooms highlighted by Wasserman and Maweu (2014b), referred to previously, where journalists have to negotiate ethnic loyalties and professional identities, including the ethical injunction to fair and independent reporting.

The constant renegotiation of journalistic roles has also been noted in the postapartheid South African context, where journalists have been redefining their relationship with government and their ethical responsibilities toward society in the new democracy (De Beer et al. 2016, 48). South African journalists do not see the "watchdog" and "developmental" roles of journalism to be binary opposites, but rather view them as roles that can be negotiated and balanced. These journalists even expressed a willingness to support government policy, moderately, alongside their responsibility to act as a watchdog over it (De Beer et al. 2016, 48).[1] This South African example illustrates that different roles for the media during conflicts do not have to be mutually exclusive, nor static and fixed. During the various moments of crisis, escalation, peacemaking, and conflict resolution and reconciliation, different ethical priorities for the media may emerge. It might be that a monitorial, watchdog role is required of the media at points in time where accountability is required of the government about the ways they seek to stem violent conflict or to ensure fair and transparent elections. At other moments in the democratization process, the imperative of social dialogue, reconciliation, and peacebuilding may require a less adversarial and more facilitative approach.

It therefore seems appropriate that alternative approaches to the monitorial role should be explored for ways in which they could provide better ways to deal with democratization conflicts in Africa or can complement the historically dominant monitorial approach.

Toward Alternatives

As the monitorial role was exported to contexts outside of its origins in Western democracies, it has often been challenged by perspectives rooted in non-Western cultures, value systems, and contexts of lived experience. These challenges sometimes broadly resonated with the alternative roles for the media in democracy that have also been identified by Christians et al. (2009), such as the *radical, collaborative,* and *facilitative* roles. Often a combination of different normative roles may be the most suitable approach to mediate African democratization conflicts. Nevertheless, the typology of radical, collaborative, and facilitative roles presents a useful matrix upon which to map alternative approaches to the monitorial, watchdog role in African democratization contexts.

While the monitorial approach usually implies that the media provides surveillance for the status quo to ensure that social configurations work properly, the *radical* role of journalists in democracies entails a challenge to the existing power structure. In the context of mediatizing democratization conflicts in African democracies, this role can be seen most prominently in the advocacy role that journalism has played toward overthrowing colonial and postcolonial authoritarian regimes (Musa and Domatob 2007, 321; Switzer and Adhikari 2000), and journalists were often harassed, threatened, or imprisoned for doing so.

Another alternative role that the media can play in democratic societies is that of *collaboration* with state power. At first glance, such a role goes against the ideals of independence, freedom, and critical distance linked to the monitorial role. However, as Christians et al. (2009, 196) point out, in many democracies around the world, such collaboration is not merely an empirical fact, but can also be a normative good. Examples of such collaboration in conflict situations could include agreeing to withhold information about operational strategies during times of war (Christians et al. 2009, 197), to exercise restraint in the publication or broadcasting of terror threats in order not to play into the hands of extremists seeking publicity (Schmid 1989, 539), or to withhold information of rescue attempts in hostage situations to avoid compromising their safety (Cohen-Almagor 2000, 251).

The notion of "development journalism" has been a particularly contentious form of collaboration between media, state, and other civic institutions in the African context. The idea that journalists' primary responsibility is to support the economic and social developmental imperatives of countries has been one of the dominant normative frameworks in postcolonial Africa. Although often seen as antithetical to the liberal framework of watchdog journalism, development journalism could be consistent with the monitorial role when governments are criticized for not meeting their development objectives (Ogan 1982, 9). The notion of "emancipatory journalism" has been proposed as a way to focus the attention on how journalism can improve people's lives on a "horizontal" level without foregrounding the "vertical" relationship between media and the state (Shah 1996). Such a reconceptualization of development journalism would be closer to the ethical concept of "listening" to the voices and experiences of marginalized, poor, and subaltern citizens, to which we will return later in this chapter.

The types of collaboration that the media may embark on within democratic societies extend beyond support for the state to that of institutions. An example of such collaboration within a transitional, postconflict democracy in Africa would be the coverage of the work of the Truth and Reconciliation Commission (TRC) in South Africa. The TRC, established by the postapartheid Parliament to conduct hearings into gross violations of human rights during the apartheid era, received "unheard-of coverage" from the South African and international media (Krabill 2010, 158). Not all of this coverage was supportive—some Afrikaans-language newspapers, such as *Die Burger*, known for their support of the regime during the apartheid years, vilified the commission. However, even these critical papers collaborated with the process as such by providing extensive coverage. A "symbiotic relationship" developed between the media and the TRC, as the commission was seen as a way of heralding the new democratic era and constructing a "common national history of the apartheid era" (Krabill 2010, 158).

Collaborations guiding journalistic practice in democratic countries not only include those between journalists and the state, or between journalists and civil society as illustrated earlier, but also take the form of cooperation between journalist organizations themselves. Recent examples where journalists have suspended their competition in favor of working together for a common cause include cross-border journalistic work, such as that leading to the Panama Papers exposé. Collaboration between journalist organizations seems to be on the rise due to massive data leaks, which requires the sharing of expertise and labor across newsrooms; the shrinking of newsrooms due to economic pressures, which makes the pooling of resources necessary; the increasing "pan-national" character of issues that need to be addressed by journalists, such as business, politics, environmental sustainability, and crime networks; and collaboration providing a way to spread the risk and exposure to threats to freedom of expression (Sambrook 2018, 1; Carson and Farhall 2018, 1899). In Africa such collaboration has also been used to counter misinformation, for instance, the fifteen Nigerian news organizations that have agreed to collaborate, supported by academics at the University of Lagos, and coordinated by the International Centre for Investigative Reporting, in the Crosscheck Nigeria project (AFP 2018). In South Africa, the pooling of resources between different media houses has also led to the successful uncovering of corruption and "state capture" in South Africa. The team that conducted the #GuptaLeaks investigation consisted of a mainstream online news portal, News24; a specialist investigative journalism outfit, AmaBhungane; and an online in-depth news analysis site, *Daily Maverick*.

The *facilitative* role of the media is based on the understanding that democratic politics requires deliberation between members of the polity, and that the media can play an important role in facilitating such "negotiation over the social, political and cultural agenda" (Christians et al. 2009, 159). A fundamental assumption underpinning this normative approach is that social conflicts in a democracy "remain the province of citizens rather than of judicial or legislative experts" (Christians et al. 2009, 159). Therefore, instead of seeing journalism in the first instance as the domain of professional experts who educate or inform the public from an elite position, the facilitative approach emphasizes the potential of the media to provide a space for debate and dialogue within an agonistic conception of democracy. Such facilitation is not the same as standing back and letting different opinions fight for dominance in a free-for-all "marketplace of ideas," but, as we will see again when discussing the notion of listening, an active attempt to create a space where journalists and citizens co-construct narrative truth.

Various manifestations of this facilitative model have been experimented with throughout media history. Most notable among them has been the public journalism movement in the United States, also referred to as civic or community journalism. Key characteristics of this approach to journalism are its ambitious attempts at understanding communities, accepting that the public has knowledge pertaining to their own situation, and framing issues in ways that are conducive to the finding of solutions (Christians et al. 2009, 161). The central orientation of this type of journalism is toward communities, seeing citizens as members of a public rather than individuals, and conceiving of journalism's ethical responsibility as that of enabling and improving the ability of communities to solve their own problems: "In journalism's facilitative role, media practitioners do not reduce social issues to financial and administrative problems for politicians but enable the public to come to terms with their everyday experiences themselves" (Christians et al. 2009, 163). The normative claim of this approach, in summary, is that "the media do not simply report on civil society's activities and institutions but seek to promote and improve them" (Christians et al. 2009, 163). In the context of conflict, such facilitative journalism can contribute to peacebuilding by creating space for open discussion and active listening, creating communicative spaces where people can engage in "disarming" conversation to break down preconceived stereotypes, and detecting incitement to violence early before it happens (Hamelink 2016, 66). One example of such an approach is that of "peace journalism."

Peace Journalism

Peace journalism can be seen as an interventionist form of journalism according to which the ethical role of journalists is not to remain at a neutral and disinterested distance when reporting on conflict, but to "participate, intervene, get involved, and promote change" (Hanitzsch 2007, 373). It has been contended that the news media makes an "excellent tool for waging war but a poor one for bringing peace" (Wolfsfeld 2018, 110) because the traditional news values of the media are oriented toward spectacular events of conflict and violence. The notion of peace journalism is an attempt to turn this situation around to focus instead on the slower, less eventful processes of reconciliation and peacebuilding.

The ultimate goal of peace journalism, Lynch and McGoldrick (2005, 5) point out, is to provide journalists with a "set of tools, both conceptual and practical, intended to equip journalists to offer a better public service." Peace journalism (and its opposite, war journalism) can be distinguished on the basis of several major criteria: its orientation to peace or conflict, its commitment to either truth or propaganda, its focus on ordinary people, and its attempts to propose solutions or war and victory (Obijiofor and Hanusch 2011, 137). Whereas war journalism covers conflict as if it were a sport where only one winner is possible, peace journalism has as its goal the de-escalation of conflict and the finding of creative solutions; peace journalism emphasizes ethical reflection on the part of journalists to understand the consequences of their reporting and to build connections with their audiences (Obijiofor and Hanusch 2011, 138). In other words, peace journalism is an explicitly normative orientation for journalists, aimed at intervening in and resolving conflicts. This approach requires journalists to reorientate their coverage in order not to identify a particular party to the conflict as the culprit, but to see conflict itself as the problem (Hanitzsch 2004, 485).

The outcomes envisaged by peace journalism can be achieved by the media informing and educating audiences about the causes of conflict; mediating between parties involved in a conflict, which requires a more interventionist stance than the conventional one of impartiality and detachment; and holding powerful role players to account for their actions and policies (Obijiofor and Hanusch 2011, 139).

This remains an idealistic normative framework, given that the dominant framing of conflicts globally still tends to be that of war journalism (Lee and Maslog 2005; Lynch 2020). Peace journalism as a normative framework "obliges media to be socially responsible and promote peace" (Hamelink 2016, 61) and orients media toward finding solutions, facilitating dialogue, and contributing to the de-escalation of conflict. Peace journalism is therefore an exception from the general rule in journalism, which is to be reactive rather than proactive (Zelizer 2017, 258).

Since peace journalism is positioned as an alternative to conventional journalism, which tends to highlight and amplify conflict, it is to be expected that it will be at odds with conventional routines and norms such as objectivity, detachment, conventional news values, and "professional" distance. For practitioners adhering to dominant normative frameworks, peace journalism could therefore be seen as a threat to professional independence and integrity. It also does not sit well with the "prevailing mode of organization and the management of media that often operate as commercial enterprises driven by an obsession with market shares, ratings, and scoops" (Hamelink 2016, 61–62).

This approach has been criticized for being romantic and idealistic to the extent that it lacks practical value in the face of severe, pervasive, and deep tensions (Hamelink 2016, 65). Implementing peace journalism would also require receptivity among audiences and a demand for a different kind of journalism than the conventional model audiences may be familiar with (Hamelink 2016, 66). A shift toward alternative models of journalism such as peace journalism therefore entails a shift away from a conception of media ethics as belonging only in the "professional" realm, as primarily or solely the obligation of media producers, to one where audiences also have a responsibility to be vigilant, critically reflect on media content, and demand alternative approaches to the mediatization of conflict.

Hanitzsch (2004, 483) suggests that although peace journalism may contribute to the de-escalation or resolution of conflicts, active intervention is the responsibility of politicians or the military and not that of journalism. As such, the intervention envisaged by peace journalism may harm the integrity of journalism. He cautions against overestimating the power of journalism to bring about a resolution of conflict, as such optimism may be based on similar assumptions as the outdated and refuted theories of linear "media effects" (2004, 483). Conversely, as Hanitzsch illustrates with reference to a civil war in Indonesia between Christian and Muslim groups, the media can also amplify polarization when journalists take sides. Instead of facilitating peace, journalists then "become combatants in a conflict, and by doing this they initiate a vicious circle of mutual reinforcement between war and journalism" (Hanitzsch 2004, 483).

It may be argued (Obijiofor and Hanusch 2011, 147) that criticism of peace journalism is based on an extension of the normative criterion of objectivity, and that peace journalism therefore falls foul of a guideline of noninterventionism that it had no intention of keeping in any case. Peace journalism's intention is to intervene in standard journalistic routines to change the frames and narratives used to report on conflict, and not to remain at a distance. Peace journalism is comfortable with the notion of attachment—to identify and support victims of conflicts, rather than a particular side.

The notion of a "journalism of attachment" has also received prominence in a somewhat different sense for the way that it has been used by the British former journalist Martin Bell (see Hanitzsch 2004, 487 for a discussion of this contrasting usage). The way Bell uses the term implies a moral responsibility for journalists to take sides in a conflict in a way that is resonant with an ethics of care and compassion, and that does away with the presumption of objectivity or impartiality. Bell proposes a journalism "that will not stand neutrally between good and evil, right and wrong, the victim and the oppressor" (1997, 8). Hanitzsch (2004, 488) takes issue with Bell's notion of attachment as well as peace journalism generally, not only for the contravention of the journalistic orthodoxy of impartiality and objectivity by assuming a social role that should be limited to the domain of politics or the military, but also because Hanitzsch sees this normative stance as based on an untenable epistemology that assumes that media has a powerful effect on audiences. Hanitzsch's criticism of the assumption of "effect" is valid to the extent that peace journalism should not be seen as having the capacity to change the outcome of conflicts in a direct, causal fashion. But his rejection (2004, 492) of peace journalism because it is derived from a normative prescription ("normative reasoning rather than empirical research") seems overstated.

A journalistic ethics narrowly conceived of in terms of rationality and professional objectivity, with disregard for the emotional dimensions of conflict, is poorly suited for mediatized conflicts. As Hamelink (2016, 21) observes, if the emotional dimensions of a conflict are ignored or neglected, the "rational solution is likely to be temporary only." Since the key drivers of the escalation of conflict are emotional in nature—anxiety, agitation, alienation, and accusation (Hamelink 2016, 21)—an ethical sensitivity toward emotion should be an important feature of journalism aimed at peacebuilding. Despite the criticism that "journalism of attachment" has received—for what is perceived as a self-aggrandizing or moralizing stance on the part of journalists that could also lead to erroneous assessments of conflicts—it can allow journalists to process traumatic events for themselves and their audiences (Tumber and Prentoulis 2003, 222, 228).

This is not to say that putting peace journalism in practice is easy to do—it would require a substantial change to the organizational models of journalism (Hamelink 2016, 65). In other words, journalism cannot be so easily divorced from the very same politico-economic conditions that give rise to the conflict-reporting frame (Cottle 2006, 103). The peaceful solutions to conflict envisaged by peace journalism might not always be available, and, as Cottle (2006, 103) argues, rather than striving for an idealistic peaceful society, journalism should aim for a broader, deeper, more contextual rendering of conflict. Instead of holding up one, alternative ideal of peace journalism, the complex set of circumstances—including the nature of the conflict, the degree of elite consensus or dissensus, and the nature of media competition (likely to influence the amount of sensationalism, personalization, and demonization employed)—should be taken into account when striving to improve the mediatization of conflict in specific settings.

From the previous overview of different normative approaches to the mediatizing of conflict, the following should become clear:

- The dominant approach of monitorial, "watchdog" journalism has serious limitations, especially in highly polarized, unequal societies such as those in African countries transitioning from authoritarianism to democracy.

- The approaches of collaboration and facilitation can contribute important perspectives on how to cover conflict in a way that can move actors toward the de-escalation of conflict and can guide the media toward a more interventionist position that can contribute to peacebuilding.
- Historically, models such as peace journalism and development journalism have emerged as exponents of facilitative and collaborative approaches that can serve as counterpoints to monitorial, watchdog approaches. The best application of these models has been in cases where such collaboration and facilitation could occur without eroding the continued importance of monitoring, which remains an important function for the media in new, postconflict democracies.

Given these limitations and criticisms, it is worth considering a new normative approach to the mediatization of conflict in emerging democracies, especially those marked by high levels of social polarization and inequality, such as is usually the case in African countries. This approach, which can be called an "ethics of listening," is what we turn to next.

Listening

One of the moral claims that journalists often make when mediating conflicts is that they "give voice" to victims of war, violence, and oppression. The notion of journalists as givers of voice assumes a certain authority on the part of journalists that allows them to bestow the right to speak for people. This assumption is problematic, for various reasons.

In contexts where conflicts result from democratization processes against a background of persisting inequalities and social or ethnic polarization, the media's claim of "giving voice" becomes complicated. The media may be viewed as siding with a particular group or may, because of their historic association with a political or social elite, be seen as biased or—at best—out of touch with the majority. The media may, in such highly polarized contexts, contribute to the escalation or perpetuation of tensions rather than their de-escalation. As discussed earlier, the concept of "professionalism" can often feed into this distance between journalists and their publics. This problem is exacerbated in conflictual, polarized contexts.

Another reason "giving voice" is a problematic notion has to do more generally with the assumption of journalistic authority. In recent years, the level of trust in journalism has been on the decline globally. This decline of journalism's position of authority has come about partly as a result of the proliferation of digital media, which have broadened participation in the media sphere and consequently undermined journalists' privileged position as arbiters of truth. Another reason has been the emergence of online "filter bubbles" or "echo chambers," which has resulted in the fragmentation of the public sphere. The propensity for these "filter bubbles" to confirm media users' pre-existing views or biases has made it more difficult for journalists to impose their authoritative interpretation of social reality on publics. Furthermore, this erosion of journalistic authority has taken place against the background of a general culture of skepticism about truth claims—the arrival of the so-called "post-truth age" (Vos and Thomas 2018, 2007).

Journalists have attempted to retain their authority as arbiters of the truth by clinging to the normative claim that journalism is crucial for the functioning of democracy. In doing so, they have attempted to rebuild the trust they used to enjoy when journalism had the monopoly over information (Vos and Thomas 2018, 2008). Waisbord (2018, 1868), however, correctly points out that these attempts to regain lost authority may be futile if they are based on the hope that journalism as an institution can control the new communication environment. In this new environment, Waisbord (2018) remarks, public expression has free rein and the old order of news production and consumption has been replaced by a chaotic, fragmented, and widely dispersed new public communication order.

The trope of "giving voice" in meta-journalistic discourse is therefore a problematic one, as Markham (2011, 101) explains:

> Giving voice to and respecting sources combine an ethos of representing the under-represented . . . with an enactment of the journalist's powers of authorial consecration, potentially alongside the ability to determine mediated identities of victimhood. There is immediately a problem with "giving" voice, as it suggests that subjects have to be authorised to speak, and the journalist's act of authorising another is first and foremost self-authorisation. The represented "other" is at best a by-product of journalistic authority claims and, at worst, a constrained, disciplined subject produced by the eliciting of expression, itself a form of coercion by the institutionalised will-to-truth that some argue journalism represents.

In transitional democracies emerging from or still undergoing conflict, competition between different voices for domination of the public sphere can result in a continuation or escalation of such conflict, especially when articulated in extreme or hate speech online. Regulation in the form of laws or codes of ethics is often seen as the way to prevent a repeat or an escalation of ethnic conflicts and tensions. Examples of these attempts include the professional journalistic codes referred to in the previous chapter and stronger measures of imposed accountability, such as insult laws or laws regulating public communication. The regulation of "professional" journalistic conduct has its limits, however. Such regulation can easily slip into a form of control that strengthens those in power and suppresses alternative, marginalized, or resistant voices. Regulation, in the "professional" mode, also limits the ethical duties of communication to those participants in public discourse who fulfill certain elite criteria. As Voltmer (2013, 195) argues, it might be more important in such contexts to create opportunities for ordinary citizens "to listen and talk to the other side." Especially in transitional democracies, the appeal to essentialized identities and the mobilization of ethnic or racial divisions are frequently used to win votes in elections. These appeals are often amplified by the media, which reinforces these divisions through stratified market strategies in which it sides with a particular grouping that it conceives of as its market (Voltmer 2016, 12). It is in these polarized and fragmented political contexts that the normative ethical value of listening could prompt an important change to the way the media engages with conflict.

The approach of "deliberative democracy" has focused on naming and framing political issues in such a way as to "engage the disparate concerns of people as opposed to polarized ideology" (Kadlec, Sprain, and Carcasson 2012, 4). This approach is a valuable alternative to the idea of an unfettered "free market of ideas" in which the strongest and most entrenched voices often get to dominate. Deliberation and collaboration can also provide a welcome counterpoint to the emphasis on procedural aspects of democracy such as elections. By attempting to obtain as wide as possible a buy-in from all stakeholders in a particular issue, deliberative democracy aims to encourage citizen participation in debates to arrive at a consensus.

A journalistic version of deliberative democracy is "public journalism," which aims to facilitate dialogue between different publics and between publics and journalists (Oelofsen 2017, 173; Amner 2011). Like deliberative democracy, public journalism is premised on the understanding that voice in itself does not necessarily resolve conflict and in fact may aggravate it—hence the need for such talk to be "moderated in such a way that cross-cutting interaction and changing one's mind are encouraged" (Voltmer 2013, 195). Public journalism could take the form of consultative meetings between journalists and members of the public, or "town hall" meetings, where journalists facilitate public debate about topical issues. The public journalism movement sought to reconnect with citizens who were disillusioned by the "gulf between daily life and public culture" to create a sense of "belonging, moral community and identity" (Cottle 2006, 112). This was done through what some critics see as a somewhat naïve return to a "resumed golden age of small-town, meeting-hall democracy in which participation and public debate and discussion could meaningfully take place and involve local communities and their agendas" (Cottle 2006, 113). However, this movement never really strayed beyond the boundaries of liberal democracy and was concerned with procedural issues rather than the substantive ones underlying the disconnect between journalism, citizens, and democratic participation, thus leaving the structural factors and social imbalances untouched (Cottle 2006, 112). Such attempts at facilitating debate also relies on a relationship of trust between audiences and the media. Where media are mistrusted—as in many African contexts marked by state ownership or intervention of the media, or elite capture of the media to serve sectional interests—such facilitation is unlikely to succeed in greater openness to different viewpoints.

Although deliberative democracy, facilitated by the media, is an attempt at creating a more inclusive democratic polity, it often fails at listening properly (Dobson 2014, 110). This is frequently because deliberation in this sense excludes certain forms of expression. A conception of deliberation premised only on rational debate, in the Habermasian sense, is bound to have very limited purchase on formal journalistic platforms. Although Habermas belongs to the tradition of deliberative democratic theory, his normative ideals focus on speaking rather than listening (Dobson 2014, 112). Missing the opportunity to listen to the voices of those who do not fit the definition of rational speech is even more problematic in highly unequal, transitional democracies, where large sections of the population have historically been excluded from public communication and still remain marginal to it. In these settings, the expression of political views and attitudes may often be characterized by rage, frustration, and protest. These "ways of speaking" are likely to be excluded from the Habermasian understanding of democratic deliberation—because they do not conform to the norms for rational speaking—and are consequently excluded from the public sphere through "failures of listening"

(Dobson 2014, 134). The notion of a rational, deliberative democracy might therefore be improved by conceiving of it rather as a "dialogic" democracy with listening at its center, as Dobson (2014, 112) suggests.

As Oelofsen (2017) shows through a case study of protests in a poor South African community, the structural conditions in an unequal setting like South Africa militate against the possibility of the voices of marginalized citizens being heard in the media. Mainstream journalists, she found, often "fall short of recognizing poor citizens as resilient and persistent political actors in mediated spaces of political deliberation" (2017, 167) because they do not recognize the expressions of voice—"where they shout, disrupt, argue, and 'bicker'" (2017, 171)—as legitimate contributions to deliberation. Consequently, these citizens often feel unheard and disconnected from the democratic polity.

An approach that extends the normative notion of deliberative democracy to include a variety of expressions beyond only the rational expressions legitimated in mainstream journalism, and that actively seeks out voices that have historically been suppressed or remain marginalized as a result of the structural factors impacting public communication and mainstream journalism, therefore has to be found. One such approach is that of "listening."

Listening as a normative approach for media in democratizing conflicts involves more than a technocratic gathering of data about audience preferences or embarking on marketing research. Nor is it the type of listening that happens routinely when journalists seek out sources for stories. Listening as an ethical strategy is aimed at expanding the reach and attention of journalists beyond their usual audiences to include those that normally appear only on the margins of media coverage (Goins 2018). But listening as an ethical value is not merely aimed at including a greater diversity of voices or faces in media coverage—what is even more important is *how* those voices appear. Listening changes the relationship of the media to citizens by treating them as constituents of a shared interpretive community rather than as consumers of interpretations handed down to them (Goins 2018). This means that ethical listening in the sense that we consider it here will not merely listen to more voices from marginalized communities only to render them in the same way as before, as victims or as objects of pity. Listening more closely to marginalized voices does not mean seeking out more examples to illustrate journalistic narratives in the same way as before, governed by the same news values.

If listening is merely incorporated as a strategy to do the same type of journalism, it may not proceed beyond a type of therapy session in which the journalist remains in control and the subject of the story remains cast in the role of victim. Journalists can continue in their familiar mode, looking for stories of drama, conflict, and suffering, without the dynamics of the relationship being altered in any significant way. This is not what is understood by listening as an ethical framework. Ethical listening, fundamentally, is about engaging with power relations in society.

Listening "provides a language" for an agonistic democratic culture by "shifting the focus from having a voice to how conventions and privilege shape who and what can be heard" (Oelofsen 2020). In this way, listening can transform not only journalism but also political culture in itself.

Listening as an ethical position requires a fundamental revision of the relationship between journalists and their publics, one in which power relations are radically revised or overturned. A more reciprocal relationship with their publics would require journalists to let go of their "desire for mastery" over the narrative, instead adopting a stance of "ethical receptivity" (Dreher 2009, 451). This is clearly very different from the kind of listening that takes place in audience research by media organizations, or even the routine interviews in which the journalist frames and controls the narrative and listens only to obtain answers to questions already formulated. Critical political listening as an ethical strategy requires a relinquishing of the control over the narrative. Of course, this does not mean that journalists no longer have any say over their reporting, nor that they don't have to take any ethical responsibility for the questions they ask. The difference in this kind of listening is that it creates a true dialogue, in the sense that the responses are allowed to alter, shift, and speak back to the original agenda rather than made to fit into it. Voltmer (2016, 16) remarks:

> Listening is more than extracting public opinion data. It involves a dialogical process that doesn't shy away from differences, but recognizes the experiences and views of the other side. As part of a dialogue, listening involves more than refraining from speaking in order to provide space for the voice of the other; it also requires a kind of response that reflects active engagement with the views of the other side.

The point of such difficult, dialogic listening is therefore not only to include a wider range of voices into the already-existing talking space but also to alter the space itself to allow for different, other, and hard-to-hear voices to appear. This is not only an attitudinal question but also a structural one. For these voices to appear in the contested, unequal, and conflictual political talking space of especially emerging and transitional democracies "requires a reconsideration of conditions that determine who and what can be heard in political talking spaces" (Oelofsen 2020).

Listening can be seen as fundamental to democratic politics (Bickford 1996, 2). This orientation toward others is not necessarily communitarian or relational, but a way to make sense of conflicts and complexities in an agonistic, contested political environment. This ethical stance of listening requires an openness to other ideas; the ability to imagine oneself in the place of another; the capacity to allow the narratives of others to emerge across the dividing lines of culture, society, or politics; and the willingness to allow one's assumptions to be challenged. Listening is an important prerequisite for a narrative ethics as described by Christians (2011, 26):

> Through stories, we constitute ways of living in common. They are symbolic frameworks that organize human experience. People tell stories about who they are and what they care about. . . . In narrative ethics, moral values are situated in the cultural context rather than anchored by philosophical abstractions. Contextual values replace ethical absolutes. The domain of ethics shifts from principles to story, from formal logic to community formation.

Opting for listening as a normative framework also acknowledges that communication in conflict situations serves not merely as a conduit for information, but also as a practice that constitutes culture and community.

While normative discourses about the media usually emphasize its transmission function (disseminating information, keeping the public informed, speaking truth to power, etc.), an ethics of listening would require an understanding of how the media can bring people together in conflict situations, heal fragmented and polarized communities, and reconcile people across shared values and interests.

As Lipari (2014a, 506) explains:

> When viewed as information transfer, communication becomes a largely mechanical routine wherein things like the accuracy of the message, the efficiency of delivery, the precision of reception, are in the foreground while

other much more interesting and important aspects of communication are missed. An altogether different way of thinking about communication derives not from the conduit metaphor, but from the cognates of the word communication, such as communion and community.

Communication in this sense is not merely transmitting information about a reality that is taken to exist independently, "out there" in the world, but an act that creates and shapes the world and our understanding of our place in it. When communication is understood as "constitutive of human life-worlds themselves" (Lipari 2014a, 511), the dialogic nature of communication, involving both speaking and listening, comes into focus more clearly. No longer the "necessary, but slightly embarrassing, dull partner" to speaking, listening is then viewed as intrinsically part of speaking, two sides of the same coin: "Every speaking is at the same time a listening, and every listening a speaking" (Lipari 2014a, 512).

When applying this insight to the mediatization of conflict, we see the media's ethical responsibility not merely as transmitting information in a monitorial mode to publics so that they can keep government to account. Nor is a view of media as facilitating deliberation or debate in the public sphere sufficient when notions of "voice" and "speaking" are emphasized without the concomitant act of listening. An ethics of listening for the media would go further than seeing the function of the media as facilitating a process of speaking and listening ("interlistening," in Lipari's [2014a] words) between members of the public. An ethics of listening would also demand that media institutions and journalists themselves engage actively in listening to their publics. This would entail that the media willingly relinquish their claim to authority over the truth, instead recognizing that truth is constructed dialogically and in relation to their publics. In practical terms, such listening may result in the co-construction of news agendas or providing community members with the opportunity to act as guest editors.

In recent years, news media organizations in various global settings have come to realize the importance of reconnecting with audiences to offset what has become a growing crisis of trust in the media. "Audience engagement," often based on an optimistic view of the capabilities of digital platforms to increase audience involvement in media work (Belair-Gagnon, Nelson, and Lewis 2018), has become a mantra often heard in newsrooms. This sometimes entails relinquishing some of the autonomy that journalists have been accustomed to as a central part of their professional identity to renew trust with their sources and audiences (Belair-Gagnon et al. 2018). Not all audience engagement, however, has the altruistic objective of deepening trust in the media to facilitate greater participation in democratic debate or building community reciprocally. While the rhetoric of audience involvement in the cocreation of news content might be the ideal, in practice the goal of such engagement is often more self-serving, namely adapting content to audience tastes so as to broaden the news outlet's market reach (Belair-Gagnon et al. 2018).

When conceived of in ethical terms, listening can serve as a normative concept to guide journalists toward changing their relationship with audiences-as-receivers to audiences-as-partners or audiences-as-interlocutors. Offline "listening sessions" can be used to build the type of reciprocal relationship that has community creation and building as its aim:

> It was clear that these journalists were evaluating the impact of their work less by the consequences of the stories they produced than by the consequences of the connections they built and maintained with their community. By listening to underreported community members in a more compassionate way, journalists felt that they were making a positive impact in the community—even if that didn't necessarily mean a positive impact on their bottom line, or on their specific audience. (Belair-Gagnon et al. 2018, 556)

Listening and Conflict

The aim of adopting listening as a normative approach in conflict settings is not only to better connect journalists with their publics but also to de-escalate and reorient conflicts so that they better contribute to democratic culture. Journalists who listen well can connect citizens horizontally with each other in order for disputes and tensions about identity, recognition, and participation to be engaged with in a constructive, agonistic, democratic, yet nonviolent space. Listening is a characteristic of good governance, especially in conflict situations. As Stremlau and Iazzolino (2017, 5) point out, "responsible leaders are able to listen to the grievances of their following and manage expectations, thus contributing to defuse escalating conflicts" by encouraging "voice" from citizens. In many African countries, patronage networks determine who gets heard. Political relationships are regulated on an informal level, through personal connections, bribes, and rent-seeking, rather than through formalized spaces where voices can be expressed and citizens may be heard regardless of their political connections. These informal, patronage relationships have been termed "veranda politics," in contrast to "air-conditioning politics," which takes place in more formal political spaces (Stremlau and Iazzolino 2017, 10).

The notion of listening resonates with the ideal of open deliberation in the public sphere, although listening would require an openness not only to rational deliberation but also to engaging with emotive expression, outrage, and protest. Mouffe (2005, 95) validates passion, emotion, and power struggles in democratic debate and takes issue with political liberalism, which offers a picture of the well-ordered society "as one from which—through rational agreement on justice—antagonism, violence, power and repression have disappeared." Bickford (2011), acknowledging critiques of rational deliberation that show its potential to entrench social hierarchies and amplify exclusions, makes a case for taking "emotion talk" seriously. For Bickford, a "conflictual and inegalitarian context" requires the acceptance of "emotion and partisan thinking as morally appropriate elements of democratic communication" (2011, 1026). Emotions should be valued as part of political communication because they signal the depth of citizens' investment in and engagement with issues: "On this view, emotion is opposed not to reason but to alienation, estrangement, and disengagement. Emotion signifies a fully alive and committed way of being in the world, and emotional experience is the fundamental element of genuine human selfhood" (Bickford 2011, 1026).

The challenge is to mediate democratic conflicts in a way that would allow these affective expressions to manifest as agonistic engagements, "a struggle among adversaries," rather than a "war between enemies" (Mouffe 2005, 31). If "antagonism is struggle between enemies, while agonism is struggle between adversaries," as Mouffe (2005, 103) argues, "the aim of democratic politics is to transform *antagonism* into *agonism*." A normative framework for the media based on listening would assist in doing this by encouraging all voices to be heard, whether they are expressed in the language of rationality or affect, deliberation or outrage. At best, what can be hoped for in such an agonistic democracy—in which the media helps citizens to listen to one another—is not the absence of conflict, but a "conflictual consensus" arising out of many different and conflicting interpretations of the "ethico-political principles" governing society (Mouffe 2005, 103).

Allowing for contesting viewpoints to emerge in an agonistic debate is the best chance the media has to facilitate the de-escalation of violence, even—and perhaps especially—in conditions of high violence, threat, and risk. Cottle (2006), for instance, argues that the media has often used labels such as "terrorism" and "terrorist" to position certain political actors outside the realm of political debate and portray them as irrational and violent. The media could play a more productive role toward pacification in giving "vent to felt grievances and publicly examining the arguments and opposing interests and identities involved" (Cottle 2006, 165).

Proposing listening as an ethical approach to solving or de-escalating conflicts does not mean that underlying substantive injustices and inequalities can be ignored or papered over in an attempt to reach consensus. Quite the contrary—listening may contribute to a better understanding of the various parties' points of view and result in the expression of marginalized or suppressed positions; conflicts do not always arise merely due to a lack of understanding. Listening as an ethical approach should therefore not exclude attempts to solve the underlying social justice issues. As Hamelink (2016, 60) points out, soberingly: "These assumptions neglect the fact that conflicts often address very real points of contention. Conflicts may be very dangerous precisely because adversaries have full information about each other's aims and motives. In fact, more information about the adversary may actually lead to more conflict."

According to Hamelink (2016, 75), the "difficult art of listening" that contributes to "meaningful dialogue" requires that participants reflect on their own positions and question their own judgments and assumptions:

> Active listening empowers the people who are listened to, allowing them to discover new choices and new possibilities. . . . Active listening also implies that people listen to each other not merely in a defensive way in order to be prepared for a rebuttal; they also listen with empathy and reflexivity in order to be able to see reality from a different perspective.

Listening as an ethical framework therefore also assumes that the media's role in democracy has to extend beyond a rationalist facilitation of democratic procedures; it has to create the conditions for people to identify with democratic values and, importantly, to experience that their voices and lived experiences are acknowledged as legitimate and paid attention to. This is a different understanding of the relationship between media and democracy, and indeed democracy itself, than in the Habermasian sense, which is predicated on reason and rational deliberation. The difference, Mouffe (2005, 70) explains with reference to Wittgenstein, is the difference between the Habermasian *Einverstand*, an agreement resulting from rational debate, and *Einstimmung*, the kind of common life and identification with democratic values that emerges from a fusion of voices made possible by a common form of life.

When we translate these insights to a normative framework for the media in contexts of conflict, it implies that the media should actively seek the inclusion of a plurality of voices and types of expression. Instead of promoting only a clinical, rational discussion of the conflict, media should listen carefully to the full range of emotions associated with human experience and consider them as valid and legitimate. The media's role would be to listen to, and amplify, the full variety of these voices: "Democratic citizenship can take many diverse forms and such a diversity, far from being a danger for democracy, is in fact its very condition of existence" (Mouffe 2005, 74). Such an agonistic understanding of democratic debate will not eschew conflict, but rather harness different understandings of democracy to coexist and grapple with each other, and embrace rather than erase diversity.

Although the listening advocated by Mouffe, Bickford, and others is related to a conception of democratic politics as agonistic and inherently conflictual, related normative approaches, such as an ethics of care and compassion (see the work of Gilligan [1982], Chouliaraki [2006], and Sontag [2003]), would resonate with this type of listening when it comes to aspects of conflict reporting that have to do with the representation of suffering and the relationship between journalists and victims of conflict. Gilligan (1982, xiii) refers to listening as an inherent part of human relationships when she describes her "ethics of care" as grounded on an understanding of human dignity based not on "abstract speculations" but on *relationships* that are *"grounded in listening."* "The most basic questions about human living—how to live and what to do," Gilligan (1982, xiv) says, "are fundamentally questions about human relations, because people's lives are deeply connected, psychologically, economically, and politically." "To have a voice," she adds (1982, xvi), "is to be human. To have something to say is to be a person. But speaking depends on listening and being heard; it is an intensely relational act."

Listening as an approach to the mediation of conflict in the first instance requires a certain ethical orientation that is more attuned to the underlying motivations of the actors; is aimed at finding solutions rather than merely reporting on clashes, disagreements, and violence in a stenographic fashion; and treats subjects of reporting with dignity and compassion. Aside from such an orientation, however, listening also requires particular practical skills and strategies. Listening requires "artfulness," Back (2007, 8) argues, because listening "isn't self-evident but a form of openness to others that needs to be crafted, a listening for the background and the half muted." Listening, therefore, is both a *virtue* and a *skill* (Dobson 2014, 172).

Of crucial importance when considering listening as an ethics of the media is that a commitment to listening does not imply an uncritical acceptance of people's stories or claims on face value. Critical media should therefore be able to hold their monitorial role in balance with their orientation as compassionate listeners. Arguing for an ethics of listening is therefore not the same as "a proposal for blind acceptance or unquestioning agreement. Being a partisan to the human story in all its manifold diversity does not exclude maintaining a critical orientation to it" (Back 2007, 8). The views revealed in people's accounting of their everyday lives may themselves be partial, biased, or prejudicial, and critical listening requires an evaluation of these narratives with the ultimate goal of understanding (Back 2007, 12).

Listening does, however, require an attunement not only to the voice of the one being listened too but also to the identity or social position of the listener, which might affect his or her listening (Lipari 2014b, 52). In the case of the media, journalists who belong to a professional, elite class therefore have to realize how their privileged social position may hamper their ability to hear what the subjects of their stories are saying and to understand what they mean. This is what Lipari (2014b, 53) refers to as a "politics of listening," relating to "who speaks and who doesn't, what is and is not said, how what is said is said, as well as, of course, to whom it is said and what is and is not heard, and *how* what is heard is heard." Listening therefore requires imagination, the practiced ability to put yourself in the shoes of another, in order to empathize with his or her situation (Dobson 2014, 113). This skill is something that could be learned and should be educated for, Nussbaum (2010, 10) implores, the sake of inclusive democracy: "The ability to imagine the experience of another—capacity almost all human beings possess in some form—needs to be greatly enhanced and refined if we are to have any hope of sustaining decent institutions across the many divisions that any modern society contains."

When people are being listened to, they experience it as having power (Dobson 2014, 171). Listening to those who are routinely ignored, silenced, or marginalized by the media is therefore also a way of overturning power relations. However, the media might also engage in a superficial kind of listening that merely obtains the input of the poor and the marginalized in a way that fits into preframed questions and narratives, without offering them the opportunity to disrupt or reframe dominant social or economic consensus. This comes down to a type of ventriloquism (Dobson 2014, 190).

Let us look at some examples of what listening as a media ethical practice may look like in African contexts of conflict.

Examples

Although most of the work done on listening in relation to media and journalism has been of a conceptual and theoretical nature, there are already examples of journalists putting these principles into practice. In the United States, several initiatives have been underway to help journalists put into practice "models, methods and workflows for listening to and building trust with the public," often using digital platforms (CLEF 2018). Some of these practices include journalists conducting neighborhood meetings to get feedback on newspaper coverage, and summits being hosted by news organizations where journalists exchange ideas on how to better connect with their communities, report with greater empathy, and shift the perspective of their stories to become more centered on people's lived experiences (Goins 2018).

In South Africa, the news website *Daily Maverick* created a subscriber base called "Maverick Insiders" who receive email newsletters, invitations to events, and special deals. During the coronavirus pandemic in 2020, the publication started sending out regular invitations to this group of subscribers to get their input on how to cover the pandemic, the national lockdown to prevent the spread of the virus, the impact of the lockdown on small businesses, and related issues. These invitations were prefaced by a message saying that the *Daily Maverick* was committed to "public interest journalism" and that this input would help the publication improve their coverage of the pandemic. The input was also used to put together webinars where journalists and invited expert panelists would answer some of the readers' questions. This is an example of how journalists can listen to their audiences and invite them to help shape the news agenda. It is, however, a rather limited form of listening—it relies only on the opinion of a select few media users to shape reporting and facilitates conversation between members of an elite group of media users rather than across the chasms of inequality and social difference.

A much more interventionist project by another South African publication, and one that set out specifically to cut across these socioeconomic divisions, is described by Garman and Malila (2018, 162). Already in 2011, *The Herald* newspaper in the coastal city of Port Elizabeth embarked on "conduct[ing] a series of listening exercises." Against the background of extremely high socioeconomic inequality, these efforts focused specifically on hearing the voices of the poor and the marginalized, who (as has been discussed at length elsewhere in this book) are still routinely excluded from mainstream news agendas. Driven by the paper's editor, Heather Robinson, working in collaboration with a local university, dialogues with communities were held over the course of four years (2011 to 2015) and took the shape of large town hall meetings, launches of books on topical issues, and smaller "fishbowl meetings" (Garman and Malila 2018, 166). These meetings had the primary aim of getting opinion leaders and citizens involved in making decisions that affected them, but the process also widened the perspectives of the editor and journalists who participated and helped them to learn from the perspectives of those they listened to. The newspaper's owners and managers, however, saw this as a commercial opportunity rather than a social or political one, and not all journalists participated, putting the sustainability of these listening exercises at risk (Garman and Malila 2018, 166).

The challenge for the newspaper—one that was not always met successfully—was to use these listening exercises to inform and ultimately change the way they report on poor communities in particular. Often the newspaper remained stuck in the monitorial role of airing the community's grievances, especially toward the local government, but did not extend this into active intervention or campaigning on behalf of those whose voices they had heard (Garman and Malila 2018, 168). At the center of these listening exercises, however, was a willingness to "stand within the community to better understand its citizens" (Garman and Malila 2018, 169), with the aim of changing journalistic practices to better serve communities in the grip of political conflict born out of socioeconomic hardships. When conducted in this way, listening is not a passive exercise, but an active one that is directly linked to the world of politics, as it enables citizens to influence news agendas, use facilitated media platforms to speak to politicians, and ultimately influence policymaking more effectively (Garman and Malila 2018, 168).

The previous example of *The Herald* demonstrates a type of listening that is premised on time-tried models of direct contact between journalists and audiences, in ways reminiscent of public journalism.

Increasingly, new digital technologies are touted as means for journalists to better connect with their audiences (often with a commercial goal in mind), but also to facilitate "social listening" (Gearhart and Maben 2019, 2) between members belonging to different constituencies. Sorensen et al. (2019) warn that, despite early optimism about the potential for social media platforms such as Twitter to enable greater democratic dialogue, these very platforms have also shown antidemocratic tendencies in the "posttruth" age of fake news and disinformation. Furthermore, the "cacophony of political voices on social media" may mask a greater apathy when it comes to the actual, active involvement of citizens in political processes such as elections. Politicians do sometimes try to use social media to engage citizens, as was the case with the South African presidency around a time of great conflict in the national Parliament. However, these attempts were limited to an elite who were connected to these platforms and remained superficial exercises that did not enable real two-way conversations or responses (Sorensen et al. 2019).

Although new technologies are often celebrated for their ability to add a wider range of voices to public debates, they may also weaken the "intimacy and directness of communication" (Dobson 2014, 184). Claims that new media platforms such as Twitter can repair or strengthen relationships between citizens and politicians, or be a conduit for dialogue, should therefore be evaluated with care (Dobson 2014, 185). The digital media ecology is aimed toward circulation—liking, sharing, and reproducing—rather than understanding (Dobson 2014, 185), which means that participation on these platforms and interaction with other users do not automatically equate to dialogue and listening.

For mainstream media wanting to use digital media to connect with their audiences, interactive platforms such as WhatsApp, Twitter, and Facebook hold potential. But while social media can help journalists find new ways to listen to their publics, they can also contribute to greater disconnection between journalists and communities. The South African journalist Niren Tolsi (2018) laments the fracturing of society as a result of the filter bubbles created by social media, and the disconnection it causes between journalists and their publics. Ultimately this process leads to a loss of empathy, the moral imagination, and therefore the ability to listen: "This atomisation uses up the oxygen required for curiosity, exploration, gaining knowledge, developing empathy and solidarity, and articulating a humane praxis. We cannot breathe. We are suffocating our personal and political imaginations and, consequently, we have stopped feeling" (Tolsi 2018).

This disconnection is amplified in contexts of inequality. Tolsi (2018) goes on to show how social media outrage or solidarity remains skewed in favor of those social groups who have access to media agendas and signifying power anyway. In that sense, social media does not necessarily—or perhaps not even usually—enable a wider listening to take place, but tends to amplify those voices that are already most audible in the media space. Add to the erosion of solidarity and the deafening of journalists through filter bubbles the economic pressures that mainstream media continue to experience, and the disconnection becomes more severe. According to Tolsi (2018), "journalists no longer embed themselves in communities because, following over two decades of retrenchments and cost-cutting, there is neither the human nor financial resources for such immersion. Often, there is no will, either." The economic imperative of chasing "clicks" may, over time, lead to a utilitarian orientation toward publics, resulting in less connection and less empathic listening, despite the celebratory claims of "connection" that these technologies afford. Moreover, the narcissistic drive for viral popularity in the "attention economy" can instill a haste in journalists that could make them unlearn ways to pay attention to, see and recognize, and listen and hear others. Again, Tolsi (2018) explains:

> Journalists have stopped looking. We have stopped looking up from our smartphones and social media platforms when we report on something. In doing this we miss the detail which elevates our story-telling. We do this because we are told our readers demand constant information. We also do it for the endorphin rush of virality, for the narcissistic kicks of affirmation from our digital networks. With our heads down, we have physically stopped looking at the world around us, its stories and its nuances.

Tolsi (2018) also expounds on "love" as an ethical virtue that underpins listening as a normative orientation. His comments resonate with the ethics of care, which has links with an ethics of listening:

> We need to start caring about the people around us. As journalists, we need to love again. For "Love," as James Baldwin observes in *The Fire Next*

Time, "takes off the masks that we fear we cannot live without and know we cannot live within." I use the word "love" here, as Baldwin does, not merely in the personal sense but as a state of being, or a state of grace—not in the infantile American sense of being made happy but in the tough and universal sense of quest and daring and growth.

In contexts where democratization processes play out amid high inequality and social polarization and against the backdrop of conflict, an ethics of listening is therefore everything but a cozy relationship built on passivity. Instead, in these contexts—online and offline—journalists and media users are called upon to take up the radical position of actively seeking out alternative perspectives, making connections, and cultivating a moral imagination based on empathy. Such an ethical orientation is the basis upon which media in contexts of conflict can build, to strengthen democracy beyond merely monitoring procedural processes and the functioning of institutions, toward a substantive contribution to the human dignity, agency, and well-being of citizens.

6

Conclusion

This book considered the role of the media in conflict from an ethical per-spective. The focus fell on the types of conflict that typically emerge from de-mocratization processes and, more specifically, how these democratization conflicts play out in Africa.

The book made three key arguments:

- First, the point of departure was that conflict cannot be completely eradicated—even more so, that conflict is a feature of democratizing processes. Although there are many examples on the African context were conflicts resulted in bloodshed and war, democratic conflicts can also be handled in a way that contributes to the deepening of democ-racy. The media's role is crucial in making this distinction between ag-onistic conflicts that can be used to solidify an open, transparent, and dialogic democracy and ones that end in destruction and violence. An ethical media can de-escalate conflict and contribute to peacebuilding while fostering a critical dialogue built on a participatory, egalitarian culture founded in social justice.
- The type of democratic culture envisaged in the aforementioned version of mediated conflict will not always look the same. The second argu-ment of the book was that African democracies, and the media's role within them, is not a one-size-fits-all system. Democracies come into being and are sustained through ongoing contestations, negotiations, and debates. There have been many examples in Africa where the de-mocratization process has relapsed into renewed authoritarianism. In these relapsed democracies, the media have often come under renewed pressure. The link between media and democracy, however, is not al-ways as self-evident as is often assumed. The book has dwelled on sev-eral examples where, even in democratic contexts in Africa, the media have remained suppressed or curtailed. Conversely, a free media does not always guarantee a deepened democratic culture. In highly unequal and socially polarized African contexts, the media may limit their focus

The Ethics of Engagement. Herman Wasserman, Oxford University Press (2021). © Oxford University Press.
DOI: 10.1093/oso/9780190917333.003.0006

to the interest of elites or be beholden to commercial interests to the extent that their democratic potential goes unfulfilled.

- For the media to fulfill this democratic potential and de-escalate conflict so that it becomes constitutive of democratic culture, it has to commit itself to ethical values and practices. The third, and central, argument of the book was that such an ethics is best thought of as collaborative and dialogic. The argument at the heart of this book was that an "ethics of engagement" implies relationship—a media that builds its practices on the values of mutuality, dialogue, and listening. This is a radical argument, requiring of media not merely to adjust or reform their values and practices, but to rethink them completely.

Why is it important to study media and conflict in Africa? And why is a focus on media ethics a particularly important approach? This book has argued that conflict provides a lens onto the intersections of media, politics, culture, and society in Africa. At this intersection, important ethical questions for journalists are raised on how to report on conflict and how their reporting may influence the development or outcome of conflict processes. In the contemporary media environment, where the lines between professional producers of media, citizen journalists, content generators, and media users are increasingly blurred, these ethical demands are applicable not only to those working for newsrooms but also to those who use media in everyday life.

When considering the intersection between media ethics, conflict, and democracy, the book identified some problems that have to be grappled with. One of the problems of imagining more ethically productive ways for the media to engage with democratization conflicts is that media ethics in African contexts is often approached and promoted (by media councils, nongovernmental organizations, and donor agencies) primarily in procedural terms. This means that the emphasis falls on the processes and institutions that are seen to establish and uphold media ethical codes, on complaints procedures, or on impartial reporting on and monitoring of elections. While these procedural aspects are important, they can also obscure the need for more substantive reflection on the media's role in African democracies, including functions such as promoting social and economic justice as well as gender, racial, and ethnic equality.

A further challenge to our thinking about the media's role in African democratization conflicts is the tendency to see conflict as a failure of democratization that needs to be resolved, instead of viewing it as part of cyclical democratic processes, to which agonistic contests are inherent. The notion that conflict is a part of democratization and therefore cannot be eradicated completely was discussed at length. This, of course, does not mean that violent conflicts should be welcomed or even tolerated. Conflict in the democratic sense does not, however, have to be violent or destructive. If democratic conflicts can be de-escalated so that they are no longer violent or destructive but rather contribute to robust deliberation and the reconfiguration of power relations, conflicts can have productive outcomes.

The starting premise of this book was that conflict is something that is often avoided, suppressed, or seen as a sign of a breakdown in relationships and peaceful coexistence. Peace and justice remain ideals the media should strive for globally, and in particular in regions of the Global South, such as Africa, where conflict, inequality, and injustice have characterized societies for centuries. Yet, if conflict is de-escalated to such a degree that it takes on the character of healthy democratic contestation rather than constructing actors as enemies, and if marginalized citizens and communities are empowered to participate in such agonistic contests instead of being relegated to the discursive sidelines, democratization conflicts could result in constructive outcomes. The media's role is crucial in determining such outcomes.

It is hoped that the discussions in this book will lead to a better understanding of how the media is implicated in democratic conflicts, and how reflection on its roles, responsibilities, and normative frameworks in these contexts can lead to the discovery of ways in which it can make a constructive contribution. At the nexus of media, democracy, and conflict, it is vital that the media does not take its own position for granted, assume an uncritical moral authority, or become complacent about its responsibilities. Meaningful mediation of conflict in African democracies will rely on ongoing reflection on the media's ethics of engagement.

Notes

Chapter 1

1. A quantified criterion for "violent" conflict is a minimum of twenty-five battle-related deaths per year, while fewer than one thousand deaths qualify as an "intermediate" violent conflict and over one thousand as a "major" violent conflict (Frère and Wilen 2015a, 1).
2. This is illustrated well by the research agendas of two major international collaborative research projects launched in recent years—Infocore (www.infocore.eu) and MeCoDEM (www.mecodem.eu)—which considered media, conflict, and democratization in African countries alongside other transitional countries in the Balkans and Central Europe.
3. I have written elsewhere (see Wasserman 2018a) about the problematic nature of considering African media through an area studies lens.

Chapter 2

1. Left outside of focus, largely for practical reasons of scope, are fictional formats such as television shows, cinema, advertising, and public relations. This is despite the fact that an interesting literature exists on the role of entertainment industries in global discourses of war and conflict (see, e.g., Burston 2003).
2. However, recent findings found weaker support for these arguments than the literature might suggest. See Baden and Tenenboim-Weinblatt (2018, 33).
3. This example is drawn from an article published previously (Wasserman 2017), where I discuss the case in the broader context of debates about "fake news."

Chapter 3

1. An example of this is the politics of the spectacle adopted by the South African opposition party the Economic Freedom Fighters (EFF). Through tactics such as wearing red overalls and berets to signify an allegiance with the working class and routinely disrupting parliamentary proceedings through interjections and walk-outs, the EFF has displayed a knack for getting media attention.
2. This section draws on Wasserman (2013, 2015). Used with permission.
3. In the days before the shooting, Ramaphosa, at the time a nonexecutive director of the mining company Lonmin, sent several emails to Lonmin executives and the ministers of police and mineral resources, in one of which he demanded "concomitant action" against the striking mineworkers (Gerber 2018).

4. The contemporary media serve as a site for the construction, definition, and contestation of what Beck referred to as the global "risk society" (1992): the industrial, technological, environmental, climactic, and other hazards that are outside human control and that pose the potential to cause great harm to global societies. The outbreak of the novel coronavirus Covid-19 that led to a global crisis in 2020 was an unprecedented and unexpected manifestation of such globalized risk. The scale and impact of these hazards were made overwhelmingly clear as Covid-19 spread around the world and were experienced by societies globally as real and devastating largely as a result of the media's ability to illuminate the crisis and raise consciousness about its effects.

5. Among these theorists, Francis Fukuyama and his notion of the "end of history" (drawing on Hegel), with liberal democracy as the end point of progress toward the ideal political organization, has probably become the most well known (and gained the most notoriety). See Fukuyama (1992), and also Ottaway (1997).

6. I discussed this example of an "act of citizenship" in relation to the Marikana massacre in South Africa elsewhere in greater detail (Wasserman 2015).

7. This section is drawn from an earlier coauthored article in which these theoretical points were illustrated with empirical data (Chuma, Wasserman, et al. 2017).

Chapter 4

1. Future research should include the effects and impact of the spread of Covid-19, which was still raging at the time of writing, on the Global South, in this conceptual framework of "slow violence." The concept might also prove useful when considering the media coverage of the pandemic in different parts of the world relative to other, long-standing problems such as poverty, inequality, and insecurity, which may have been exacerbated by the pandemic.

2. The outbreak of Covid-19 again emphasized the importance of trustworthy, science-based reporting against the onslaught of misinformation, which could have dangerous health consequences.

Chapter 5

1. Although the situation was still evolving at the time of writing, the South African media's response to the government's handling of the Covid-19 crisis in 2020 seemed to display a similar balance between monitorial and collaborative roles. While scrutinizing the government's plans and policies and reporting on abuses of power by the military and police during the national lockdown, the media also largely collaborated with government's appeals to citizens to adhere to lockdown regulations and comply with health and safety advice such as handwashing and social distancing.

References

Abrahamsen, R. 2004. "A Breeding Ground for Terrorists? Africa and Britain's 'War on Terrorism.'" *Review of African Political Economy* 31 (102): 677–84.

Adekanye, J. B. 1995. "Structural Adjustment, Democratization and Rising Ethnic Tensions in Africa." *Development and Change* 26 (2): 355–74.

AFP (Agence France-Presse). 2018. "Nigeria Media Unite against Fake News ahead of the 2019 Elections." *Business Day*, November 28. Accessed December 10, 2018. https://www.businesslive.co.za/bd/world/africa/2018-11-28-nigeria-media-unite-against-fake-news-ahead-of-2019-elections/.

Alexander, P., T. Lekgowa, B. Mmope, L. Sinwell, and B. Xeswi. 2012. *Marikana: A View from the Mountain and a Case to Answer*. Johannesburg: Jacana Media.

Amner, R. 2011. "Paper Bridges: A Critical Examination of the *Daily Dispatch*'s Community Dialogues." *Ecquid Novi: African Journalism Studies* 32 (1): 25–48.

Andresen, K., A. Hoxha, and J. Godole. 2017. "New Roles for the Media in the Western Balkans." *Journalism Studies* 18 (5): 614–28.

Back, L. 2007. *The Art of Listening*. London: Bloomsbury.

Baden, C. 2014. "Constructions of Violent Conflict in Public Discourse." Infocore Working Paper 2014/10. Accessed March 12, 2018. http://www.infocore.eu/wp-content/uploads/2016/02/Conceptual-Paper-MWG-CA_final.pdf.

Baden, C., and K. Tenenboim-Weinblatt. 2018. "The Search for Common Ground in Conflict News Research: Comparing the Coverage of Six Current Conflicts in Domestic and International Media over Time." *Media, War & Conflict* 11 (1): 22–45.

Barber, K. 2017. *A History of African Popular Culture*. Cambridge: Cambridge University Press.

BBC. 2018. "Kenya TV Stations to Remain Off-Air after Odinga 'Inauguration.'" Accessed February 5, 2018. http://www.bbc.com/news/world-africa-42888904.

Beck, U. 1992. *Risk Society*. London: Sage.

Belair-Gagnon, V., J. L. Nelson, and S. C. Lewis. 2018. "Audience Engagement, Reciprocity, and the Pursuit of Community Connectedness in Public Media Journalism." *Journalism Practice* 13 (5): 558–75.

Bell, M. 1997. "TV News: How Far Should We Go?" *British Journalism Review* 8 (1): 7–16.

Berger, G. 2002. "Theorizing the Media–Democracy Relationship in Southern Africa." *Gazette* 64 (1): 21–45.

Berger, G. 2008. "A Paradigm in Process: What the Scapegoating of Vusi Mona Signalled about South African Journalism." *Communicatio* 34 (1): 1–20.

Bertrand, J-C. 2000. *Media Ethics and Accountability Systems*. New Brunswick, NJ: Transaction Publishers.

Bickford, S. 1996. *The Dissonance of Democracy: Listening, Conflict and Citizenship*. Ithaca, NY: Cornell University Press.

Bickford, S. 2011. "Emotion Talk and Political Judgment." *Journal of Politics* 73 (4): 1025–37.

Biznews. 2017. "Bell Pottinger White Monopoly Capital Plot: Damning EVIDENCE of Gupta Conspiracy #Guptaleaks." Accessed July 4, 2017. http://www.biznews.com/guptaleaks/2017/06/09/bell-pottinger-white-monopoly-capital/.

Black, J., B. Steele, and R. D. Barney. 1995. *Doing Ethics in Journalism: A Handbook with Case Studies*. Boston: Allyn and Bacon.

Bocha, G. 2018. "How International Media Reported Kenya TV Shutdown." *Daily Nation*, February 5. Accessed March 27, 2018. https://www.nation.co.ke/news/International-media-report-on-Kenya-TV-shutdown/1056-4292234-pd48ou/index.html.

Bosch, T. 2016. "Twitter and Participatory Citizenship: #FeesMustFall in South Africa." In *Digital Activism in the Social Media Era*, edited by B. Mutsvairo, 159–73. London: Palgrave Macmillan.

Bosch, T., H. Wasserman, and W. Chuma. 2018. "South African Activists' Use of Nanomedia and Digital Media in Democratisation Conflicts." *International Journal of Communication* 12: 1–18.

Boyle, K. 2005. *Media and Violence: Gendering the Debates*. London: Sage.

Brown, B. 2017. *Braving the Wilderness*. New York: Random House.

Bruce, P. 2017. "The Price of Writing about the Guptas." *Business Day*, June 29. Accessed July 5, 2017. https://www.businesslive.co.za/bd/opinion/columnists/2017-06-29-peter-bruce--the-price-of-writing-about-the-guptas/.

Bunce, M. 2014. "International News and the Image of Africa: New Storytellers, New Narratives?" In *Images of Africa: Creation, Negotiation and Subversion*, edited by J. Gallagher, 42–62. Manchester: Manchester University Press.

Burston, J. 2003. "War and the Entertainment Industries: New Research Priorities in an Era of Cyber-Patriotism." In *War and the Media*, edited by D. K. Thussu and D. Freedman, 163–75. London: Sage.

Carson, A., and K. Farhall. 2018. "Understanding Collaborative Investigative Journalism in a 'Post-Truth' Age." *Journalism Studies* 19 (13): 1899–911.

Cebulski, A. 2018. "Mitchells Plain and Siqalo residents hold crisis meeting." GroundUp, May 3. Accessed May 5, 2018. https://www.groundup.org.za/article/mitchells-plain-and-siqalo-residents-meet-defuse-conflict/.

Cheeseman, N. 2015. *Democracy in Africa: Successes, Failures, and the Struggle for Political Reform*. Cambridge: Cambridge University Press.

Cheeseman, N. 2018. "African Leaders Are More Constrained by Democratic Rules Than You Think." The Conversation, April 17. Accessed April 18, 2018. https://theconversation.com/african-leaders-are-more-constrained-by-democratic-rules-than-you-think-94999.

Cheeseman, N., M. Collord, and F. Reyntjens. 2018. "War and Democracy: The Legacy of Conflict in East Africa." *Journal of Modern African Studies* 56 (1): 31–61.

Chibuwe, A., and O. Ureke. 2016. "'Political Gladiators' on Facebook in Zimbabwe: A Discursive Analysis of Intra-Zimbabwe African National Union-PF Cyber Wars; Baba Jukwa versus Amai Jukwa." *Media, Culture and Society* 38 (8): 1247–60.

Chiumbu, S. 2015. "Social Movements, Media Practices and Radical Democracy in South Africa." *French Journal for Media Research* 4 : 1–20.

Chouliaraki, L. 2006. *The Spectatorship of Suffering*. London: Sage.

Christians, C. 2011. "Cultural Diversity and Moral Relativism in Communication Ethics." In *Ethical Issues in International Communication*, edited by A. G. Nikolaev, 23–34. New York: Palgrave Macmillan.

Christians, C. G., T. L. Glasser, D. Mcquail, K. Nordenstreng, and R. A. White. 2009. *Normative Theories of the Media: Journalism in Democratic Societies.* Urbana: University of Illinois Press.

Christians, C. G., and K. Nordenstreng. 2004. "Social Responsibility Worldwide." *Journal of Mass Media Ethics* 19 (1): 3–28.

Christians, C. G., S. Rao, S. J. Ward, and H. Wasserman. 2008. "Toward a Global Media Ethics: Exploring New Theoretical Perspectives." *Ecquid Novi: African Journalism Studies* 29 (2): 135–72.

Chuma, W., T. Bosch, and H. Wasserman. 2017. "The Media, Civil Society and Democracy in South Africa: The Case of the State of the Nation Address 2015." *Communicatio* 43 (2): 93–108.

Chuma, W., H. Wasserman, T. Bosch, and R. Pointer. 2017. "Questioning the Media–Democracy Link: South African Journalists' Views." *African Journalism Studies* 38 (10): 104–28.

City Press. 2012. "Watch—Marikana: Who Shot First?" *City Press*, August 21. Accessed August 21, 2018. https://www.news24.com/Archives/City-Press/Watch-Marikana-Who-shot-first-20150429.

City Press. 2014a. "Fourth Person Dies after Mothutlung Protests." *City Press*, January 20. Accessed August 21, 2018. https://www.news24.com/Archives/City-Press/Fourth-person-dies-after-Mothutlung-protests-20150429.

City Press. 2014b. "Man Shot Dead in Housing Protest." *City Press*, January 23. Accessed August 21, 2018. https://www.news24.com/Archives/City-Press/Man-shot-dead-in-housing-protest-20150429.

Clarke, H., and B. Duggan. 2018. "Kenya TV Stations Shutdown Enters 5th Day as Government Defies Court Order." CNN, February 3. Accessed March 27, 2018. https://edition.cnn.com/2018/02/03/africa/kenya-tv-stations-shutdown/index.html.

CLEF (Community Listening and Engagement Fund). 2018. "Community Listening and Engagement Fund." Accessed April 26, 2019. https://www.lenfestinstitute.org/community-listening-engagement-fund/.

Cohen-Almagor, R. 2000. "The Terrorists' Best Ally: The Quebec Media Coverage of the FLQ Crisis in October 1970." *Canadian Journal of Communication* 25 (2): 251–84.

Cottle, S. 2006. *Mediatized Conflict.* Maidenhead: Open University Press.

Dahir, A. L. 2017. "Internet Shutdowns Are Costing African Governments More Than We Thought." Quartz Africa, September 28. Accessed March 5, 2018. https://qz.com/1089749/internet-shutdowns-are-increasingly-taking-a-toll-on-africas-economies/.

Dahir, A. L. 2018. "WhatsApp Is the Most Popular Messaging App in Africa." Quartz Africa, February 14. Accessed July 13, 2018. https://qz.com/1206935/whatsapp-is-the-most-popular-messaging-app-in-africa/.

Daily Maverick. 2016. "Paid Twitter: Manufacturing Dissent, Helping Guptas." Daily Maverick, November 10. Accessed July 24, 2017. https://www.dailymaverick.co.za/article/2016-11-10-paid-twitter-manufacturing-dissent-helping-guptas.

Davids, C. A. 2018. "The Water Point." Africa Is a Country. Accessed February 15, 2018. http://africasacountry.com/2018/02/the-water-point/.

De Beer, A. S., V. Malila, S. Beckett, and H. Wasserman. 2016. "Binary Opposites—Can South African Journalists Be Both Watchdogs and Developmental Journalists?" *Journal of African Media Studies* 8 (1): 35–53.

De Waal, M. 2011. "Remembering Andries Tatane, Not Forgetting Police Brutality." *Daily Maverick*, April 18. Accessed March 26, 2018. http://dailymaverick.co.za/article/2011-04-18-remembering-andries-tatane-not-forgetting-police-brutality.

De Waal, M. 2012. "Marikana: What Really Happened? We May Never Know." *Daily Maverick*, August 23. Accessed August 21, 2018. http://dailymaverick.co.za/article/2012-08-23-marikana-what-really-happened-we-may-never-know.

Dimitrakopoulou, D., and S. Boukala. 2018. "Exploring Democracy and Violence in Burundi: A Multi-methodical Analysis of Hegemonic Discourses on Twitter." *Media, War & Conflict* 11 (1): 125–48.

Dobson, A. 2014. *Listening for Democracy: Recognition, Representation, Reconciliation.* Oxford: Oxford University Press.

Dodson, B. 2010. "Locating Xenophobia: Debate, Discourse, and Everyday Experience in Cape Town, South Africa." *Africa Today* 56 (3): 2–22.

Dreher, T. 2009. "Listening across Difference: Media and Multiculturalism beyond the Politics of Voice." *Continuum* 23 (4): 445–58.

Duncan, J. 2012. "Marikana and the Problem of Pack Journalism." Abahlali baseMjondolo, October 11. Accessed August 25, 2018. http://abahlali.org/node/9253/.

Duncan, J. 2016. *Protest Nation: The Right to Protest in South Africa.* Durban: University of KwaZulu-Natal Press.

Elbadawi, E., and N. Sambanis. 2000. "Why Are There So Many Civil Wars in Africa? Understanding and Preventing Violent Conflict." *Journal of African Economies* 9 (3): 244–69.

Elliott, C., W. Chuma, Y. El Gendi, D. Marko, and A. Patel. 2016. "Hate Speech." MeCoDEM Working Paper. Accessed March 16, 2018. http://www.mecodem.eu/wp-content/uploads/2015/05/Elliot-Chuma-ElGendi-Marko-Patel-2016_Hate-Speech.pdf.

Ellis, S. 1989. "Tuning into Pavement Radio." *African Affairs* 88 (352): 321–30.

Entman, R. M. 2007. "Framing Bias: Media in the Distribution of Power." *Journal of Communication* 57: 163–73.

Etheridge, J. 2016. "Penny Sparrow Suffers Another Setback in Court." News 24, March 11. Accessed March 29, 2018. https://www.news24.com/SouthAfrica/News/penny-sparrow-suffers-another-setback-in-court-20161103.

EWN. 2017. "Ennerdale Residents Just Want Same as Black People Have Been Given." Eyewitness News, May 9. Accessed April 30, 2018. https://www.youtube.com/watch?v=Un05lchPOhc.

Fengler, S. 2012. "From Media Self-Regulation to 'Crowd-Criticism': Media Accountability in the Digital Age." *Central European Journal of Communication* 5 (2): 175–89.

Findlay, K. 2016. "Running Interference: The Fake 'White Monopoly Capital' Propaganda Community on Twitter." Superlinear, November 18. Accessed July 24, 2017. http://www.superlinear.co.za/running-interference-the-fake-white-monopoly-capital-propaganda-community-on-twitter/.

Fraser, N. 1999. "Social Justice in the Age of Identity Politics. In *Culture and Economy after the Cultural Turn*, edited by L. Ray and A. Sayer, 25–52. Thousand Oaks, CA: Sage.

Frère, M-S. 2007. *The Media and Conflicts in Central Africa.* London: Lynne Rienner.

Frère, M-S. 2011. *Elections and the Media in Post-Conflict Africa: Votes and Voices for Peace?* London: Zed Books.

Frère, M-S., and N. Wilen. 2015a. Infocore Definitions: Conflict. Brussels: ULB. Accessed March 12, 2018. http://www.infocore.eu/wp-content/uploads/2016/02/def_conflict.pdf.

Frère, M-S., and N. Wilen. 2015b. Infocore Definitions: Violent Conflict. Brussels: ULB. Accessed March 12, 2018. http://www.infocore.eu/wp-content/uploads/2016/02/def_violent-conflict.pdf.

Frère, M-S., and N. Wilen. 2015c. Infocore Definitions: Conflict Phases. Accessed March 12, 2018. http://www.infocore.eu/wp-content/uploads/2016/02/def_conflict-phases.pdf.

Frère, M-S., and N. Wilen. 2015d. Infocore Definitions: Escalation/De-escalation. Accessed March 12, 2018. http://www.infocore.eu/wp-content/uploads/2016/02/def_escalation-de-escalation.pdf.

Friedman, S. 2011. "Whose Freedom? South Africa's Press, Middle-Class Bias and the Threat of Control." *Ecquid Novi: African Journalism Studies* 32 (2): 106–21.

Fröhlich, R., and M. Jungblut. 2018. "Between Factoids and Facts: The Application of 'Evidence' in NGO Strategic Communication on War and Armed Conflict." *Media, War & Conflict.* 11 (1): 85–106.

Fukuyama, F. 1992. *The End of History and the Last Man.* New York: Free Press.

Garman, A. 2005. "Teaching Journalism to Produce 'Interpretive Communities' Rather Than Just 'Professionals.'" *Ecquid Novi: African Journalism Studies* 26 (2): 199–211.

Garman, A., and V. Malila. 2018. "When an Editor Decides to Listen to a City: Heather Robertson, *The Herald* and Nelson Mandela Bay." In *Critical Perspectives on Journalistic Beliefs and Actions: Global Experiences,* edited by E. Freedman, R. S. Goodman, and E. Steyn, 162–72. New York: Routledge.

Gearhart, C. C., and S. K. Maben. 2019. "Active and Empathetic Listening in Social Media: What Do Stakeholders Really Expect." *International Journal of Listening.* doi: 10.1080/10904018.2019.1602046.

George, C. 2013. "Diversity around a Democratic Core: The Universal and the Particular in Journalism." *Journalism* 14 (4): 490–503.

Gerber, J. 2018. "Ramaphosa 'Determined to Atone' for Marikana Massacre." News 24, February 20. Accessed May 2, 2018. https://www.news24.com/SouthAfrica/News/ramaphosa-determined-to-atone-for-marikana-massacre-20180220.

Gilligan, C. 1982. *In a Different Voice: Psychological Theory and Moral Development.* Cambridge, MA: Harvard University Press.

Goba, N. 2017. "Mob Attacks Top Journalists." *Times Live,* June 30. Accessed August 8, 2018. https://www.timeslive.co.za/news/south-africa/2017-06-30-mob-attacks-top-journalists/.

Goins, C. 2018. "How a Culture of Listening Strengthens Reporting and Relationships." American Press Institute, September 4. Accessed April 16, 2020. https://www.americanpressinstitute.org/publications/how a-culture-of-listening-strengthens-reporting-and-relationships/.

Gronvall, J. 2014. "De-coupling of Journalism and Democracy: Empirical Insights from Discussions with Leading Nordic Media Executives." *Journalism* 16 (8): 1027–44.

Guptaleaks. 2018. Accessed March 17, 2018. http://www.gupta-leaks.com.

Haffajee, F. 2017. "Ferial Haffajee: The Gupta Fake News Factory and Me." *Huffington Post,* June 6. Accessed July 24, 2017. http://www.huffingtonpost.co.za/2017/06/05/ferial-haffajee-the-gupta-fake-news-factory-and-me_a_22126282/.

Hallin, D. C., and P. Mancini. 2004. *Comparing Media Systems: Three Models of Media and Politics.* Cambridge: Cambridge University Press.

Hallin, D. C., and P. Mancini, eds. 2012. *Comparing Media Systems beyond the Western World.* Cambridge: Cambridge University Press.

Hamelink, C. 2016. *Media and Conflict: Escalating Evil.* London: Routledge.

Hanitzsch, T. 2004. "Journalists as Peacekeeping Force? Peace Journalism and Mass Communication Theory." *Journalism Studies* 5 (4): 483–95.

Hanitzsch, T. 2007. "Deconstructing Journalism Culture: Toward a Universal Theory." *Communication Theory* 17: 367–85.

Hanitzsch, T., F. Hanusch, J. Ramaprasad, and A. S. de Beer, eds. 2019. *Worlds of Journalism: Journalistic Cultures around the World.* New York: Columbia University Press.

Hanitzsch, T., and T. Vos. 2016. "Journalism beyond Democracy: A New Look into Journalistic Roles in Political and Everyday Life." *Journalism* 19 (2): 146–64.

Harding, A. 2013. "Facebook Character Stirs up Zimbabwe Politics." BBC News, May 24. Accessed May 4, 2018. http://www.bbc.com/news/world-africa-22661079.

Hawkins, V. 2002. "The Other Side of the CNN Factor: The Media and Conflict." *Journalism Studies* 3 (2): 225–40.

Heller, P. 2009. "Democratic Deepening in India and South Africa." *Journal of Asian and African Studies* 44 (1): 123–49.

Herrero-Jiménez, B., C. A. Calderón, A. Carratalá, and R. Berganza. 2018. "The Impact of Media and NGOs on Four European Parliament Discourses about Conflicts in the Middle East." *Media, War & Conflict* 11 (1): 65–84.

Hirsch, J. B. 2013. "Meaning and the Horizon of Interpretation: How Goals Structure Our Experience of the World." In *The Experience of Meaning in Life: Classical Perspectives, Emerging Themes, and Controversies*, edited by J. A. Hicks and C. Routledge, 129–39. Dordrecht: Springer.

Hoskins, A., B. Richards, and P. Selb. 2008. Editorial. *Media, War & Conflict* 1 (1): 5–7.

Houeland, C., and S. Jacobs. 2016. "The 'Big Man' Syndrome in Africa." Africa Is a Country, November 3. Accessed July 26, 2018. https://africasacountry.com/2016/03/the-big-man-syndrome-in-africa/.

Hoxha, A., and T. Hanitzsch. 2018. "How Conflict News Comes into Being: Reconstructing 'Reality' through Telling Stories." *Media, War & Conflict* 11 (1): 46–64.

Hsu, Y. 2008. "Acts of Chinese Citizenship: The Tank Man and Democracy-to-Come." In *Acts of Citizenship*, edited by E. F. Isin and G. M. Nielsen, 247–65. London: Zed Books.

Hughes, S., and Y. Vorobyeva. 2019. "Explaining the Killing of Journalists in the Contemporary Era: The Importance of Hybrid Regimes and Subnational Variations." *Journalism.* https://journals.sagepub.com/doi/pdf/10.1177/1464884919885588.

Huntington, S. 1991. *The Third Wave: Democratization in the Late Twentieth Century.* Norman: University of Oklahoma Press.

Isin, E. F., and G. M. Nielsen. 2008. "Introduction." In *Acts of Citizenship*, edited by E. F Isin and G. M. Nielsen, 1–12. London: Zed Books.

Jacobs, S., and H. Wasserman. 2018. "Siqalo Shows How Social Media Is Reshaping Protest Narratives." News 24, May 11. Accessed July 13, 2018. https://www.news24.com/Analysis/siqalo-showed-how-social-media-is-reshaping-protest-narratives-20180511.

Joseph, R. 1997. "Democratization in Africa after 1989: Comparative and Theoretical Perspectives." *Comparative Politics* 29 (3): 363–82.

Josephi, B. 2005. "Journalism in the Global Age: Between Normative and Empirical." *Gazette* 67 (6): 575–90.

Josephi, B. 2013. "How Much Democracy Does Journalism Need?" *Journalism* 14 (4): 474–89.

Kadlec, A., L. Sprain, and M. Carcasson. 2012. "Framing for Democracy: Exploring the Impacts of Adversarial and Deliberative Framing, Understanding the Longer-Term Benefits of Deliberation." Kettering Foundation Working Paper

2012–2. Accessed August 14, 2018. https://www.kettering.org/catalog/product/framing-democracy-exploring-impacts-adversarial-and-deliberative-framing.

Kalyango, Y. 2011. *African Media and Democratization: Public Opinion, Ownership and Rule of Law*. New York: Peter Lang.

Knight, A., C. George, and A. Gerlis. 2008. "Who Is a Journalist?" *Journalism Studies* 9 (1): 117–31.

Krabill, R. 2010. *Starring Mandela and Cosby: Media and the End(s) of Apartheid*. Chicago: University of Chicago Press.

Kruger, F. 2009. *Media Courts of Honour: Self-Regulatory Councils in Southern Africa and Elsewhere*. Research report. Windhoek: Fesmedia.

Krüger, F. 2017. "What Should Journalism Do in a New Democracy?" *Communicatio* 43 (2): 23–38.

Ledwaba, L. 2013. "Marikana: Medical Tests to Ascertain Muti Ritual Scars." *City Press*, March 6. Accessed August 21, 2018. https://www.news24.com/Archives/City-Press/Marikana-Medical-tests-to-ascertain-muti-ritual-scars-20150430.

Lee, S., and C. C. Maslog. 2005. "War or Peace Journalism? Asian Newspaper Coverage of Conflicts." *Journal of Communication* 55 (2): 311–29.

Lipari, L. 2014a. "On Interlistening and the Idea of Dialogue." *Theory and Psychology* 24 (4): 504–23.

Lipari, L. 2014b. *Listening, Thinking, Being: Towards an Ethics of Attunement*. University Park: University of Pennsylvania Press.

Lodamo, B., and T. Skjerdal. 2009. "Freebies and Brown Envelopes in Ethiopian Journalism." *Ecquid Novi: African Journalism Studies* 30 (2): 134–54.

Luescher, T., L. Loader, and T. Mugume. 2016. "#FeesMustFall: An Internet-Age Student Movement in South Africa and the Case of the University of the Free State." *Politikon* 44 (2): 231–45.

Lynch, J. 2020. "Peace Journalism." In *Oxford Research Encyclopedia of Journalism Studies*, edited by Henrik Örnebring, 1288–99, vol. 3. Oxford: Oxford University Press. https://oxfordre.com/communication/view/10.1093/acrefore/9780190228613.013.856

Lynch, J., and A. McGoldrick. 2005. *Peace Journalism*. Stroud: Hawthorn Press.

Magder, T. 2003. "Watching What We Say: Global Communication in a Time of Fear." In *War and the Media*, edited by D. K. Thussu and D. Freedman, 28–44. London: Sage.

Makinana, A. 2016. "Suspended SABC Journalist Speaks Out." *City Press*, July 2. Accessed January 24, 2018. http://city-press.news24.com/News/suspended-sabc-journalist-speaks-out-20160703.

Mäkinen, M,, and M. W. Kuira. 2008. "Social Media and Postelection Crisis in Kenya." *International Journal of Press/Politics* 13 (3): 328–35.

Malila, V. 2014. "Tracing the ANC's Criticism of South African Media." *Rhodes Journalism Review* 34: 13–15.

Malila, V., M. Oelofsen, A. Garman, and H. Wasserman. 2013. "Making Meaning of Citizenship: How 'Born Frees' Use Media in South Africa's Democratic Evolution." *Communicatio* 39 (4): 415–31.

Mano, W. 2007. "Popular Music as Journalism in Zimbabwe." *Journalism Studies* 8 (1): 61–78.

Mano, W. 2012. "Why Radio Is Africa's Medium of Choice in the Global Age." In *Radio in Africa: Publics, Cultures, Communities*, edited by L. Gunner, D. Ligaga, D. Moyo, T. Bosch, M. Chibita, and D. B. Coplan, 102–16. Johannesburg: Wits University Press.

Maphunye, K. J. 2018. "Weaning African Leaders Off Addiction to Power Is an Ongoing Struggle." The Conversation, April 16. Accessed April 17, 2018. https://theconversation.com/weaning-african-leaders-off-addiction-to-power-is-an-ongoing-struggle-94196.

Mare, A. 2016. "Facebook, Youth and Political Action: A Comparative Study of Zimbabwe and South Africa." PhD diss., Rhodes University.

Marchant, E., and N. Stremlau. 2020. "A Spectrum of Shutdowns: Reframing Internet Shutdowns from Africa." International Journal of Communication 14 (2020): 4327–42.

Marinovich, G. 2012. "The Murder Fields of Marikana. The Cold Murder Fields of Marikana." Daily Maverick, September 8. Accessed August 25, 2018. https://www.dailymaverick.co.za/article/2012-09-08-the-murder-fields-of-marikana-the-cold-murder-fields-of-marikana/.

Markham, T. 2011. The Politics of War Reporting: Authority, Authenticity and Morality. Manchester: Manchester University Press.

Maromo, J. 2013. "Marikana Commission: Strikers Used Muti, Believed They Were Invincible." Mail & Guardian, November 26. Accessed August 21, 2018. http://mg.co.za/article/2013-11-26-marikana-commission-strikers-used-muti-believed-they-were-invincible.

Martin, L. 2018. "Coverage of Sierra Leone's Election Reflected Stereotypes, Not Reality." The Conversation, April 22. Accessed April 23, 2018. https://theconversation.com/coverage-of-sierra-leones-election-reflected-stereotypes-not-reality-95322.

Mathekga, R. 2018. "The Poor Have Survived Day Zero for Years." News 24, January 29. Accessed March 16, 2018. https://www.news24.com/Columnists/Ralph_Mathekga/the-poor-has-survived-day-zero-for-years-20180129.

Meyer, C. O., C. Baden, and M-S. Frère. 2018. "Navigating the Complexities of Media Roles in Conflict: The INFOCORE Approach." Media, War & Conflict 11 (1): 3–21.

Meyer, C. O., E. Sanger, and E. Michaels, E. 2018. "How Do Non-governmental Organizations Influence Media Coverage of Conflict? The Case of the Syrian Conflict, 2011–2014." Media, War & Conflict 11 (1): 149–71.

Mohammed, O. 2015. "WhatsApp Is Now the Primary Platform for Political Trash Talk in Tanzania's Election Campaign." Quartz Africa, September 27. Accessed July 13, 2018. https://qz.com/510899/whatsapp-is-now-the-primary-platform-for-political-trash-talk-in-tanzanias-election-campaign/.

Moore, J. 2017. "Political Clashes in Kenya Leave Several Dead." New York Times, November 17. Accessed March 27, 2018. https://nyti.ms/2jzQLKm.

Moore, J. 2018. "Kenyans Name 'a People's President', and TV Broadcasts Are Cut." New York Times, January 30. Accessed March 27, 2018. https://www.nytimes.com/2018/01/30/world/africa/raila-odinga-kenya.html.

Mouffe, C. 2005. The Democratic Paradox. London: Verso.

Moyo, D. 2007. "Alternative Media, Diasporas and the Mediation of the Zimbabwe Crisis." Ecquid Novi: African Journalism Studies 28 (1–2): 81–105.

Moyo, L. 2011. "Blogging Down a Dictatorship: Human Rights, Citizen Journalists and the Right to Communicate in Zimbabwe." Journalism 12 (6): 745–60.

Msimang, S. 2016. "South Africa Has No Patience for Penny Sparrow's Apartheid Nostalgia." The Guardian, January 7. Accessed March 29, 2018. https://www.theguardian.com/commentisfree/2016/jan/07/south-africa-penny-sparrow-apartheid-nostalgia-racist.

Muendo, M. 2017. "Kenya Targets WhatsApp Administrators in Its Fight against Hate Speech." The Conversation, August 31. Accessed July 13, 2018. https://theconversation.com/kenya-targets-whatsapp-administrators-in-its-fight-against-hate-speech-82767.

Musa, B. A., and J. K. Domatob. 2007. "Who Is a Development Journalist? Perspectives on Media Ethics and Professionalism in Post-colonial Societies." *Journal of Mass Media Ethics* 22 (4): 315–31.

Mutsvairo, B., and L. Sirks. 2015. "Examining the Contribution of Social Media in Reinforcing Political Participation in Zimbabwe." *Journal of African Media Studies* 7 (3): 329–44.

Myburgh, P. 2017. "#GuptaEmails: Read the Documents Here." News 24, May 28. Accessed July 24, 2017. http://www.news24.com/SouthAfrica/News/guptaemails-read-the-documents-here-20170528.

Ndangam, L. 2006. "'Gombo': Bribery and the Corruption of Journalism Ethics in Cameroon." *Ecquid Novi: African Journalism Studies* 27 (2): 179–99.

Ndlela, N. 2005. "The African Paradigm: The Coverage of the Zimbabwean Crisis in the Norwegian Media." *Westminster Papers in Communication and Culture* November: 71–90.

Neocosmos, M. 2010. *From "Foreign Natives" to "Native Foreigners": Explaining Xenophobia in Post-apartheid South Africa: Citizenship and Nationalism, Identity and Politics.* Dakar: CODESRIA.

Nielsen, R., and L. Graves. 2017. "'News You Don't Believe': Audience Perspectives on Fake News." *Reuters Institute Factsheet,* October. Accessed March 5. 2018. https://reutersinstitute.politics.ox.ac.uk/sites/default/files/2017-10/Nielsen%26Graves_factsheet_1710v3_FINAL_download.pdf.

Nixon, R. 2011. *Slow Violence and the Environmentalism of the Poor.* Cambridge, MA: Harvard University Press.

Nussbaum, M. C. 2010. *Not for Profit: Why Democracy Needs the Humanities.* Princeton, NJ: Princeton University Press.

Nyabola, H. N. 2017. "Media Perspectives: Social Media and New Narratives: Kenyans Tweet Back." In *Africa's Media Image in the 21st Century: From the "Heart of Darkness" to "Africa Rising,"* edited by M. Bunce, S. Franks, and C. Paterson, 113–15. London: Routledge.

Nyambura, Z. 2017. "In Kenya, Politics Split on Ethnic Divide." *Deutsche Welle.* Accessed February 6, 2018. http://www.dw.com/en/in-kenya-politics-split-on-ethnic-divide/a-37442394.

Nyamnjoh, F. 2005. *Africa's Media: Democracy and the Politics of Belonging.* London: Zed Books.

Nyamnjoh, F. 2011. "De-Westernizing Media Theory to Make Room for African Experience." In *Popular Media, Democracy and Development in Africa,* edited by H. Wasserman, 19–31. New York: Routledge.

Obi, C. 2006. "Terrorism in West Africa: Real, Emerging or Imagined Threats?" *African Security Review* 15 (3): 87–101.

Obijiofor, L., and F. Hanusch. 2011. *Journalism across Cultures: An Introduction.* Basingstoke: Palgrave MacMillan.

Oelofsen, H. M. 2017. "Hearing the Citizens: Inequality, Access to Journalists and the Prospects for Inclusively Mediated Spaces of Political Deliberation in South Africa." PhD diss., Rhodes University.

Oelofsen, H. M. 2020. "Listening for the Quiet Violence in the Unspoken." In *Post-conflict Hauntings—Transforming Collective Memories,* edited by Pumla Gobodo-Madikizela, Jeff Prager, and Kim Wale, 177–202. New York: Palgrave MacMillan.

Ogan, C. 1982. "Development Journalism/Communication: The Status of the Concept." *International Communication Gazette* 29 (1–2): 3–9.

Ottaway, M. 1997. "African Democratization and the Leninist Option." *Journal of Modern African Studies* 35 (1): 1–15.

Pajnik, M., and J. Downing. 2008. "Introduction: The Challenges of Nano-media." In *Alternative Media and the Politics of Resistance: Perspectives and Challenges*, edited by M. Pajnik and J. Downing, 7–16. Ljubljana: Peace Institute.

Palmer, L. 2019. *The Fixers: Local News Workers and the Underground Labor of International Reporting.* New York: Oxford University Press.

Paterson, C. 2013. "Journalism and Social Media in the African Context." *Ecquid Novi: African Journalism Studies* 34 (1): 1–6.

Paterson, C. 2018. "The Afghanistan-ization of Africa." Africa Is a Country, March 23. Accessed March 26, 2018. https://africasacountry.com/2018/03/the-afghanistan-ization-of-africa.

Paterson, C., A. Gadzekpo, and H. Wasserman, eds. 2018. "Special Issue: Journalism and Foreign Aid." *African Journalism Studies* 39 (2).

Pijoos, I. 2018. "Police, Army Will Help Secure Day Zero Water Distribution Points—Zille." News 24, January 24. Accessed February 27, 2018. https://www.news24.com/SouthAfrica/News/police-army-will-help-secure-day-zero-water-distribution-points-zille-20180124.

Pithouse, R. 2007. "The University of Abahlali baseMjondolo. Voices of Resistance from Occupied London." Accessed October 31, 2017. http://abahlali.org/node/2814/.

Plaut, M. 2012. "South Africa's Lonmin Marikana Clashes Killed 34." BBC News Africa, August 17. Accessed August 21, 2018. http://www.bbc.co.uk/news/world-africa-19292909.

Pohjonen, M., and S Udupa. 2017. "Extreme Speech Online: An Anthropological Critique of Hate Speech Debates." *International Journal of Communication* 11: 1173–91.

Pointer, R., T. Bosch, W. Chuma, and H. Wasserman. 2016. "Civil Society, Political Activism and Communications in Democratisation Conflicts." MeCoDEM Working Paper. Accessed March 16, 2018. http://www.mecodem.eu/wp-content/uploads/2015/05/Pointer-et-al-2016_Civil-society-political-activism-and-communications-in-democratisation-conflicts.pdf.

Poppick, L. 2018. "What's behind Cape Town's Water Woes?" Smithsonian.com. Accessed February15,2018.https://www.smithsonianmag.com/science-nature/day-zero-looms-cape-town-water-crisis-may-signify-new-normal-180968128/.

Quintal, G. 2012. "Journo's Marikana Story Questioned." *Business Report*, August 31. Accessed August 21, 2018. https://www.iol.co.za/business-report/companies/journos-marikana-story-questioned-1373775.

Rao, S., and H. Wasserman. 2007. "Global Journalism Ethics Revisited: A Postcolonial Critique." *Global Media and Communication* 3 (1): 29–50.

Reid, J. 2014. "Third-Party Complaints in the System of Press Regulation: Inviting the Reader to Take Part in Journalistic Accountability and Securing Press Freedom." *African Journalism Studies* 35 (2): 58–74.

Reid, J. 2017. "The Audience-Centred Approach to Media Policymaking: A Critical Analysis of the South African Press Freedom Commission as a Participatory Process of Review." *African Journalism Studies* 38 (3–4): 74–97.

Republic of South Africa. 1996. The Constitution of the Republic of South Africa. Accessed April 24, 2018. http://www.justice.gov.za/legislation/constitution/SAConstitution-web-eng.pdf.

Roberts, L. 2018. "Politics, Poverty, and Climate Change: Stories from Cape Town's 'Day Zero.'" Overseas Development Institute. Accessed March 16, 2018. https://www.odi.org/comment/10616-politics-poverty-and-climate-change-stories-cape-town-s-day-zero.

Rodny-Gumede, Y. 2017. "Questioning the Media and Democracy Relationship: The Case of South Africa." *Communicatio* 43 (2): 10–22.

SABC. 2017. "SABC Embarks on Editorial Policies Review Process." Accessed January 24, 2018. http://web.sabc.co.za/sabc/home/editorialpolicies/multimedia/details?id=22b756ca-a569-47ed-b616-dd5b69e2b735&title=SABC%20Embarks%20on%20Editorial%20Policies%20Review%20Process.

Sambrook, R., ed. 2018. *Global Teamwork: The Rise of Collaboration in Investigative Journalism.* Oxford: Reuters Institute for the Study of Journalism.

Schmid, A. P. 1989. "Terrorism and the Media: The Ethics of Publicity." *Terrorism and Political Violence* 4 (1): 539–65.

Scott, M., M. Bunce, and K. Wright. 2019. "Foundation Funding and the Boundaries of Journalism." *Journalism Studies* 20 (14): 2034–52. doi: 10.1080/1461670X.2018.1556321.

Seaton, J. 2003. "Understanding Not Empathy." In *War and the Media*, edited by D. K. Thussu and D. Freedman, 45–54. London: Sage.

Shah, H. 1996. "Modernization, Marginalization, and Emancipation: Toward a Normative Model of Journalism and National Development." *Communication Theory* 6 (2): 143–66.

Sibanda, T. 2015. "Baba Jukwa Case Collapses." *NewsDay*, May 30. Accessed April 23, 2018. https://www.newsday.co.zw/2015/05/baba-jukwa-case-collapses/.

Siebert, F. S., T. Peterson, and W. Schramm. 1956. *Four Theories of the Press*. Urbana: University of Illinois Press.

Silverstone, R. 2007. *Media and Morality: On the Rise of the Mediapolis*. Cambridge: Polity.

Singer, J. 2006. "The Socially Responsible Existentialist." *Journalism Studies* 7 (1): 2–18.

Skjerdal, T. S. 2010. "Research on Brown Envelope Journalism in the African Media." *African Communication Research* 3 (3): 367–406.

Smith, G. 2018. "Protesting the Only Language Authorities Understand." Eyewitness News, May 2. Accessed May 2, 2018. http://ewn.co.za/2018/05/02/protesting-the-only-language-authorities-understand.

Smith, Z. K. 2000. "The Impact of Political Liberalisation and Democratisation on Ethnic Conflict in Africa: An Empirical Test of Common Assumptions." *Journal of Modern African Studies* 38 (1): 21–39.

Smith-Spark, L., and K. Polglase. 2017. "2 Men Guilty in South Africa Coffin Assault Case." CNN, August 25. Accessed March 29, 2018. https://edition.cnn.com/2017/08/25/africa/south-africa-coffin-assault-verdict/index.html.

Sontag, S. 2003. *Regarding the Pain of Others*. London: Penguin.

Sorensen, L., H. Ford, W. Al-Saqaf, and T. Bosch. 2019. "'Dialogue of the Deaf': The Performance of Listening on Twitter during the 2015 South African State of the Nation Address." In *Media, Communication and the Struggle for Democratic Change*, edited by K. Voltmer, C. Christensen, I. Neverla, N. Stremlau, B. Thomass, H. Wasserman, and N. Vladisavljevic. New York: Palgrave MacMillan.

Sparks, C. 2009. "South African Media in Transition." *Journal of African Media Studies* 1 (2): 195–220.

Spivak, G. 1988. "Can the Subaltern Speak?" In *Marxism and the Interpretation of Culture*, edited by C. Nelson and L. Grossberg, 271–316. Urbana: University of Illinois Press.

Steele, J. 2018. *Mediating Islam: Cosmopolitan Journalisms in Muslim Southeast Asia*. Seattle: University of Washington Press.

Stoddard, E. 2018. "Explainer: South Africa Aims to Expropriate Land without Compensation." Reuters, March 14. Accessed March 16, 2018. https://www.reuters.com/article/us-safrica-land-explainer/explainer-south-africa-aims-to-expropriate-land-without-compensation-idUSKCN1GQ280.

Straus, S. 2007. "What Is the Relationship between Hate Radio and Violence? Rethinking Rwanda's 'Radio Machete.'" *Politics and Society* 35 (4): 609–37.

Strauss, A., and J. Corbin. 1994. "Grounded Theory Methodology: An Overview." In *Handbook of Qualitative Research*, edited by N. Denzin and Y. S. Lincoln, 273–85. Thousand Oaks, CA: Sage.

Stremlau, N., and G. Iazzolino. 2017. "Communications, Power and Governance in Democratisation Conflicts." MeCoDEM Working Paper. Accessed April 12, 2018. http://www.mecodem.eu/wp-content/uploads/2017/04/Stremlau-Iazzolino-2017_Communications-power-and-governance-in-democratisation-conflicts.pdf.

Strömbäck, J. 2005. "In Search of a Standard: Four Models of Democracy and Their Normative Implications for Journalism." *Journalism Studies* 6 (3): 331–45.

Swailes, B., and B. Adebayo. 2018. "South African Woman Recorded Racially Abusing Police Officer Jailed for 3 Years." CNN, March 29. Accessed March 29, 2018. https://edition.cnn.com/2018/03/29/africa/south-african-vicki-momberg-sentencing/index.html.

Switzer, L., and M. Adhikari, eds. 2000. *South Africa's Resistance Press: Alternative Voices in the Last Generation under Apartheid*. Athens: Ohio University Center for International Studies.

Tettey, W. J. 2006. "The Politics of Media Accountability in Africa." *International Communication Gazette* 68 (3): 229–48.

Thamm, M., and J. Le Roux. 2017. "In the Non-surprise of the Year, WMCLEAKS.com Smear Campaign Tracked to a Gupta Associate." *Daily Maverick*, June 22. Accessed July 5, 2017. https://www.dailymaverick.co.za/article/2017-06-22-scorpio-in-the-non-surprise-of-the-year-wmcleaks.com-smear-campaign-tracked-to-a-gupta-associate/#.WV0Q4dOGPZs.

Thussu, D. K. 2003. "Live TV and Bloodless Deaths: War, Infotainment and 24/7 News." In *War and the Media*, edited by D. K. Thussu and D. Freedman, 117–32. London: Sage.

Thussu, D. K., and D. Freedman, eds. 2003. *War and the Media*. London: Sage.

Times Live. 2013. "Marikana Inquiry Told Human Tongue, Chin Used in Muti." Times Live, March 11. Accessed August 21, 2018. http://www.timeslive.co.za/local/2013/03/11/marikana-inquiry-told-human-tongue-chin-used-in-muti.

Tolsi, N. 2018. "Starting the Fire. Ruth First Memorial Lecture." University of the Witwatersrand, Johannesburg, October 18. Accessed October 19, 2018. http://journalism.co.za/2018-ruth-first-memorial-lecture-delivered-by-niren-tolsi-full-paper/.

Tuchman, G. 1972. "Objectivity as Strategic Ritual: An Examination of Newsmen's Notions of Objectivity." *American Journal of Sociology* 77 (4): 660–79.

Tuchman, G. 1978. "The Symbolic Annihilation of Women by the Mass Media." In *Hearth and Home: Images of Women in the Mass Media*, edited by G. Tuchman, A. K. Daniels, and J. Benet, 3–38. New York: Oxford University Press.

Tully, M., and B. Ekdale. 2014. "Sites of Playful Engagement: Twitter Hashtags as Spaces of Leisure and Development in Kenya." *Information Technologies and International Development* 10 (3): 67–82.

Tumber, H., and M. Prentoulis. 2003. "Journalists under Fire: Subcultures, Objectivity and Emotional Literacy." In *War and the Media*, edited by D. K. Thussu and D. Freedman, 215–30. London: Sage.

Tveit, M. 2014. "Facebook and Politics in Zimbabwe: Who Is Baba Jukwa?" Africa Is a Country, July 19. Accessed May 4, 2018. https://africasacountry.com/2014/07/facebook-politics-in-zimbabwe-who-is-baba-jukwa.

Udupa, S. 2017. "Viral Video: Mobile Media, Riot and Religious Politics." In *Media as Politics in South Asia*, edited by S. Udupa and S. D. McDowell, 190–205. London: Routledge.

Ugland, E., and J. Henderson. 2007. "Who Is a Journalist and Why Does It Matter? Disentangling the Legal and Ethical Arguments." *Journal of Mass Media Ethics* 22 (4): 241–61.

UNESCO. n.d. "Professional Journalistic Standards and Code of Ethics." Accessed June 21, 2018. http://www.unesco.org/new/en/communication-and-information/freedom-of-expression/professional-journalistic-standards-and-code-of-ethics/.

Vladisavljević, N. 2015. "Media Framing of Political Conflict: A Review of the Literature." MeCoDEM Working Paper. Accessed February 16, 2018. http://www.mecodem.eu/wp-content/uploads/2015/05/Vladisavljevi%C4%87-2015_Media-framing-of-political-conflict_-a-review-of-the-literature.pdf.

Voltmer, K. 2006. "The Mass Media and the Dynamics of Political Communication in Processes of Democratization: An Introduction." In *Mass Media and Political Communication in New Democracies*, edited by K. Voltmer, 1–20. London: Routledge.

Voltmer, K. 2013. *The Media in Transitional Democracies*. Cambridge: Polity.

Voltmer, K. 2016. "Media and Conflict in Transitional Democracies: Polarization, Power and the Struggle for Recognition." Keynote Address, Forum für Media Entwicklung (FoME) Symposium (Observer, Agitator, Target: Media and Media Assistance in Fragile Contexts), Berlin, November 3–4, pp. 9–17. Accessed October 5, 2018. https://fome.info/wp-content/uploads/2017/03/FoME-Observer-Agitator-Target-2016.pdf.

Voltmer, K. 2019. "Introduction: Democratization Conflicts as Communicative Contestations." In: *Media, Communication and the Struggle for Democratic Change* edited by K. Voltmer, C. Christensen, I. Neverla, N. Stremlau, B. Thomass, N. Vladisavljević, and H. Wasserman, 1–31. Cham: Palgrave MacMillan.

Voltmer, K., and H. Wasserman. 2014. "Journalistic Norms between Universality and Domestication: Journalists' Interpretations of Press Freedom in Six New Democracies." *Global Media and Communication* 10 (2): 177–92.

Vos, T. P., and R. J. Thomas. 2018. "The Discursive Construction of Journalistic Authority in a Post-truth Age." *Journalism Studies* 19 (13): 2001–10.

Wadekar, N. 2018. "Kenya's Dangerous Path toward Authoritarianism." *New Yorker*, February 9. Accessed March 27, 2018. https://www.newyorker.com/news/news-desk/kenyas-dangerous-path-toward-authoritarianism.

Waisbord, S. 2013. *Reinventing Professionalism: Journalism and News in Global Perspective*. Oxford: Polity.

Waisbord, S. 2018. "Truth Is What Happens to News." *Journalism Studies* 19 (13): 1866–78.

Wallensteen, P. 2007. *Understanding Conflict Resolution*. London: Sage.

Ward, S. J. A. 2005. *The Invention of Journalism Ethics: The Path to Objectivity and Beyond.* Montreal: McGill-Queens University Press.

Ward, S. J. A. 2018. *Disrupting Journalism Ethics.* Abingdon: Routledge.

Ward, S. J. A., and H. Wasserman, eds. 2010. *Media Ethics beyond Borders.* New York: Routledge.

Ward, S. J. A., and H. Wasserman. 2015. "Open Ethics: Towards a Global Media Ethics of Listening." *Journalism Studies* 16 (6): 834–39.

Wasserman, H. 2006. "Tackles and Sidesteps: Normative Maintenance and Paradigm Repair in Mainstream Media Reactions to Tabloid Journalism." *Communicare* 25 (1): 59–80.

Wasserman, H. 2007. "Is a New World Wide Web Possible? An Explorative Comparison of the Use of ICTs by Two South African Social Movements." *African Studies Review* 50 (1): 109–31.

Wasserman, H. 2010b. *Tabloid Journalism in South Africa: True Story!* Bloomington: Indiana University Press.

Wasserman, H. 2011a. "Mobile Phones, Popular Media and Everyday African Democracy: Transmissions and Transgressions." *Popular Communication* 9 (2): 146–58.

Wasserman, H. 2011b. "Towards a Global Journalism Ethics via Local Narratives." *Journalism Studies* 12 (6): 791–803.

Wasserman, H. 2013. "Journalism in a New Democracy: The Ethics of Listening." *Communicatio* 39 (1): 67–84.

Wasserman, H. 2014. "Media Ethics Theories in Africa." In *International Handbook of Media and Mass Communication Theory*, edited by R. Fortner and M. Fackler, 781–97. Hoboken, NJ: Wiley-Blackwell.

Wasserman, H. 2015. "Marikana and the Media: Acts of Citizenship and a Faith in Democracy-to-Come." *Social Dynamics* 41 (2): 375–86.

Wasserman, H. 2017. "Fake News from Africa: Panics, Politics and Paradigms." *Journalism: Theory, Practice, Critique* 21 (1): 3–16.

Wasserman, H. 2018a. *Media, Geopolitics and Power: A View from the Global South.* Urbana: University of Illinois Press.

Wasserman, H. 2018b. "The Social Is Political: Media, Protest and Change as a Challenge to African Media Research." In *Palgrave Handbook for Media and Communication Research in Africa*, edited by B. Mutsvairo, 213–24. New York: Palgrave MacMillan.

Wasserman, H., and N. Benequista. 2017. *Pathways to Media Reform in Sub-Saharan Africa: Reflections from a Regional Consultation.* Washington, DC: Center for International Media Assistance. Accessed January 9, 2018. https://www.cima.ned.org/wp-content/uploads/2017/12/CIMA-Media-Reform-in-SSA_web_150ppi.pdf.

Wasserman, H., T. Bosch, and W. Chuma. 2016. "Voices of the Poor Are Missing from South Africa's Media." The Conversation, January 22. Accessed August 14, 2018. https://theconversation.com/voices-of-the-poor-are-missing-from-south-africas-media-53068.

Wasserman, H., T. Bosch, and W. Chuma. 2018. "Communication from Above and Below: Media, Protest and Democracy." *Politikon.* https://doi.org/10.1080/02589346.2018.1446482.

Wasserman, H., and A. S. de Beer. 2005. "A Fragile Affair: An Overview of the Relationship between the Media and State in Post-apartheid South Africa." *Journal of Mass Media Ethics* 20 (2–3): 192–208.

Wasserman, H., and D. Madrid-Morales. 2019. "An Exploratory Study of "Fake News" and Media Trust in Kenya, Nigeria and South Africa." *African Journalism Studies* 40 (1): 107–23.

Wasserman, H., and J. M. Maweu. 2014a. "The Freedom to Be Silent? Market Pressures on Journalistic Normative Ideals at the Nation Media Group in Kenya." *Review of African Political Economy* 41 (142): 623–33.

Wasserman, H., and J. M. Maweu. 2014b. "The Tension between Ethics and Ethnicity: Examining Journalists' Ethical Decision-Making at the Nation Media Group in Kenya." *Journal of African Media Studies* 6 (2): 165–79.

WHO (World Health Organization). 2020. 1st WHO Infodemiology Conference. Accessed August 17, 2020. https://www.who.int/news-room/events/detail/2020/06/30/default-calendar/1st-who-infodemiology-conference.

Willems, W. 2010. "Beyond Dramatic Revolutions and Grand Rebellions: Everyday Forms of Resistance during 'the Zimbabwe Crisis.'" *Communicare* 29 (1): 1–17.

Willems, W. 2011. "Comic Strips and 'the Crisis': Postcolonial Laughter and Coping with Everyday Life in Zimbabwe." *Popular Communication* 9: 126–45.

Willems, W. 2014. "Beyond Normative Dewesternization: Examining Media Culture from the Vantage Point of the Global South." *Global South* 8 (1): 7–23.

Willems, W., and W. Mano. 2017. "Decolonizing and Provincializing Audience and Internet Studies: Contextual Approaches from African Vantage Points." In *Everyday Media Culture in Africa: Audiences and Users*, edited by W. Willems and W. Mano, 1–26. London: Routledge.

Wolfsfeld, G. 2018. "The Role of the Media in Violent Conflicts in the Digital Age: Israeli and Palestinian Leaders' Perceptions." *Media, War & Conflict* 11 (1): 107–24.

Wolfsfeld, G., D. Segev, and T. Sheafer. 2013. "Social Media and the Arab Spring: Politics Comes First." *International Journal of Press/Politics* 18 (2): 115–37.

Wright, K. 2018. *Who's Reporting Africa Now? Non-Governmental Organizations, Journalists, and Multimedia*. Bern: Peter Lang.

Yang, G. 2016. "Narrative Agency in Hashtag Activism: The Case of #BlackLivesMatter." *Media and Communication* 4 (4): 13–17.

Zelizer, B. 2017. *What Journalism Could Be*. Cambridge: Polity.

Zenebe, B. 2012. "The Role of Media in Ethnic Violence during Political Transition in Africa: The Case of Rwanda and Kenya." PhD diss., University of Nebraska.

Index